LIBR
WITHDRAW

THE SCRAP

A true story from the 1916 rising

Gene Kerrigan

Doubleday Ireland

TRANSWORLD IRELAND PUBLISHERS
28 Lower Leeson Street, Dublin 2, Ireland
www.transworldireland.ie

Transworld Ireland is part of the Penguin Random House
group of companies whose addresses can be found at
global.penguinrandomhouse.com

Penguin
Random House
UK

First published in the UK and Ireland in 2015
by Doubleday Ireland
an imprint of Transworld Publishers

Copyright © Gene Kerrigan 2015

Gene Kerrigan has asserted his right under the Copyright, Designs
and Patents Act 1988 to be identified as the author of this work.

Every effort has been made to obtain the necessary permissions with
reference to copyright material, both illustrative and quoted. We
apologize for any omissions in this respect and will be pleased to
make the appropriate acknowledgements in any future edition.

A CIP catalogue record for this book
is available from the British Library.

ISBN 9781781620359

Typeset in 11¼/14½pt Sabon by Kestrel Data, Exeter, Devon.
Printed and bound by Clays Ltd, Bungay, Suffolk.

Penguin Random House is committed to a sustainable
future for our business, our readers and our planet. This book
is made from Forest Stewardship Council® certified paper.

MIX
Paper from
responsible sources
FSC® C018179

1 3 5 7 9 10 8 6 4 2

From witness statements at the Bureau of Military History

The Countess told me about a fortnight before the rising that the scrap was definitely fixed for Easter.
Marie Perolz, WS246

One of them told me the scrap was starting and that they were going to the GPO.
Catherine Rooney, WS648

When passing through Upper Fitzwilliam Street we heard the sound of rifle firing. Tannam turned to me and said, 'The scrap is on'.
Seamus Murray, WS308

There was a bit of a scrap there with some British troops and a number of them were killed.
Thomas Harris, WS320

MacBride turned and bade each of us goodbye . . . 'All we can do is have a scrap and send it on to the next generation'.
Christopher M. Byrne, WS1014

This is for Derek Speirs

Contents

Introduction

This is the true story of members of F Company, 2nd Battalion, Dublin Brigade of the Irish Volunteers, and their experience of the rising at Easter 1916. It's based on first-hand evidence.

In the 1940s, the Bureau of Military History took statements from hundreds of witnesses to the 1913–23 struggle for Irish independence. The remarkable detail they left allows us to construct a close-up view of a major turning point in British and Irish history.

The idea behind the book was to choose a small unit of ordinary rebels, pretty much at random, and follow them through the rising – along with the people they encountered and alongside whom they fought. We see the rebellion as they saw it, in the context of some of the major events of that week.

Members of F Company were active in the GPO, in Jacob's factory and in the frightening and heartbreaking last phase of the rising, in Moore Street. People such as Patrick Pearse, James Connolly, Tom Clarke and Michael Collins became the stuff of legends and monuments – here we see them through the eyes of the rank and file, junior officers, nurses and others.

This is a writer's work, not an historian's – so there are

no footnotes. But if in this story there are tears in a man's eyes it's not made up. If sparks fly from horses' hooves when Lancers gallop on cobblestones, it's not poetic licence. It's there in the remarkable military archives.

The story of F Company reflects the larger one: a small band of mostly young men and women challenged an empire that comprised a fifth of the world's population – and lost. And then won.

Main characters

Charlie Saurin – student, F Company, aged 20

Frank Henderson – clerk, captain, F Company, aged 30

Oscar Traynor – professional footballer, lieutenant, F Company, aged 30

Arthur 'Boss' Shields – Abbey Theatre actor, F Company, aged 20

Harry Colley – rate collector, F Company, aged 25

Seamus Daly – fitter, F Company, aged 32

Harry Boland – merchant and tailor, F Company, aged 29

Vincent Poole – sewer worker, captain, Irish Citizen Army, aged 36

Nora O'Daly – nurse, Cumann na mBan, aged 33

Joe Good – electrician, London Volunteer, aged 21

Helena Molony – union organizer, Citizen Army, aged 31

Kathleen Lynn – doctor, Citizen Army, aged 42

Mattie Connolly – Citizen Army, aged 16

Matt Stafford – Fenian, aged 64

A note on sources

Scenes in the narrative are built sometimes from one or two statements, often from several viewpoints, with additional detail from secondary sources. Where the memories of witnesses differed I cross-checked accounts and made judgements about the sequence of events most likely to be accurate.

Where speech is within quote marks it's taken directly from witness statements. Where speech is without quote marks it's from indirect speech as recalled by participants.

Where one person might be variously called James, Jim, Jimmy or Seamus, I've used the least confusing version of names, depending on circumstances. I've adopted in most cases the casual form of names, as used by friends and comrades – i.e. Tom, Joe and Katie, not Thomas, Joseph and Catherine, etc.

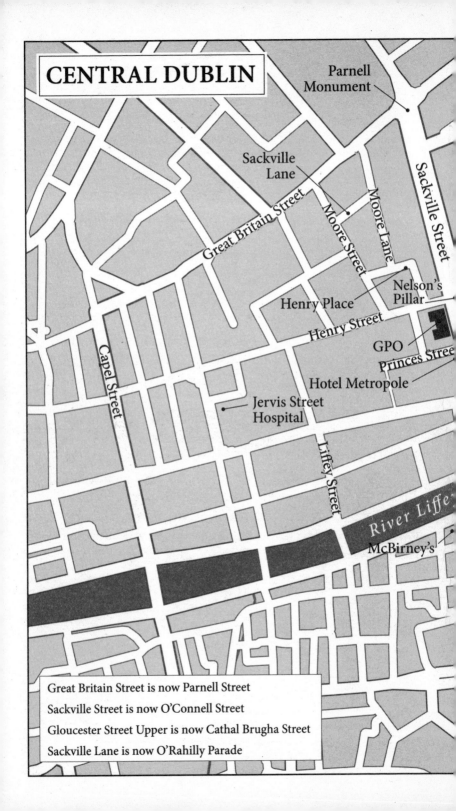

CENTRAL DUBLIN

Parnell Monument

Sackville Lane

Great Britain Street

Moore Street

Moore Lane

Sackville Street

Henry Place

Nelson's Pillar

Henry Street

GPO

Princes Street

Hotel Metropole

Capel Street

Jervis Street Hospital

Liffey Street

River Liffey

McBirney's

Great Britain Street is now Parnell Street

Sackville Street is now O'Connell Street

Gloucester Street Upper is now Cathal Brugha Street

Sackville Lane is now O'Rahilly Parade

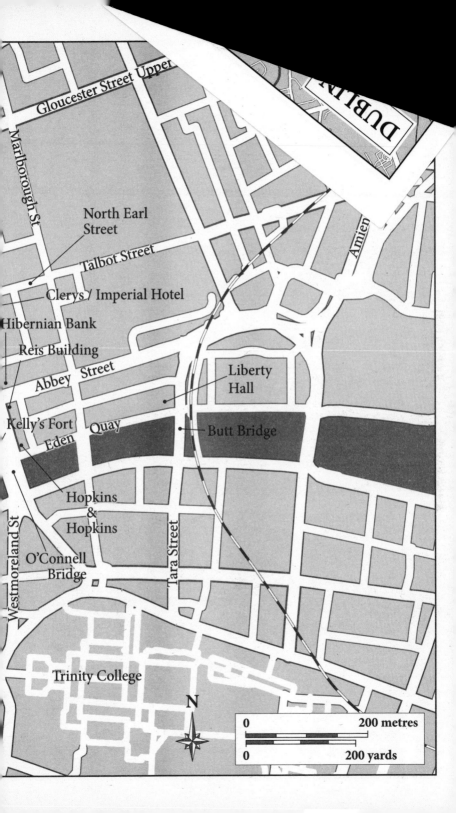

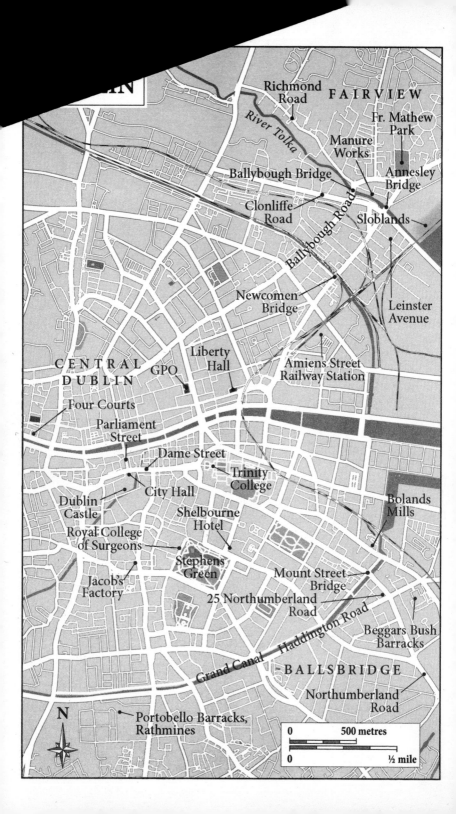

Part One

April 1916

1

The bullet wound in his arm was fresh. It was understood, without anyone having to say anything, that this was a special case, to be handled sensitively.

He didn't tell the nursing staff at Dublin's Mater Hospital how the wound happened. They guessed it had something to do with drilling and training. Anyone who knew Mr Clarke knew he was the kind of man who probably did a bit of drilling and training.

Tom Clarke was thin, with the frail appearance of an old man, although he was just fifty-eight. It was the fifteen years in jail did that to him. The beatings, the torture.

He was taken to St Vincent's ward. A senior surgeon, Denis Farnan, a man of strong nationalist sympathies, examined the patient's wound.

It was standard practice for a patient in a Catholic hospital undergoing a serious procedure to receive the sacraments of Confession and the Eucharist. Clarke refused the sacraments, causing unease among the nursing sisters, who were aware that any procedure could go wrong.

Dr Farnan took out the bullet and dressed the wound.

Ideally, such a procedure would be followed by a

period of recuperation. Clarke left the hospital in a hurry, his arm in a sling. He had things to do. The arrangements for the rising were almost complete, the wording of the Proclamation of the Republic had yet to be agreed.

The hospital chart disappeared and no record of the visit was entered in the hospital register.

Tom MacDonagh was a romantic poet, but when he addressed his officers this evening he spoke of raincoats, leggings and marching boots.

Needles and thread, too.

Pins, bandages, rations for several days.

Arms and ammunition, of course.

Horlicks malted milk tablets, for quick nourishment.

Tinned beef, chocolate and cheese.

A box of matches.

The good soldier is equipped for every eventuality.

MacDonagh was a poet, novelist and teacher, Officer Commanding 2nd Battalion, Dublin Brigade of the Irish Volunteers. He had recently been appointed the seventh member of the secret Military Council that was planning the rising. His was the final appointment, joining Tom Clarke, Patrick Pearse, Eamonn Ceannt, Sean MacDermott, Joe Plunkett and James Connolly.

In front of him in the packed room sat the men who would carry through their plans – the junior officers of the Dublin Brigade.

MacDonagh, a cheery, emotional man of thirty-eight, was on personal terms with many of the officers here this evening. None more so than Frank Henderson and Oscar Traynor, the captain and lieutenant of F Company, 2nd Battalion. The company was informally known among some of the Volunteers as 'MacDonagh's Own'.

It was a Saturday evening early in April 1916. The

meeting was held in the headquarters of the Irish Volunteers, at 2 Dawson Street, Dublin. The rumours had multiplied in recent weeks. Everyone in the audience believed the scrap was coming soon, few knew exactly when.

When MacDonagh was finished, another member of the Military Council, Eamonn Ceannt, rose. You will receive your orders, he said. 'I myself don't know when that order may come, but I do know it can't be far distant.'

Ceannt said he'd made his will.

'We've organised a fund in America to look after the wives and dependants of those who will go down. And each man is to hand in the names of his dependants to his Company Captain immediately. Prepare yourselves for the day and put your souls in order.'

The audience having been warmed up, the star turn made his appearance.

Patrick Pearse, wearing a greatcoat and a slouch hat, a green uniform with yellow tabs to indicate senior officer status, moved towards the top of the room. A teacher, a non-practising barrister, a poet in his mid-thirties, Pearse was a self-consciously romantic figure, his life totally consumed by the idea of Irish independence from the Empire. He ran a school, St Enda's, in Rathfarnham. Tom MacDonagh worked alongside him there.

When he reached the top of the room Pearse turned and faced the officers. He passed his slouch hat to his brother Willie. His brother helped him take off the heavy overcoat.

Pearse stood, amid complete silence, his head lowered.

He let the tension build. The seconds ticked by – ten, twenty, thirty – and he stood there, silent, poised, head down.

He raised his head quickly and said, 'Is every man here prepared to meet his God?'

He spoke not loudly but with great intensity.

In the audience, the words hit Oscar Traynor like an electric jolt. He was aware that the men around him were similarly moved.

'I know that you've been preparing your bodies for this great struggle that lies before us, but have you also been preparing your souls?'

Again, a long pause.

Then came the core message of Pearse's appearance here – the warning, without specifics or times or places, that the drilling and training were almost over.

For any man not in earnest, Pearse said, this is the time to get out.

The rest of his speech merely repeated earlier suggestions about practical preparations for the battle. It was the opening lines, the drama of that moment, which stuck in the minds of his audience.

Raincoats and leggings, needles and thread, make your will and cleanse your soul. The movement had always been a mixture of the secular and the divine, the mundane and the romantic. It would continue so into its climax, and long beyond.

2

The authorities at Dublin Castle knew rebellion was a possibility. There were two schools of thought about how to deal with the paramilitary pretensions of the Irish nationalists. Crack down on them, or let them march and drill like toy soldiers.

The Irish Volunteers were one small part of the nationalist movement, which in turn was just one element in a country securely held for the Empire. One point of view said such dissidence could be easily overwhelmed by the force of the British Army, shot, locked up and intimidated out of existence.

The other point of view was that cracking down might provoke the insurrection the authorities were hoping to avoid. It would inflame other nationalists, who weren't members of the Volunteers, who might be radicalized by the suppression. Leave the Volunteers alone, let them burn up their anger and ambition in playing at being soldiers. The extremists among them were, after all, a bunch of amateurs with little support among the people.

The day after the officer meeting addressed by Pearse, police raided the Volunteer training ground at Fr. Mathew Park, off Philipsburg Avenue, in Fairview. They wanted to search for a consignment of guns received from Volunteers in Wexford.

F Company's lieutenant, Oscar Traynor, quickly organized a defence and the police were held off at gunpoint: 'Not one step further or I order fire.'

Word spread. Captain Frank Henderson was among the F Company men who rushed to the park and forced the police to back down.

One thing the authorities could do, they decided, was stop the printing and sale of seditious literature. A range of small newspapers openly championed everything from intellectual rejection of the Empire to detailed analysis of the tactics of insurrection. The police raided printworks in Capel Street and Liffey Street, then hurried down Eden Quay and raided the shop in Liberty Hall, offices of the Irish Transport and General Workers Union, where the papers were sold.

On the outbreak of the Great War in 1914 the Irish Citizen Army had decorated the front of Liberty Hall with a large banner: 'We serve neither King nor Kaiser, but Ireland'.

Two policemen entered the union's Co-op shop. They told Rosie Hackett they were taking the newspapers. Already a veteran trade unionist at the age of twenty-three, Hackett was also a member of the Irish Citizen Army. 'Wait 'til I get the head,' she told them and sent a printer to find James Connolly.

By the time Connolly came down, Helena Molony, secretary of the Irish Women Workers' Union, had entered the shop. She was a separatist, a socialist, a feminist and a member of the Citizen Army. She also on occasion acted at the Abbey Theatre.

When Connolly arrived he was armed, and accompanied by the shop manager, Jenny Shanahan.

The police had already begun confiscating the seditious newspapers. The *Workers' Republic* was currently carrying educational articles by Connolly, describing how a small army might engage an occupying force in street fighting.

One policeman told Connolly, 'We've come to seize the paper.'

'You can't,' Connolly said.

'I have my orders.'

Connolly raised his gun. 'Drop them,' he said, 'or I'll drop you.'

Behind the police, Helena Molony had drawn her revolver. Caught between the two, the police officers backed down and left the shop.

Connolly knew they'd be back. And this time they'd likely be out to suppress more than the newspapers. Already, plainclothes policemen routinely watched the building.

He hurried upstairs to his office. Minutes later, he came out on to the landing and spotted Jimmy O'Shea, a member of the Citizen Army. 'Come up at once to No. 7.'

The Irish Citizen Army had originated as a group formed to protect strikers from the beatings they regularly received from police batons. Over the previous two years, under James Connolly, it had become an armed force of about three hundred that drilled regularly and intensely. Jimmy O'Shea, who worked in a foundry that built Guinness barges, was one of the Citizen Army's most committed members.

When O'Shea entered room No. 7 he saw Constance Markievicz, nationalist, suffragette and member of the Citizen Army. Markievicz had become a countess when she married a Polish aristocrat. Now, she was writing quickly on a series of small pieces of paper. Nearby, Nora

Connolly – the union leader's daughter – was doing the same. There was a .45 revolver on the table in front of James Connolly. Markievicz too had a gun beside her.

Connolly asked O'Shea if he could evade the detectives watching the building and deliver these mobilization papers.

O'Shea said he'd try.

There was a standing order in the Citizen Army: if any member received a mobilization paper signed by Connolly they had to leave wherever they were – work, bed, home – and get to the place specified on the paper.

After the raid on the Co-op shop, and the resistance to the confiscation of the newspapers, Connolly feared that the police would return in force to close down the building and carry out arrests.

Three months earlier, Connolly had secretly become a member of the Military Council planning the rising – a socialist along with six nationalists. While Patrick Pearse had assumed the position of commander-in-chief, it was agreed that Connolly would direct military operations in Dublin. Knowing how close the rising was, he feared that a successful police assault on Liberty Hall would put the Citizen Army out of business – disrupting the plans, perhaps fatally. To prevent that, he now decided that Liberty Hall, up to the day of the insurrection, would become a fortress.

Within a few minutes the mobilization papers were ready. Connolly told Jimmy O'Shea to get them to the Citizen Army mobilizing officer, Tom Kain, who had a shop on Arran Quay.

Constance Markievicz put the papers down the back of O'Shea's shirt.

At the office downstairs, knowing the detectives watching from outside could see him, O'Shea made a show of paying his union subs. He'd been working at the foundry that morning and was streaked with grime, so he looked the part. Resisting the urge to hurry, he strolled past the detectives, lighting a cigarette. He crossed over to the quayside and walked up towards Marlborough Street. Only when he was out of sight of the detectives did he break into a run. He didn't stop until he had run a mile alongside the Liffey, to Capel Street Bridge.

At a premises there, O'Shea passed the mobilization papers to Tom Kain, who began circulating them to Citizen Army members, who in turn alerted others.

Jimmy O'Shea continued on to Emmet Hall, in Inchicore, where Mike Mallin, James Connolly's second in command, lived. O'Shea and Mallin armed themselves with rifles and bandoliers and set out for Liberty Hall.

They came to the union offices, scores of armed men, from foundries, fitting shops, forges and construction sites. These weren't casual members of the Citizen Army, in the way that many nationalists were casual members of the Irish Volunteers. They were committed, often hardened, soldiers.

Some carters had time to stable their horses, others brought them to Liberty Hall. Men arrived at the union hall in their greasy smocks, some with whips hanging from their belts, many flecked with coal, mud or cement.

Sean Connolly was there, captain in the Citizen Army, dressed in accordance with his job as a clerk in the rates department of City Hall.

Whatever their working clothes, they came with bandoliers and weapons. Each window and entrance was allocated an armed guard.

Everyone else went to a large room inside Liberty Hall, where James Connolly addressed them. The police had attempted to raid the building today, he said. They may come again, and we have to be prepared for anything. From here on, guards will be posted day and night. Each man will do two nights a week, plus Saturday and Sunday. Those who are unemployed will take the day shifts.

In the days that followed, there were armed members on landings and in corridors, women preparing knapsacks, young boys collecting bread from bakeries, large hams being cooked for when they'd be needed.

You walk into a room and there's someone with a blowtorch heating a French bayonet, to bend it to fit a rifle for which it was never meant. Someone else is brewing tea on one side of a glowing fireplace; on the other side of the fireplace there's a pot of melted lead, to make bullets. The building was now not so much a union hall as a military barracks in the days before a battle.

In the early hours of Wednesday, 19 April, Tom Clarke arrived at his home in Richmond Road. He told his wife Kathleen about tonight's meeting of the Military Council, at which the wording for the Proclamation of the Republic had finally been agreed.

Clarke had been a nationalist activist since his teens, a nineteenth-century Fenian – believing the Empire wouldn't release its grip on Ireland without an armed fight. At age twenty-six he had been sentenced to jail, convicted of planning to blow up London Bridge. On release, after fifteen years, he went to the United States. He lived there for ten years and he and Kathleen married there. In 1907 he returned to Ireland, where he opened a tobacco shop in the centre of Dublin. Now, his record as an activist, and his selfless dedication to the cause, had won him a solid reputation among nationalists.

Pearse had this evening produced a draft version of

the Proclamation. The Military Council discussed and amended it. Clarke was the first of the men to sign. He initially refused that honour, but Tom MacDonagh praised the Fenian's courage and example to the younger men. 'No man will precede you with my consent.'

The Proclamation addressed 'Irishmen and Irish-women'. It took a stand with the suffragettes, endorsing 'the suffrages of all her men and women'. That was Connolly, a supporter of feminism. One of the seven signatories opposed the inclusion of equal opportunities and votes for women. Six of them supported it. Clarke told his wife which of the men had rejected the idea, but she would never reveal the name – other than to say it wasn't Tom.

On Holy Thursday, F Company paraded at Fr. Mathew Park and was addressed by Tom MacDonagh. He tried to prepare the rank-and-file Volunteers without telling them outright that they were within days of the rising. He spoke for longer than usual. The training manoeuvres that were to be held on Sunday were very important, he said. Any man who wasn't up for a fight should drop out now, and no one would think less of them. If you choose to fight, don't worry about your families. Our friends in America have provided sufficient funds to ensure they'll be looked after.

Tomorrow, he said, was Good Friday; Sunday was Easter, a time of resurgence.

When the parade finished, MacDonagh said he wanted to have a chat with Frank Henderson. The captain put him off – he had a couple of hours of company work to do. Would it be all right if . . .

Of course, said MacDonagh. Sure, we'll talk again.

They never did.

*

Even now there would be obstacles and setbacks, but nothing could stop the rising. The Citizen Army would throw two or three hundred people into the fight; there were perhaps three thousand Irish Volunteers around the country.

In the event, two-thirds of those Volunteers would not come out, due to conflict among their leaders and to lack of arms. Those who did come out would have few modern weapons. Some would carry old guns more dangerous to themselves than to the enemy.

Somewhere in Dublin, preparing to take on the Empire within the next few days, a Volunteer from Dublin's 4th Battalion was patiently improvising a bayonet. He drilled a single blade from a pair of garden shears, then banded and bolted it to his shotgun.

They were taking on tens of thousands of troops, many of them battle-hardened in an army experienced in suppressing opposition throughout the Empire. An army with unlimited access to modern rifles, machine guns and artillery.

Part Two

The politics that created F Company

3

Sean O'Casey was singing 'Herself and Myself', a gentle romantic song about an old couple dancing at the wedding of a young friend and recalling their own youth.

It was 1912, O'Casey was aged thirty-two. It would be another five years before he would begin writing plays, and eleven years before the Abbey Theatre would first accept one of his works – leading to his emergence as an internationally acclaimed writer. For now, he was Sean, the Dublin labourer with the perpetually sore eyes, enjoying himself at another social evening at the St Laurence O'Toole hurling club.

The club was named after a twelfth-century archbishop of Dublin, the songs sung there were of lost heroes and lost loves – 'Jackets Green' or 'The Old Rustic Bridge by the Mill'.

This apparently placid cultural moment was a tiny part of a political shift taking place within Ireland, and between Ireland and its imperial owner. The governance of Ireland had become an issue, after a century in which Ireland was administered arrogantly and disastrously. In 1841 there were six and a half million people on the island. Then came famine and its consequences. By 1911, starvation and flight had cut the population to just over three million.

The imperial government felt strongly about not interfering with the free market. And Irish farmers and merchants felt equally strongly about their right to sell to the highest bidder, regardless of the consequences. In the words of the Earl of Clarendon, Lord Lieutenant of Ireland: 'No-one could now venture to dispute the fact that Ireland had been sacrificed to the London corn-dealers . . . and that no distress would have occurred if the exportation of Irish grain had been prohibited.'

Every day, as people starved to death, shiploads of food left Irish ports.

For an age, Ireland had been held firmly within the Empire. The imperial power – despite its ideological hang-up about intervening in the free market – imposed oppressive controls on land; put limits on industrial and commercial development; suppressed political and administrative control; and responded with rigid and disastrous policies to the famines. In every aspect of government, what always counted was what best suited the interests and beliefs of those who ran the Empire.

By the end of the nineteenth century, the result was a battered, deferential country, annually paying extortionate amounts of tax to the Empire. According to Sir Robert Giffen, chief statistical adviser to the UK government, 'Ireland ought to pay about £3,500,000 and it pays nearly £7,000,000.'

Ireland was also submissive culturally – speaking the language of the Empire, playing its games, singing its songs, performing and listening to its music. The history taught in schools was history as seen by the Empire. The Irish had adopted the mindset of the colonized, in which subservience to a foreign monarch was the natural order of things.

The shift that was occurring in political attitudes would continue throughout the next decade, culminating in the wrenching of Ireland from the grasp of the British Empire, and the partition of the island into Catholic nationalist and Protestant unionist enclaves.

One of the strands in that shift in attitudes was cultural. As a counter to the culture of the Empire, there had been an upsurge of interest in Ireland's Gaelic past. The Gaelic League promoted the Irish language, music and dance. The Gaelic Athletic Association promoted native games. The Abbey Theatre promoted national drama, and would in time see the emergence of a generation of celebrated writers – including O'Casey, J. M. Synge, Lady Gregory and W. B. Yeats.

The St Laurence O'Toole club was run by the GAA. Like the great number of such clubs, it held social evenings to encourage interest in Irish culture, as well as concerts, dances and open-air festivals where a range of activities were staged.

Frank Henderson, the future captain of F Company, was master of ceremonies at the St Laurence O'Toole social club and a friend of Sean O'Casey's. He was aged twenty-six, a member of the GAA and the Gaelic League, an avid reader of the political newspapers that flowered in the atmosphere of Celtic revival.

Henderson shared with O'Casey a sympathy for the trade union efforts to reduce the squalor of working-class life. He flirted with socialist ideas: 'The common people were downtrodden at the time and under heavy oppression and there was no relief forthcoming but by uniting together and striking a blow against their bosses.'

But Henderson believed that breaking the imperial

bond was more important than socialism: 'political freedom was a better objective and to break the connection with English rule in Ireland.' Besides, someone told him socialists would never tolerate his devotion to Catholicism, so he drew back.

Politically, the shift in nationalist attitudes was dominated by the Irish Parliamentary Party – led by John Redmond MP. After campaigning for thirty years, the Irish Party had finally in 1912 got a Home Rule Bill enacted by the British parliament. It was due to be brought into effect within two years. This would set up an Irish parliament, with limited powers, within the Empire.

There was another strand of nationalism, stemming from the old Fenian tradition, which said the British would concede no real power without a fight. They would have to be kicked out.

Behind the scenes, the secretive Irish Republican Brotherhood was spreading the doctrine of physical force. The organization had been founded half a century earlier, among Irish emigrants in America, and had for several years been burrowing away covertly inside the nationalist cultural and political movement. By 1912 it had about 1,700 members in Ireland.

However, it wasn't the nationalists whose activities caused the Empire the most worry. Between 1912 and 1914 there was a real fear of conflict between the Empire and its loyal subjects in Ireland.

The violent events of 1912–16 would be driven largely by the unionists' preparations to resist Home Rule. Their resolute leader, Sir Edward Carson, a southern unionist, a widely respected lawyer with a successful practice in London, began organizing armed militias in 1912, with the explicit intent to resist the will of parliament. These eventually became the Ulster Volunteer Force. Having fought and lost their case politically, the unionists threatened civil war rather than allow the UK government to implement parliament's Home Rule legislation.

Like Patrick Pearse would later do, Carson presided over a Military Council. By the summer of 1914, he and his comrades had formally constituted a provisional government.

The British establishment didn't seek to put down this incipient rebellion. They were deeply respectful of the upper-class figures involved. Treasonous British Army officers at the Curragh camp warned that they would not obey any order to act against the unionists, and were treated respectfully by the authorities.

Imitating the example of the unionists, nationalists held a rally in Dublin and set up the Irish Volunteers. They armed themselves as best they could and engaged in intensive training. The Empire's toleration of Carson's seditious forces now made it difficult for the British to act aggressively against the Irish Volunteers.

The titular head of the Volunteers was Professor Eoin MacNeill, from University College Dublin, an academic specializing in early and medieval Irish history. Behind the scenes, the IRB subtly nudged here and pushed there – a quiet word, a planted idea.

Like the unionists, the Volunteers bought guns in Germany. The Kaiser's people, anticipating war with the United Kingdom, hoped that by providing weapons to both sides they might create an Irish civil war that would distract the British.

Frank Henderson and his brother Leo were involved in organizing the rally that saw the creation of the Volunteers. They enlisted in B Company, 2nd Battalion, Dublin Brigade. The 2nd Battalion training ground at Fr. Mathew

Park was just across the road from their home at Windsor Villas.

Sean O'Casey was a member of the IRB. He approached Frank Henderson and invited him to join. This was an honour, a sign of trust and high regard by the hidden inner circle of Irish nationalism.

Frank's brother Leo – seven years younger – was already a member of the IRB, but Frank was not. He thought about it for a week, then said no. On the one hand he believed that there would never be an effective rebellion against the Empire unless there was some secretive body working away in the background – an open organization would be prey to spies and informers. However, the Catholic bishops had issued a Pastoral letter in which they ruled that it was sinful for Catholics to join secret, oath-bound societies. Frank's nationalism clashed with his strong Catholic beliefs, and his deep religious commitment won out.

Charlie Saurin and his friend Arthur Shields had grown up together on Vernon Terrace, Clontarf, a few doors away from one another. Saurin was a student. Shields, who attended Maguire's Business College, had just begun a career as an actor with the Abbey Theatre. They had young men's interests, and they didn't get involved in politics.

Oscar Traynor was a professional footballer. Born in Dublin, he played in goal for Belfast Celtic, a highly successful club. After the team won the inaugural Gold Cup and Charity Cup in 1911/12, they toured Europe, winning five of six matches in Prague, and drawing the sixth.

Although inclined towards separatism, Traynor wasn't too enthusiastic about the nationalist organizations of the

day, and his job as a footballer kept him too busy to get
involved.

Harry Colley, a young man who worked as a rate
collector, was interested in politics but he had a slight
hearing defect that made it difficult for him to hear the
orders during drilling sessions, so after a brief time in the
Volunteers he dropped out.

When Carson's unionists brought twenty-five thousand
rifles ashore at Larne in April 1914, the British authorities turned a blind eye.

Three months later, the Irish Volunteers brought
nine hundred ancient Mauser rifles ashore at Howth. A
detachment of the King's Own Scottish Borderers tried
but failed to confiscate the guns and were jeered by a
nationalist crowd at Bachelors Walk in the centre of
Dublin. The soldiers shot dead three unarmed civilians
and wounded thirty-eight.

The lesson was plain – unionists could organize and
arm to resist parliament, with no comeback. Nationalists
organized and their supporters got shot. The killings
sent a storm of rage through nationalist Ireland, and the
Volunteers recruited in large numbers.

Among those recruited in the wake of the killings at
Bachelors Walk were Charlie Saurin, Arthur Shields,
Oscar Traynor and Harry Colley. Saurin and Shields were
then eighteen, Traynor was ten years older, Colley was
twenty-three. Charlie Saurin's younger brother Frank,
aged thirteen, joined the Fianna, a kind of nationalist
Boy Scouts.

Soon the Volunteers numbered about 180,000. It became such a significant force that John Redmond, head
of the Irish Party, used his clout to demand a leadership
role.

Dublin's 2nd Battalion now had A, B, C, D and E

companies. B Company had so many members it was split in two, and the new unit was designated F Company. It was based around the Fairview–North Strand–Ballybough area of the city, but some members of the company lived in Clontarf, others as far away as Dollymount.

Charlie Saurin, Arthur Shields, Oscar Traynor and Harry Colley ended up in F Company, with Frank Henderson. As Henderson moved up the ranks to become captain of the company, Oscar Traynor moved up to become lieutenant.

In a society in which duties and rights were strictly divided by gender, nationalist men who wanted to get involved joined the Volunteers. Boys joined the Fianna. And women joined Cumann na mBan (the Women's Association). The Irish Citizen Army was alone in not being segregated.

The Irish Citizen Army grew out of the 1913 Lockout, when Dublin employers tried to break the trade unions and the unions fought back by withdrawing their labour, in sympathetic strikes. The Dublin Metropolitan Police acted as the employers' enforcers, swinging batons, breaking heads, occasionally killing strikers. The Citizen Army started as a protective force. Then, under union leader James Connolly, it became a potential insurrectionary army.

It and the Volunteers were at first belligerent, then wary, then cooperative. At a recent *aeridheacht* – open-air festival – at Pearse's school in Rathfarnham, the Citizen Army had twice beaten the Volunteers in drilling competitions. It was smaller than the Volunteers, but it trained just as intensely and many of its members were considerably tougher.

Vincent Poole, for example. Aged thirty-six, he was

a hard, experienced man from Dublin's inner city. He'd been in the British Army, fighting against the Boers. Once out of the army, back home in 1910, he'd found work with Dublin Corporation, in the sewers beneath the city, at a wage of £1 a week.

Mature, seasoned, Vincent Poole was aware of the place assigned to him as a subject of the Empire. He was also aware of his place as a working-class man in a city where the Lockout resulted in a victory for the employers, who were unsparing in the cruelty of their conquest. It was inevitable that he would join the Citizen Army. He was made a captain. His brothers Kit, Patrick and John also joined.

He was small, about five foot three, but he knew how to look after himself. 'Truculent' was a word applied to Vincent. Some preferred 'irascible'. Quick to take offence, fond of a drink, he had eighteen criminal convictions. The last one was in 1915, when he got into trouble at a British Army recruitment meeting outside the Custom House. He got six months for making 'statements prejudicial to the recruitment of His Majesty's forces'.

A few months before the rising, Poole's truculence led to a row and he left the Citizen Army – whether he was kicked out or left by agreement is unclear. Sometime before the rising he rejoined, still as a captain.

While the Citizen Army was born out of class conflict – and James Connolly saw the rising as a first step towards a social revolution – the political leanings of the Irish Volunteers were diverse. Frank Henderson, for instance, detested the foul conditions people had to endure in the tenements. He admired the likes of Connolly, Jim Larkin and Bill O'Brien, who led the trade union fightback. Other Volunteers, such as William Cosgrave – future founder and leader of Fine Gael – were far over to the right. In between, there were all kinds of views.

Dublin had become a place of riches and slums. Famine had driven the starving to the city, in search of shelter, food and work. As the decades passed, the prosperous middle classes moved to independently governed townships like Rathmines, Pembroke and Rathgar, where they didn't have to pay municipal rates for the upkeep of such facilities as hospitals and workhouses. The old Georgian mansions they left behind decayed and were bought up cheaply by landlords. Hungry for multiple rents, the landlords subdivided the tenements into tiny rooms and rented them to families desperate for shelter – a family per room. Dozens of people lived in each tenement – houses once the homes of single families. There was usually one foul toilet in the back yard, shared by everyone in the house. The yard also had a single tap to provide water to all.

Thirty per cent of Dubliners lived in the slums, where damp oozed from the walls, and poisonous fumes seeped into basements from sewage pipes. About twelve thousand people per year died of the tuberculosis that raged through the over-crowded tenements.

The slums provided a reserve army of cheap and eager labour, which could be hired and discarded as required, despite the efforts of the trade unions to improve conditions.

The steadily growing nationalist movement had little to say about such social squalor. There were some among the nationalists who spoke movingly of their desire for Irish freedom and who at the same time benefited, as landlords or as employers of cheap labour, from relentlessly oppressing their fellow Irish people.

There was little agreement – or even debate – on what shape Irish freedom would take. The assumption was that the creation of an Irish parliament – whether within the Empire, under Home Rule, or after complete separation – would constitute freedom. The gross inequality that resulted in the slums was to many within nationalism as natural as the rising and setting of the sun.

Meanwhile, there were global political forces at play, and they were about to tear apart the Irish Volunteer movement.

4

Within days of the gun-running at Howth, the Great War started. Soon, there would be a continent-wide bloodbath as empires sought to preserve their territories, alliances and the spoils of imperialism.

John Redmond and the Irish Party rowed in behind the British government recruitment campaign. About two hundred thousand Irish men would go to fight the Germans, many of them from the slums, many of them at the urging of Redmond.

Redmond and his party believed in defending the Empire, but even had they not felt that way they had little choice. They were committed to Home Rule, and any position other than urging their supporters to fight for the Empire would have killed the Home Rule project.

As it was, Home Rule was formally put on hold for the duration of the war.

The Volunteers split. About 170,000 went with Redmond into what was called the National Volunteers, and about 11,000 stayed with the Irish Volunteers. The issue was decided at meetings of the rank and file. When the discussion ended, the Volunteers went to different sides of the room, voting with their feet. Men shed tears as friends took opposing sides.

Of the hundred or so members of F Company, about sixty went with Redmond and forty stayed. And, as time went by, many of those forty drifted away, some joining Redmond's outfit. At one stage F Company was down to a dozen men or fewer. Among them were Frank Henderson, Charlie Saurin, Arthur Shields, Harry Colley, Harry Boland, Seamus Daly, Michael McDonnell, Frank Murtagh, Jim Slattery and Oscar Traynor. Around this nucleus, F Company would have to gradually build anew.

The IRB now had a much smaller Volunteer organization within which to work, but a more cohesive, single-minded outfit, committed to Irish separatism. And it was more easily manipulated. Immediately, the IRB Military Council resolved that before this war ended – and no one thought it would last four years – the Brotherhood would launch an insurrection. Joe Plunkett was given the job of drawing up detailed military plans for a rising.

Frank Henderson was for a second time invited to join the IRB. Again, his religious conviction against secret oath-bound societies led him to say no.

By 1916, the expectations of a rebellion were high. Patrick Pearse announced plans for training manoeuvres on Easter Sunday and many with IRB connections expected the rising to be triggered by those manoeuvres.

Sir Roger Casement, knighted for his humanitarian work exposing the effects of colonialism in Africa, was now in Germany seeking guns for a rising. The IRB had bought another twenty thousand rifles from Germany, and they were scheduled to arrive by boat off the coast of Kerry at Easter. James Connolly had been taken on to the Military Council, and the Volunteers were now working with the Citizen Army – Liberty Hall had become the hub of preparation.

On Thursday of Easter Week, three days before the

expected rising, Frank Henderson was at home at Windsor Villas when Volunteer Michael O'Hanrahan came visiting. He, like Frank's brother Leo, was a member of the IRB.

'Well, Michael,' Frank asked, 'are we going out on Sunday and not coming back again?'

'Yes, we're going out,' O'Hanrahan answered. 'And not coming back.'

The following evening, Good Friday, young Charlie Saurin was helping Seamus Daly, also from F Company, a fitter, make primitive bombs at the house where Daly lived, on the seafront down in Clontarf. They had been at it most of the week. Daly, a dozen years older, was in the IRB. He confided in Saurin that the Sunday manoeuvres would be 'the real thing'. The exercise would begin at 3pm and the rising would kick off at 6pm.

Saurin's friend Arthur Shields was in England, touring with the Abbey Theatre. He was due back on Sunday morning, just in time for the manoeuvres.

On Saturday, Harry Colley had some business in Summerhill and he separately bumped into two F Company men, Matty Parnell and Paddy Mahon.

Everyone's saying it's tomorrow, Matty told him.

Is tomorrow the day, do you think? Harry asked Paddy Mahon.

Yes, Paddy said, tomorrow is indeed 'der tag'.

That morning, Patrick Pearse and his brother Willie went to Dominick Street church. They went up to the altar rail and asked an altar boy to get a priest. A Fr Ryan came out and spoke with them.

Further down the church, Volunteer Sean Price, waiting to attend Confession, watched as Patrick seemed to argue with the priest. After a while, the priest went into the sacristy and returned with a chalice. He gave them both Communion and the two men left.

*

Even as individual Volunteers prepared for the day and Pearse put his soul in order, divisions within the leadership of the Volunteers – unknown to the rank and file – were in the process of aborting the rising.

That Saturday evening, after F Company had completed a drill session at Fr. Mathew Park, Captain Frank Henderson took Lieutenant Oscar Traynor aside.

'Do you know anything?' Henderson asked.

'I know there's going to be trouble, but that's all I know.' Traynor was a member of the IRB, but not a senior one.

Henderson said, 'There's going to be an insurrection tomorrow.'

'Are you sure of that?'

'I'm certain of it.'

The headquarters staff is split, Henderson said. 'Some are in favour of the rising and some are against it. And it may be necessary to arrest some of the members of the staff.'

'An extraordinary state of affairs,' said Traynor. 'Do you know what Pearse's attitude is?'

'Strongly in favour.'

Traynor said, 'That's good enough for me.'

Liberty Hall was so crowded that someone pasted a notice on the stairs: 'Please Keep to the Right'.

As he prepared to sleep, James Connolly gave strict instructions that under no circumstances should he be woken. It might, he said, be the last night's sleep he'd ever have.

5

Bulmer Hobson was a major figure within the IRB. He'd been a member since 1904 and served on its Supreme Council. He'd helped found the Irish Volunteers and he'd played a key role in organizing the Howth gun-running.

And, now, as the rising approached, he was an outsider.

When John Redmond and the Irish Party had demanded control of the Irish Volunteers, Hobson wanted to avoid splitting the movement, so he gave in and supported Redmond. For this, Clarke, Pearse and the other IRB leaders considered him a traitor to the Brotherhood.

As April 1916 approached, and rumours multiplied, Hobson concluded the hardliners were about to launch an insurrection. He believed it would be a disaster – there simply wasn't any way that a poorly armed force of three thousand or so Volunteers could shift the British Empire.

Hobson wasn't against armed action – he believed the Volunteers could use arms to resist conscription of Irish men to fight the Empire's Great War. Or to defend themselves in the event of a state crackdown. He believed that when the Volunteers had grown in numbers and in arms they might legitimately fight a revolutionary war that would wear the enemy down. Such a war would be fought using guerrilla tactics.

To stage a set-piece insurrection, taking buildings and waiting for a greatly more powerful enemy to attack, was, Hobson believed, madness. He suspected that people like Pearse were infatuated with the need to go down in history as having given their all for Ireland. In a recent speech, without naming anyone, Hobson had damned the blood-sacrifice faction: 'No man has a right to risk the fortunes of the country in order to create for himself a niche in history.'

Hobson's views were largely shared by other Volunteer leaders, such as Eoin MacNeill and Michael O'Rahilly.

For the Pearse faction – including Tom Clarke, Sean MacDermott and Tom MacDonagh – the rising had two aims. The first – almost certain to fail – was that of removing the British. They knew the Volunteers couldn't hold Dublin for long. Plans for an insurrection outside Dublin were hazy. They had vague ideas of retreating to the countryside to continue the fight, but victory was extremely unlikely.

The second aim was perhaps achievable. The rising would challenge the anglicized state of mind that dominated the country – one that accepted that the natural order of things was that Ireland was forever a subservient colony, to be used according to the needs of the Empire.

To change this state of mind they were ready to give their lives. The Hobson faction believed it wasn't just a waste of life, but a squandering of the movement that had been built up, and which in time might have a reasonable chance to achieve more.

Apart from figuring out how best to take on the Empire, the seven men on the Military Council had to prepare to deal with those within the movement who would oppose the rising. Without the support of Professor Eoin MacNeill, the rebellion would be undermined. And, if Bulmer Hobson was available to stiffen MacNeill's backbone, the whole thing could collapse all the more quickly.

The solution was simple: lie to MacNeill and kidnap Hobson.

It was probable that Joe Plunkett forged what became known as the Castle Document. There may have been a contingency document, drawn up by the British, indicating likely targets if it was ever decided to crack down on the drilling and parading of the nationalists. It would have been negligent had there not been such a document. If one didn't exist, Plunkett and his chums invented it; if it did exist, they – in a phrase that would be used in a later generation – sexed it up.

The cover story was that a nationalist sympathizer read the document in the Castle and decoded it, and gave it to the IRB, and they printed it. The Castle Document, which the forgers called 'this dastardly plan', listed anyone even vaguely related to nationalism – including the Catholic bishops – and marked them for arrest. It said the arrests were imminent.

This was brought to MacNeill, who immediately fell for it. He equipped himself with a revolver, for when the British came to take him.

Luckily, the IRB told him, the Volunteers are due to mount manoeuvres this Sunday.

And, as it happens, we've got twenty thousand rifles coming in off the Kerry coast at the weekend.

And we also have a strategic plan for taking the centre of Dublin.

Throw in with us, before the British sweep the lot of us into jail – or watch the Volunteers become another in the long list of failed nationalist projects.

MacNeill committed himself to the rising.

Friday afternoon, Bulmer Hobson was called to a meeting in a house at Cabra Park, the home of Volunteer Martin Conlon. When he arrived, the IRB arrested him.

Later that day, the plan went off the rails. The British captured the ship with the twenty thousand rifles. The German captain scuppered it before it could be towed to port.

MacNeill panicked. The rising was off, he said. Without the rifles, the Volunteers hadn't a chance.

The IRB, though, was determined to press on. Neither faction managed to convince the other. The result was chaos.

When Michael O'Rahilly found out that Hobson had been kidnapped he drew a gun on Pearse, who convinced him to put it away. Hobson, Pearse claimed, had exceeded his authority.

MacNeill tried to get other Volunteers to persuade Pearse and his allies to change course, but that went nowhere. Eventually, he despatched emissaries – including O'Rahilly – to bring orders down the country, calling off the manoeuvres. He put a notice in the *Sunday Independent* to that effect.

6

Easter Sunday morning, Captain Frank Henderson returned home from eight o'clock Mass and sat down to breakfast. A member of F Company, Conway McGinn, arrived at the house. 'Have you seen this?'

He showed Henderson the *Sunday Independent*, with the notice from Professor MacNeill cancelling the Volunteer manoeuvres.

Henderson had seen the announcement. He'd also had a note from a local priest, asking him to obey MacNeill's cancellation. He was uncertain how to respond. He respected MacNeill, but was used to responding to orders through the chain of command.

Volunteer Harry Colley arrived at the Henderson house. He'd been coming from Mass and had bought the newspaper and read MacNeill's notice.

What's this about?

Henderson said he was waiting for exact instructions. It was best if Colley went home and stood to arms. Wait for orders.

Less than two miles away, in Parnell Square, hundreds of Volunteers had mobilized and paraded, awaiting orders to launch the rising. A young man bearing despatches arrived and the Volunteers were dismissed and sent home.

*

At his home at 6 Vernon Terrace, Clontarf, Charlie Saurin read the MacNeill order in the *Sunday Independent*, but he wanted to check things out for himself. Sometime before noon he went along to Fr. Mathew Park. His brother Frank insisted on going too.

Charlie met Captain Frank Henderson at the park and asked him what was happening.

I don't know, Henderson said. We stay close to home, we wait to be mobilized, if that's what's going to happen.

Charlie had a nagging worry. His brother Frank was fifteen. Anytime twenty-year-old Charlie got his equipment together and set out for a parade, a manoeuvre or a meeting, young Frank insisted on coming along. Frank had been in the Fianna since he was thirteen. A week ago he'd transferred to F Company. Charlie didn't want him involved in any fighting and he asked Henderson to keep the lad out of the action. Henderson agreed to warn him off.

Matt Stafford, an old Fenian, turned up at Fr. Mathew Park, ready for whatever the day would bring. Almost fifty years earlier, as a boy, Matt had answered the call during the half-cocked 1867 rising. Now, a member of 2nd Battalion, he was told to stand to arms.

Nora O'Daly of Cumann na mBan, married to Seamus Daly of F Company, arrived at the park convinced the cancellation was a hoax. O'Daly had been involved in the Howth gun-running – where she collected and saved eight rifles. At Fr. Mathew Park, she found Frank Henderson and asked him if it was true the manoeuvres had been called off, or was it a hoax? He told her it was no hoax.

Lieutenant Oscar Traynor read MacNeill's statement in the *Sunday Independent* and immediately went to Fr.

Mathew Park. Watching the Volunteers come and go, with no purpose, no certainty, little semblance of military discipline, he despaired.

Bordering on chaos, he concluded.

The leaders of the insurrection responded to MacNeill's order according to their personalities. Sean MacDermott displayed a cold, controlled fury. Constance Markievicz promised to shoot MacNeill on sight. Commandant Thomas Hunter of 2nd Battalion threw his arms around a friend, Marie Perolz. He said, 'We're fooled again' and burst into tears.

James Connolly was putting on a brave face. When he got word of the cancellation tears ran down his cheeks. The last few years had been tough. The wearying Lock-out, the despair when so many workers abandoned their own interests and rushed to obey the war cries of the clashing empires. And now – the infighting among the Irish nationalists.

Some within the Citizen Army got the impression that Connolly, frustrated by the nationalists and their dis-array, was about to order that day a rising of just his own tiny army.

Volunteer Michael Cremen heard that Pearse was attending Mass at the Jesuit church in Gardiner Street. He went there, found him and asked him if this *Sunday Independent* notice was bogus. Was it a British ruse?

No, Pearse said. It's genuine, MacNeill's work.

Although stunned that what he'd worked for had fallen apart before it began, Pearse was planning a response. You'll have further orders later on, he told Cremen.

After Mass, Pearse went to Liberty Hall, to the meeting of the Military Council he'd already arranged. There, they examined the arguments for and against proceeding with the rising. If they went ahead, might not the British, alerted by MacNeill's intervention, be expecting a rebellion? Or, might the British – following MacNeill's cancellation – be assuming all was quiet?

The argument that could not be trumped was the bluntest of them all – it's now or never.

Trusted Volunteers received despatches from Pearse that said: 'Postponed until twelve o'clock tomorrow'.

That Sunday evening, Claire Cregan, fiancée of Bulmer Hobson, called to Liberty Hall, where the Military Council was meeting. She asked did anyone know where Bulmer was. She hadn't seen him since Friday.

No, they shook their heads, no idea.

She turned to John MacDonagh, Tom's brother, and asked him did he know anything.

Behind her back, Diarmuid Lynch, a member of the IRB Supreme Council, put a finger to his lips.

John MacDonagh said no, he had no information on Bulmer.

The guards at Cabra Park had to call for help in dealing with Bulmer Hobson. He was getting troublesome, noisy. Volunteer Maurice Collins warned him to calm down, to stay quiet. It was clear the tension was getting to the captive.

That evening, and into the night, the Military Council talked through the possibilities. MacNeill's intervention had ensured that the turnout would be smaller than planned – the scale of the rising had to be adjusted; some of the buildings they intended to occupy would now have to be forgone. The chances of a national rising were reduced – they had no way of knowing how many

Volunteers would obey MacNeill and how many would come out.

And the twenty thousand rifles at the bottom of the Atlantic left them desperately short of weapons.

Nevertheless, the Volunteers, the Citizen Army and Cumann na mBan were designated to be a single body – the Irish Republican Army – and the rising was set for noon on Easter Monday.

Tom MacDonagh hurried home and said goodbye to his family. His son Donagh didn't wake from his sleep. His daughter Barbara reached up and hugged him.

Part Three

The scrap begins

7

Captain Frank Henderson finally slept. It was past six o'clock on the morning of the rising and he'd spent the night supervising the Volunteer shifts guarding Fr. Mathew Park – in case of raid or theft. The park's pavilion held the arms and ammunition accumulated over years.

He was just drifting into sleep when he was woken. Commandant Thomas Hunter wanted to know if F Company could provide eight or nine cyclist scouts. No, Henderson said, the company had only two available. He went back to sleep.

Hunter, second in command of 2nd Battalion, was trying to improvise. The plan to launch the rising out of Sunday's manoeuvres was dead. There were fewer Volunteers available, objectives had to be changed, the scale of the rising had to be reduced, resources had to be assessed and allocated on the run. Hunter was sending as many cycle scouts as he could find to rouse and mobilize Volunteers.

A couple of hours later Frank Henderson was woken again. A message from Commandant Hunter. He wanted F Company assembled in St Stephens Green by 10am.

Henderson sought out Hunter and told him it wasn't

possible. It was already around 9am – the mobilization mechanism had to inform all members of F Company of Hunter's orders, those Volunteers had to ready themselves, make their way to Fr. Mathew Park, then cross to the far side of the city – all in the space of an hour.

'Do your best,' Commandant Hunter said, 'and get as many men as you can.'

Frank Henderson set off for the home of Volunteer John McQuaid. McQuaid was F Company's 'pivot', a central role in mobilizing Volunteers in a city where phones were a luxury.

Having alerted Sergeant McQuaid, Henderson dropped in to his own home, to freshen up after spending most of the night awake. On his way, crossing Ballybough Bridge, a preoccupied Tom Clarke passed Henderson without acknowledgement. The old Fenian was walking to Liberty Hall, from where the rising would be launched.

Meanwhile, Frank Henderson's brother Leo, just promoted from lieutenant to captain of B Company, was at Amiens Street railway station with a case of ammunition. There he met Cathleen Ryan. The Ryan family, from Clonliffe Road, were staunch supporters of the Volunteers. Some of the Howth rifles had been hidden in their house. That morning, two of Cathleen's sisters were up near the Magazine Fort, in the Phoenix Park, counting British soldiers going in and out.

Leo had a rail ticket ready for Cathleen. He put her on the nine o'clock train for Omagh and shoved the case of ammunition under her seat. When you get to Omagh station, he told her, go to Baxter's Hotel. The boys will be there, waiting for you.

If anyone asks you where you're going, he said, you're going north to take up a position as a priest's housekeeper.

Cathleen Ryan was fifteen. She usually wore her hair in two long plaits. That morning her mother had tucked them around her ears, using hairpins, so she looked a little older.

Charlie Saurin had just finished breakfast when his mobilization order arrived. He put on his uniform, ammunition pouches, full pack and water bottle. He was armed with a Martini-Henry single-shot rifle and a sword bayonet. He had just twenty-eight rounds of ammunition for the rifle and about thirty rounds for his .38 revolver. He also wore a large sheath knife on his belt.

Saurin left the house, and to his irritation his young brother Frank tagged along.

After some rainy weather, Easter Monday was a lovely day, with strong sunshine and a clear blue sky.

In the city centre, inside Liberty Hall, Joe Plunkett had arrived for a meeting of the Military Council. Plunkett was frail, his health wrecked by tuberculosis, a bandage concealing an open wound on his throat following an operation. He was accompanied by two men of very different sensibilities.

Volunteer Michael Collins was twenty-six and from Cork. The previous year he'd moved back to Ireland from London, where he had been working – and where he had become a member of the IRB. He'd quickly gained a reputation as an organizer and was now an aide to Plunkett.

Volunteer William Brennan-Whitmore, from Enniscorthy, in Wexford, was a former sergeant in the British Army, who had served in India and left the army in 1907. Such people were treasured for their experience – a number of ex-British Army personnel, and some

American ex-soldiers, provided the Volunteers with valuable training.

Brennan-Whitmore was a controversial figure, with a unique talent for rubbing people up the wrong way. He had written an unpublished textbook on street fighting. Joe Plunkett read it and asked him to come to Dublin as an aide to the HQ staff.

Among his other writings was a piece in a publication called *An Gael*, published two months before the rising, which warned that Irish Catholicism was under threat from Jews and Freemasons.

Brennan-Whitmore arrived in Dublin on Good Friday, just two days before the scheduled rising. He had been officer commanding the Enniscorthy Volunteers until recently, when he resigned following a clash with brigade staff in Wexford. The clash arose from the fact that Volunteers in Enniscorthy were fond of going to dances. In those days, you took what few pleasures were available. Work, for many – if they had it – was usually backbreaking and poorly paid. Somewhere between the religious duties of Sodality on Thursday, fish on Friday, Confession on Saturday and Mass on Sunday you might get in a bit of dancing.

Brennan-Whitmore, however, reckoned the Volunteers should give up the dancing and save their money to buy weapons and equipment. He wanted to take disciplinary action against those who refused. When he lost out in the ensuing row, with a brigade staff less committed to austere living, he resigned as officer commanding.

Now, his supposed talents as a military strategist had given him access to the leaders at the heart of the rebellion. He and Collins helped the ailing Plunkett climb the stairs to an attic room.

While Plunkett joined Pearse and Connolly in the

room, Brennan-Whitmore was left outside. After a moment, Pearse emerged and shook Brennan-Whitmore's hand, then invited him in.

Plunkett was taking a seat, chatting with the others.

Brennan-Whitmore looked around the attic room. There was a stack of posters on a table and he glanced at the top one. It was the Proclamation of the Republic, to be delivered today, by Pearse, at the GPO. It had been printed just the previous night, with some difficulty. The printers were short of fonts, and had to improvise. They didn't have enough Es, so they used sealing wax to make Fs into Es.

Brennan-Whitmore turned the poster around so that he could more easily read it. He read the lines of the first paragraph, which spoke of Ireland, God and the dead generations, about summoning the nation's children to the flag.

It was the second paragraph that galvanized him. 'Having organised and trained her manhood through her secret revolutionary organisation, the Irish Republican Brotherhood . . .'

He stared at the poster, startled and frozen.

'. . . and through her open military organisations, the Irish Volunteers and the Irish Citizen Army . . .'

For so long, Brennan-Whitmore, a member of Sinn Fein, had argued in public speeches and in articles that the Irish Volunteers would succeed where other organizations had failed. And it would succeed because it was an open body that declared its policies, without a secret organization working away in the background.

He sat there, shocked by the reality behind his own rhetoric.

8

Having stopped by his home for a short time, Captain Frank Henderson came back to Fr. Mathew Park. About half the available members of 2nd Battalion, including a number from F Company, crossed the city to Jacob's factory, under Commandant Thomas Hunter.

Those who were left would stay at the park to guard the battalion's arms and munitions, in case of a police raid. What they would do after that was left hazy. Out of touch with the rising's leaders, without transport for the arms, the officers of 2nd Battalion were operating on the blind.

Volunteers were still coming into Fr. Mathew Park. Around 10.30am, Arthur Shields, the Abbey Theatre actor, just back from the tour of England, arrived. When Arthur was a baby a doting aunt remarked, 'Doesn't he look the little boss', and from then on, to family and friends – and to his fellow members of F Company – he was Boss Shields.

He asked Frank Henderson for permission to go to the Abbey: he had to check if he was needed for a matinee that afternoon.

Shields also wanted to collect a rifle he'd hidden under the Abbey stage.

Having been given permission, he left the park and met his friend Charlie Saurin on Philipsburg Avenue, on the way to report for duty.

Charlie's young brother Frank was still tagging along. Charlie and Matty Parnell were assigned to a sentry position, on a raised bank with a view of one of the gateways to the park. Other rank and file were assigned to cover other gates. Charlie and Matty took the opportunity to have a stretch on the grass, enjoying the April sunshine.

Meanwhile, Frank Henderson again gave young Frank Saurin a direct order to go home, and the boy left the park.

On the other side of the city, at St Stephens Green, another Irish Volunteer officer spotted another eager youngster. What was Vinny Byrne doing here? He was a child. Lieutenant Jimmy Shiels intercepted the boy.

Where are you going?

I'm going on parade, sir, Vinny Byrne said. I've been mobilized.

You'd better go home, young Byrne, Lieutenant Shiels said. Vinny's protests couldn't persuade him to withdraw the order.

Making his way reluctantly down Grafton Street, the fifteen-year-old Vinny felt emotion welling up.

He'd been a member of E Company, 2nd Battalion, Dublin Brigade, for the past fifteen months. Parading, training, drilling. Vinny attended James Connolly's lectures on street fighting. He went to Dr Kathleen Lynn's classes in first aid. Always preparing for the day when the Volunteers would rise up against the Empire. Now, on a day when something seemed to be happening, he was being treated as a child.

Slowly moving down Grafton Street, the boy began to cry.

*

While youngsters sought to join in whatever military action was on the cards, an old man sat in his home on Drumcondra Road, waiting for orders. He had a responsible position, knew the importance of military discipline and needed to be where his captain could reach him.

Matt Stafford, the Fenian who had been out in the failed rising of 1867, was in his mid-sixties. As a member of B Company, 2nd Battalion, Dublin Brigade, Matt trained with the others, but on one occasion, as the Volunteers were moving at the double around the training ground at Fr. Mathew Park, he fell out of the ranks, physically unable to continue the demanding drill. Other Volunteers marvelled at the determination of the old Fenian to stay active.

On Monday, Matt Stafford was working. When he learned from his son Jack, at around 3pm, that the Volunteers were mobilizing he quit work – he was self-employed – and went home to await orders. He had a total of £29.17 shillings of company money. In the event of action there would be calls on those funds – for food, blankets, ammunition, whatever.

Matt Stafford would stay at his home in Drumcondra throughout the day, primed to respond to orders. Only the well-off had phones; there were no radio stations. Whatever urge Matt had to leave the house and find out what was happening, his duty was to be available in case the company needed access to funds. He sat and he waited.

On his way down Grafton Street, visibly upset, fifteen-year-old Vinny Byrne met Mick Colgan, a section commander from E Company. Mick asked him what was wrong.

Vinny said that Lieutenant Shiels had told him to go home. He was too young.

Mick Colgan didn't approve. 'Come along out of that, and don't mind him,' he said. He brought Vinny back up to Stephens Green, where someone handed the boy a .22 rifle and he joined the rest of his company as they paraded.

It was almost noon. Some members of the Citizen Army had taken up positions. Vinny heard one of them shout out through the railings of the Green: 'Now or never, boys!'

The excitement among the ranks was bubbling. Vinny turned to Joe Doyle, from B Company. What's going on?

'There's a scrap on now,' Doyle said.

The rebels closed the gates of the park and ushered civilians away.

After a while, Commandant Thomas Hunter came along and inspected the troops. B Company formed up alongside other members of 2nd Battalion, including members of F Company. On command, young Vinny Byrne and his comrades began to march. The destination was Jacob's biscuit factory in Bishop Street.

As they left, Volunteers and members of the Irish Citizen Army were digging trenches in Stephens Green.

9

Down at Liberty Hall, James Connolly was handing out revolvers to women members of the Citizen Army. Some of the women weren't experienced with weapons. 'Don't use them except in the last resort,' Connolly said.

Helena Molony had her own revolver. Connolly told her, 'You go with Sean,' indicating Captain Sean Connolly. Molony and Sean Connolly were old friends and had acted together at the Abbey Theatre. Molony knew the rising was on, but she had no idea where they were going.

Boss Shields was supposed to return to Fr. Mathew Park and report back to F Company. Having gone to the Abbey Theatre and retrieved his rifle from under the stage, he reckoned it was too late to go back to Fairview – F Company would surely have left there by now. So, he arrived instead at Liberty Hall and introduced himself to James Connolly.

'If you're as good a man as your father, you'll be all right,' Connolly said.

Adolphus Shields was a composer, long part of the trade union struggle. Twenty years earlier, he had been a leading activist in the fight for the eight-hour working day.

Boss Shields found himself in the group of rebels assigned to take over the GPO.

James Connolly and the other leaders went upstairs to room No. 7. Armed with his rifle, Citizen Army man Jimmy O'Shea guarded the door. This was the final meeting of the leaders, about an hour or so before the rising was to start. O'Shea was told there were to be no interruptions – and if anything drastic happened, like someone rushing the door to the room, his orders were to shoot.

Shortly afterwards, a well-dressed young woman came down the passage towards the door. O'Shea stopped her at bayonet point and asked her business. She said she had to see James Connolly.

He's engaged, I'm sorry, that's not possible.

Please, she begged, please.

No, O'Shea repeated, it wasn't possible.

She burst into tears. She said she had to see someone. She was desperate.

Bulmer Hobson, she told him, is my fiancé. He's disappeared. He's been arrested by our people, our army – your army – and he's going to be put to death. Just one second is enough, she said – one second, they all know me – I know them, one second, to ask them.

Jimmy O'Shea saw himself as a hardened revolutionary. Claire Cregan saw him as a boy. She pressed on, demanding, imploring.

Eventually, moved by her distress, O'Shea said okay, he'd pass a message in. But she had to go back down to the end of the passage and stay there.

She said yes, she would, and she showered blessings on him.

O'Shea knocked on the door and an irritated James

Connolly answered. No interruptions, he said – but a frantic Claire Cregan was already rushing back down the passage to the door.

Where's Bulmer, what's to happen to him?

Connolly said he didn't know where Hobson was.

'You know he's been arrested?'

Yes, Connolly said.

'Why was he arrested? Was he not a perfectly honest man?'

He might have interfered with the plans for a rising, Connolly said. He seemed surly, spoke grudgingly.

'Pearse might know something about it, will you send him out to me?'

Cregan wouldn't go away until Pearse came out. When he did he was kind to her and concerned, but just as uninformative. She insisted on seeing Sean MacDermott – it was Bulmer who had brought Sean MacDermott to Dublin; they'd known each other a long time. He and Bulmer had together seen Tom Clarke as a father figure.

MacDermott came out. He was sympathetic and assured Cregan that Bulmer was safe. No need to worry. He took her by the arm affectionately and told her they knew Bulmer was a man of integrity.

Bulmer had long thought MacDermott was slippery. Now, Claire saw only slyness in him. He shook her hand and said goodbye.

She cried, offered prayers, but MacDermott was unmoved.

Embarrassed and feeling sorry for her, Jimmy O'Shea moved away down the corridor.

The last meeting of the Military Council was over. Claire Cregan had been sent away. Mike Mallin – James Connolly's second in command – asked Jimmy O'Shea if he was ready. With MacNeill calling off the manoeuvres, Mallin said, the Citizen Army might have to fight without the Volunteers.

O'Shea said he was ready.

'It will be short and sharp,' Mallin said. 'We'll be all dead in a short time.'

O'Shea joined his comrades outside Liberty Hall. It was like the start of any parade or manoeuvre, a bit of chat between friends, nothing dramatic.

Ten minutes to noon.

Sharp commands rang out around Beresford Place. Sean Connolly's contingent from the Citizen Army, a third of them women, set off across Butt Bridge. Among them was Jimmy O'Shea's young friend Charlie D'Arcy – the two had gone to Confession together the previous evening.

As he waited in the ranks, standing at ease, O'Shea noticed an old man on the pavement. O'Shea figured him for a Fenian. All the makings. Tall and stout, black soft hat and flowing beard.

Good luck, the old man said to O'Shea. And God's help in your terrible task.

He gripped O'Shea's hand, his palm calloused and dry. There were tears on his cheeks.

Volunteer Joe Good had left Kimmage that morning with some dozens of his comrades, heading for the city centre, all carrying weapons. They travelled by tram. Upstairs, Joe's friend Johnny O'Connor played his flute and others sang. Passengers on trams going the other way jeered, and the Volunteers cheered.

The Kimmage unit was made up of members from British-based Volunteer companies – Irish, or of Irish descent – who had been active in nationalist politics in Britain. Faced with being conscripted to fight for the

Empire, many had decided they'd rather fight for a cause they chose themselves, and left for Ireland before controls were put on the ports.

The Kimmage garrison – which included Michael Collins – was known within the Volunteers as 'the refugees', and occasionally 'the Foreign Legion'.

Joe Good and Johnny O'Connor were from London, both electricians, and both had left to avoid conscription into a war they didn't believe in. Joe had a London accent. Johnny was always 'blimey this' and 'blimey that', so much so that he was commonly known as Blimey.

Their captain, George Plunkett, brother of Joe Plunkett, insisted on paying the tram fares: 'Fifty-nine two-penny fares, please.'

Volunteer Michael Cremen rode a bicycle ahead of the tram, scouting for trouble. If he spotted army or police activity he would alert the others to be ready to fight.

The journey was uneventful and they disembarked near Sackville Street and marched to Liberty Hall.

Outside the union building, members of the Citizen Army and the Volunteers had formed fours. There were two horse-drawn lorries loaded with weapons and tools – sledgehammers and crowbars. Joe Plunkett, accompanied by Brennan-Whitmore, stood beside Patrick Pearse.

Plunkett was dressed in high tan leather boots and spurs. He wore pince-nez spectacles and carried a sword-stick. He looked, Joe Good thought, like any British brass-hat staff officer.

A comrade whispered to Joe Good: 'Ludendorff', the name of a prominent and ostentatious German general.

James Connolly looked drab beside Plunkett. He was wearing a bottle-green, thin serge uniform.

Two different ideas of freedom, Joe Good thought.

Margaret Skinnider, from the Citizen Army, ran up to

the Kimmage garrison and sought out her friend Seamus Robinson. 'It's on,' she said.

'What's on?'

'The rebellion, of course.'

He wasn't the only one who had gone out that Monday unaware that the day had come. Given the warnings, the lectures and the hints of the previous weeks – with Volunteers told that anyone not willing to fight should drop out now – Robinson, and just about everyone else, was aware that a rising was imminent. Most of them didn't know exactly when or how it would happen.

Joe Plunkett drew the blade from his sword-stick and tossed away the sheath.

About then, a luxurious De Dion-Bouton touring car pulled up outside Liberty Hall. Out stepped Michael O'Rahilly – loyal to Eoin MacNeill, having skipped sleep two nights in a row to spread MacNeill's cancellation orders to Volunteer units down the country.

O'Rahilly, who grandly called himself 'The O'Rahilly' – thereby claiming leadership of the O'Rahilly clan – wasn't a typical member of the Volunteers. From Kerry, a merchant's son, with a wealthy background and a private income, privately educated at Clongowes, living in a large house in Herbert Park, he had travelled Europe and lived in the USA.

Some years earlier, he had fallen in love with an American woman visiting Ireland, Nancy Brown. When in 1898 he discovered an American rival had proposed to Nancy he went to Amsterdam and bought a diamond ring, then he sailed to New York, proposed to her and she accepted. After a nine-month-long honeymoon in Europe, they lived in Ireland for a while, and then Philadelphia, before settling back in Ireland in 1909, when The O'Rahilly was thirty-three.

Having learned Irish and in 1914 having joined the Irish Volunteers, he became totally committed to Irish independence. He devoted much of his income to the cause. One of his contributions was financing the import of arms.

In recent weeks, aware of the split in the movement and the rising tension, The O'Rahilly had become morose. A premature rising, he felt, would lead to disaster. He believed armed struggle was inevitable, and the British would not voluntarily grant true independence – but the grand gesture of taking the battle to the enemy from a position of weakness he considered madness.

At one stage he remarked to a friend that food might be hard to come by, in the middle of a rebellion. He was thinking of stocking up, in case it was a prolonged effort. Then, he said, maybe not – that wouldn't be fair to those who couldn't afford to do the same. He'd take his chances along with everyone else.

And now, having hurried back to Dublin, he turned up at Liberty Hall, armed and ready for action. He didn't want a rising, but if a rising was to go ahead he believed he should be there with his comrades. For two years he'd helped arm the Volunteers. If they were about to use those arms, he thought, it would be unbecoming of him not to be with them.

Outside Liberty Hall, The O'Rahilly's sister Anna approached Patrick Pearse and pinched his arm in a way that was meant to hurt. 'This is all your fault,' she said.

The headquarters contingent shaped up to begin the short march along the quays to Sackville Street and the GPO.

10

Captain Sean Connolly led his party of the Irish Citizen Army across the Liffey, towards Dublin Castle – about twenty men and ten women. Connolly was aged thirty-three. His father and his brothers Joe, Eamon and George were also in the Citizen Army. His sister Kate, too – she was among the contingent he was leading.

Passing Tara Street fire station, they got a wave from his fireman brother Joe, who was leaving his workplace to join his Citizen Army comrades at Stephens Green.

A few paces behind Sean Connolly was his sixteen-year old brother Mattie, clutching a rifle, a bugle dangling from a strap across his chest.

All this had the appearance of the marching man-oeuvres the people of Dublin, and the police, had become used to seeing on the city streets. As the Citizen Army group moved up Dame Street the bells of the noon Angelus began ringing out from the city churches.

Because of his frailties, Tom Clarke was driven to the GPO. He was accompanied by Sean MacDermott, who had suffered from polio and now walked with the aid of a cane. On the way they passed a police detective named Hoey, from G Division, the police section that specialized in surveillance of nationalists.

One of the men in the car suggested they take the opportunity to shoot Hoey. Sean MacDermott was so irate at the proposal that he cursed the man who made it. The notion of coldly assassinating a policeman was repulsive.

Clarke and MacDermott were outside the GPO when the headquarters group, headed by Pearse, Connolly and Joe Plunkett, arrived.

The detachment formed two lines facing the Post Office. Michael Collins and Brennan-Whitmore linked arms with the frail and sickly Joe Plunkett. George Plunkett, Joe's brother, gave the order: 'Charge!'

The rebels took the GPO, to the bewilderment of the customers and staff inside.

Within a minute, the civilians having been ordered out, Connolly gave instructions to break the glass from the windows. In seconds, the footpath outside the GPO was thick with broken shards. Connolly's lectures on street fighting had stressed the dangers of leaving window glass unbroken – it was a potential source of deadly flying splinters when the enemy attacked with machine guns or explosives. The windows were barricaded with furniture, sandbags and mailbags.

In anticipation that the supply would be turned off, every useful vessel was filled with water. Weapons and tools from the horse-drawn lorries were unloaded and taken inside the GPO.

Volunteers moved upstairs to secure the building. On a landing, several were surprised by a unit of seven British soldiers, covering them with rifles. The Volunteers fired their handguns and a sergeant fell, his forehead grazed by a bullet. The other six British soldiers put down their rifles and put their hands up. The seven soldiers, the only army defence of the GPO, had no ammunition.

Having marched to the GPO, Joe Good now found himself, on the command of George Plunkett, running back down Sackville Street, towards O'Connell Bridge, along with the rest of his unit. He had no idea where they were running, or why.

The leader of the unit, Peadar Bracken, was under orders to take Kelly's gunpowder shop at the end of Sackville Street – on the corner of Bachelors Walk – and jewellers Hopkins & Hopkins, on the opposite side of Sackville Street. This would give the Volunteers command of the southern entrance to Sackville Street, overlooking O'Connell Bridge.

Joe Good, with two others, was sent on to the bridge, with orders to prevent the enemy crossing. Good stood on the island in the middle of the wide bridge, a companion on either side, his back to Sackville Street. The three had shotguns.

Outside Hopkins & Hopkins, Seamus Robinson was in charge of Volunteers working to open the steel shutters. A giant of a policeman arrived and Robinson showed him his gun. The policeman backed away. This isn't any of my business, he insisted – this is military business.

Stand still, Robinson ordered.

The policeman kept backing away. Robinson told him again to stand still. He wanted him here, until the Volunteers got into the buildings, not running off to raise the alarm.

Military business, the policeman said, backing away. Nothing to do with me.

Robinson pointed the shotgun at him and, in a savage

tone, very explicitly told the policeman what would happen if he didn't stand still. The policeman stood still.

Sean Connolly's unit broke up as they approached Dublin Castle, small detachments taking over the Henry & James tailor's shop and the offices of the *Daily Express*. Young Mattie Connolly was among a group that went through a side entrance into City Hall.

Sean Connolly turned left on to Cork Hill and rushed for the main gate of Dublin Castle. There had been a plan to take the Castle, but James Connolly had concluded that it was too big and too hard to hold with the forces available. The plan now was to take City Hall and some outposts, along with the Castle guardhouse.

The policeman on duty at the Castle, James O'Brien, a big man in his mid-forties, realized this was something more than a routine Volunteer march. He began to push the gate shut and reached out to stop Sean Connolly, who instinctively raised his rifle and fired the first fatal shot of the rising, killing the unarmed policeman.

From a second-floor window, Peter Folan, head constable of the Royal Irish Constabulary, saw Constable O'Brien being shot. One of the Citizen Army people raised a rifle – Folan threw himself on the floor. The window glass above him shattered.

The Citizen Army contingent split – some ran towards the guardhouse, fired at it and threw a bomb inside. It failed to go off, but the several soldiers inside were overwhelmed – they were tied up and the guardhouse was taken.

Sean Connolly and his detachment turned to City Hall, beside the Castle. Connolly knew his way around the building, having worked as a clerk for Dublin Corporation, and he had keys. He and the others made their way to the roof. He assigned four or five men to take positions along and behind the parapet. He directed his young brother Mattie to go further up, climbing a ladder to the sloping area of the roof, which gave a good view down Parliament Street.

Mattie's orders were to keep watch for the approach of British troops. Individual unarmed British soldiers, Sean warned, should not be fired on.

On Grafton Street, an elderly British Army soldier, on horseback, gestured with his sword. 'Why, damn your soul, I've a right to put this through you.'

Volunteer Peter Reynolds, a courier on a motorbike, had advised the old gent not to go any further down the street – it was dangerous.

Reynolds pointed his Parabellum pistol at the old man. Then he thought better of it and put the gun away. 'Oh, all right, go on, someone else will do it.'

Some men from E Company, 4th Battalion, moved out of Liberty Hall and began tunnelling their way along Eden Quay, towards Hopkins & Hopkins, on the corner of Sackville Street.

'Boring through' would become a standard tactic of the rising. When rebels took over a building they broke through the wall into the next building, and continued boring through all along the block. When they were finished tunnelling they had hidden access from one end of the block to the other – safe from enemy eyes and bullets.

It wasn't a straight-line series of bored holes, for two reasons. One: floor levels differed; two: the holes had to be staggered or an enemy finding one hole could fire the length of the block.

At Eden Quay, the E Company unit came through one wall and found themselves in a pub. Acting on instructions to remove potential occasions of sin, they turned on the beer taps and left them running, and they poured bottles of spirits down the sink.

Having delivered his despatches from the GPO headquarters to the Citizen Army at Stephens Green, Volunteer Peter Reynolds revved up his motorbike and set off back down Grafton Street. The sound of gunfire now echoed up the street. The crowds had melted away.

Passing through College Green, Reynolds saw on the cobblestones, outside the gates of Trinity, the body of the old soldier with his sword, near his dead horse.

Nora O'Daly was having a late breakfast when a mobilization order reached her at her home in Clontarf. She was to report to 2nd Battalion at Stephens Green. She took her knapsack, equipped with bandages, iodine and suchlike, and set off by tram. Her husband, Seamus Daly, had already left the house and reported to F Company at Fr. Mathew Park.

Arriving in Sackville Street, Nora heard the cheers from the GPO and knew the rising had started. She took another tram to Stephens Green and met the other members of Cumann na mBan, but 2nd Battalion was nowhere to be found.

At this stage, Captain Hunter had taken 2nd Battalion, including much of F Company, to Jacob's factory. The rest of F Company and others from 2nd Battalion were still assembling back in Fr. Mathew Park.

Mike Mallin's second in command, Constance Markievicz, came along. She suggested to the Cumann na mBan women that, since they couldn't find 2nd

Battalion, 'Throw in your lot with ours.'

It seemed the logical thing to do. O'Daly made her way to the first aid station at the summerhouse in the middle of the Green, listening to distant shots ringing out from around the city. Members of the Citizen Army were digging trenches.

O'Daly was worried. She wasn't a military person, but this business of digging trenches in a twenty-acre park overlooked by high buildings – well, it seemed to her to be something of a death trap.

At the GPO, on James Connolly's orders, two flags were being run up flagpoles on the roof – a tricolour, and a green flag with 'Irish Republic' in gold letters.

Part Four

Troop trains

11

With the rising under way, the officers of 2nd Battalion at Fr. Mathew Park prepared to move their stockpile of weapons and ammunition into the city centre.

A lorry that was supposed to carry the material hadn't turned up. Captain Tom Weafer approached F Company's Seamus Daly, maker of bombs and grenades. 'Here, long fellow, come here. Get me a couple of wagons.'

'Where'll I get them?'

'Get them wherever you can, but get them quick. Any sort of conveyance at all – drays or lorries or anything you can get.'

Daly called Charlie Saurin, his occasional assistant in bomb making, who was nearby, and told him to come along: they had a mission.

At this point, some people were approaching Fr. Mathew Park with the intention of confusing matters even further. Supporters of MacNeill and Hobson had arrived and were spreading the word that the rising had been aborted. As Charlie Saurin and Seamus Daly left the park, they met a woman who told them she had a message from James Connolly.

'It's all off,' she said.

She went into the park and Saurin and Daly paused,

unsure whether to continue. They went back to the park.

The woman passed Harry Colley. 'We're not going out,' she said. He recognized her. Name of Ryan – she worked in the Volunteer HQ, in Dawson Street. She was secretary to Professor Eoin MacNeill.

The woman found the officer in charge, Captain Tom Weafer, and told him the same. It was only the Citizen Army that was going out.

Others, including journalist Sean Lester of the *Evening Mail*, approached Frank Henderson. The message was that there was rioting in the city centre, but that only the Citizen Army had gone into action. A mob had run wild and set about killing people.

Indecision ruled. This new information – if it was true – turned everything on its head. No one knew to what extent the rising was proceeding. No one knew what role – if any – the remnants of 2nd Battalion were to play. Blundering on, into unknown circumstances, was out of the question.

Among the officers, Frank Henderson felt at a disadvantage, given that he was the only one who was not a member of the IRB – and thereby couldn't know what orders others might be following. Henderson proposed that the indecision be resolved by the senior officer present, Captain Tom Weafer. This was agreed.

Weafer, born in Enniscorthy, married and living in Dublin, was in his mid-twenties. He decided he should go into the city centre and seek out the leaders – perhaps Pearse or Connolly – to find out what was expected of them. The others agreed and Tom Weafer set off.

The waiting Volunteers were told to stand down for the moment. Disperse in small groups to houses nearby – anyone from outlying districts should stay with comrades who lived closer to Fr. Mathew Park.

There was some dissent – Seamus Daly was seething – but orders were orders.

Dr Kathleen Lynn drove to Dublin Castle, bringing with her a range of first aid equipment and medicine. As she left the car she saw the body of James O'Brien, the Dublin Metropolitan policeman shot dead by Sean Connolly.

Lynn crossed to the gate of City Hall. It was locked. She climbed the gate with her equipment, went inside and found Sean Connolly. He suggested that the Volunteers firing from the rooftop might need medical help. Lynn found Jenny Shanahan, the Citizen Army manager of the Co-op shop, and the two brought medical supplies up to the roof.

With time to kill, the Volunteers at Fr. Mathew Park spread out to nearby homes. Four of them went to the house of M. W. O'Reilly, former captain of F Company. One of the four – Paddy Shortis, from Ballybunion, in Kerry – was one of those Irish people who had left England to escape conscription into the blood mills on the continent. He'd been active in Irish independence circles in England and joined the Volunteers on reaching Dublin. Not having a place to stay, he had gratefully accepted temporary accommodation from M. W. O'Reilly and his wife Catherine, and was lodging with them in Foster Terrace, off Ballybough Road.

It had been a long time since breakfast. While the officers were getting orders from Liberty Hall, Shortis invited his three F Company comrades – Charlie Saurin, Seamus Daly and Harry Coyle – to have a bite to eat.

Catherine O'Reilly had already left the house with her four children, and Shortis began preparing food for himself, Saurin, Daly and Coyle.

*

The *Irish Times* later parodied what happened at the GPO, as Patrick Pearse read aloud the Proclamation of the Republic. Noblett's sweet shop, on the corner of North Earl Street, had been looted. 'Nearly all rushed across the street to join in the spoil.' Those remaining to listen to Pearse were, the newspaper said, 'a few old men and women who had lost their desire for sweets'.

'Isn't Clerys broken into yet?'

'Hivens, it's a great shame Clerys isn't broken.'

Apart from the stage Irish dialect and the sneering contempt, it was an accurate enough account of the early reaction to the rising.

Some within the nationalist community were taken aback that such names as Professor MacNeill and Sinn Fein's Arthur Griffith were missing from the Proclamation. How could any rising go ahead without the imprimatur of such eminent nationalist leaders? Especially since the signatories included the likes of James Connolly, a socialist held in low regard by middle-class nationalists who frowned on the activities of trade unions. And this fellow Pearse – a jumped-up schoolmaster, full of romantic notions.

The response of the people from the tenements was no less dismissive. Many had men in the British Army, fighting in France.

For others, the rising opened up unprecedented opportunities.

With the police out of the picture, thanks to the lads with rifles on the roof of the GPO, people who lived in grinding poverty, with no prospect of rising above subsistence level, had only to smash a window to grab armfuls of what they could never afford, no matter how long and how hard they worked. The Volunteers tried appealing to the patriotic nature of the looters, they tried firing shots over their heads. But the temptation of free goods – whatever they might be, whether needed or not – was too strong.

Youths smashed windows and stood inside, skimming hats out to anyone who wanted to catch them. Some kids got their hands on cricket balls and bats. In other shops, men and women sat and tried on shoes until they found the right size. The more practical people went straight for what their families needed most, and stole food.

Down in Gorman's shop on Moore Street, looters left with about 3,500 cigarettes, more than half of them the cheap Woodbine brand. Cases of John West salmon and Skipper sardines were taken from another shop, along with Oxo cubes, butter and jam. Homes in which biscuits were a rare treat that evening had whole tins of them.

At the storage sheds on Sir John Rogerson's Quay, some entrepreneurs were making off with no fewer than twenty-eight bags of Egyptian onions. At the other end of the scale, more than one piano was seen being wheeled through streets broad and narrow.

A medical student with time on his hands arrived in Sackville Street to see what the fuss was about. He saw boys playing cowboys and Indians with toy guns, and little girls hugging teddy bears and dolls. The children of the slums had access, for a brief moment, to simple pleasures usually beyond their hopes.

The element of fun ended when several dozen Lancers rode their horses down Sackville Street, from the north end. It wasn't so much a charge as a canter, soldiers sent to find out what the fuss was about and assert the authority of the Empire. They were met with a deadly rattle of rifle fire from the GPO, which left four dead soldiers and two dead horses lying on the city's bloodstained main street.

*

Up in Cabra Park, at Martin Conlon's house, the Volunteers guarding Bulmer Hobson were getting restless. They knew the rising was under way and they were irritated at being stuck here guarding this bloody prisoner.

It didn't help that Hobson was fretting, and seemed on the verge of a fainting fit.

One of the guards suggested they put a bullet into the bastard and dump him somewhere. Martin Conlon wasn't sure if they were serious, or just blowing off steam. He told them he had a revolver and he'd use it if they tried anything of that sort.

Jervis Street Hospital was receiving its first casualties from the rising. Four dead soldiers, and a woman shot dead near her own door in Capel Street. At the Richmond Hospital, a priest from Church Street carried in a child, shot through the head.

At the wicker gate blocking entry to Jacob's biscuit factory in Bishop Street, Mick McDonnell of F Company was swinging an axe. He was at the head of 150 Volunteers, mostly from 2nd Battalion. The gate gave way to McDonnell's attack and the Volunteers surged forward to take their objective.

Jim Slattery from F Company was detailed to take some men around to the back of the factory, to New Street, and build a barricade.

There were British Army barracks dotted around the outskirts of the city – Beggars Bush in the south-east, Portobello and Wellington in the south, Richmond in the south-west, Islandbridge in the west, Royal, Marlboro and Linenhall north of the river.

The barracks weren't sited randomly. They were carefully placed to ensure that troops would be available anywhere in the city at short notice. The populace might have been quiescent for decades, but the British were aware of the possibilities, and prepared accordingly.

As the Volunteers rushed to occupy the factory, a shotgun went off close to Major John MacBride, hero of the Irish Transvaal Brigade in the Boer War, erstwhile husband of Maude Gonne, the nationalist muse of W. B. Yeats. From somewhere, the Volunteers had acquired a consignment of temperamental American shotguns. The slightest bump and they went off. Affecting to pick pellets out of his waxed moustache, MacBride drawled, 'Shotguns should be treated carefully.'

Two units of Lancers rode up along Burgh Quay and turned on to O'Connell Bridge. Unaware of the rising, unaware that others of their regiment had already been shot dead just yards away in Sackville Street, they were escorting a consignment of ammunition.

Joe Good, still standing in the middle of the wide bridge flanked by the other two Volunteers from the Kimmage garrison, felt ridiculous. He said to one of his companions, 'Will we wipe out this lot, Arthur?'

Arthur Agnew grinned. Two units of cavalry versus three young men with shotguns.

Good casually raised his shotgun so it was resting on his left forearm, pointing in the general direction of the Lancer officer. If the action started, Joe decided, he'd fire one shot then dive into the river.

Outside Hopkins & Hopkins, Seamus Robinson and some of his men saw the Lancers. The game is up, at least one of them thought. Robinson lay down on the pavement on the corner of Sackville Street, his shotgun aimed.

A car stopped near the soldiers and a passenger got out. He gestured up towards the GPO. The Lancer officer declined to show interest. He had escort duty to perform.

The officer wore a monocle. He looked disdainfully down at Joe Good as he rode slowly across the bridge. Several of the troopers smiled. It was as though they had come across some clowns, sent to entertain them.

The Lancers wheeled left on to Bachelors Walk and rode leisurely up along the Liffey towards the Phoenix Park. On the way, they would have to pass the Four Courts, which Ned Daly's 1st Battalion had just taken over.

The biggest fools have the best of luck, a relieved Joe Good told himself. Outside Hopkins & Hopkins, an equally relieved Seamus Robinson rose to his feet and went into the jewellery shop.

At M. W. O'Reilly's home on Foster Terrace, house guest Paddy Shortis had a small automatic pistol going spare, along with some ammunition. He gave it to Charlie Saurin.

The four Volunteers – having eaten – each took a room, to keep watch in case the authorities had a round-up in mind. From an upstairs room at the back of the house, Charlie Saurin watched a train pass along the viaduct behind Clonliffe Road, towards the city. It was packed with khaki-clad British troops.

That stuff about it being all off – from what Charlie Saurin saw it certainly didn't look like that was true. After a while, they got word to return to Fr. Mathew Park.

Captain Tom Weafer, having spoken to James Connolly, was back at Fr. Mathew Park with orders to load up all weapons and ammunition and bring them into the centre of the city, where Connolly would give further instructions.

Charlie Saurin and Seamus Daly resumed their mission to find transport to carry the guns and ammo. Daly knew of a furniture removal business at Summerhill, so they headed there. The place was closed, it being a bank holiday. They began to force open the door, at which point a yardman appeared and asked what the hell they wanted.

They found two carts and yoked a horse to each, the yardman all the while threatening to get the police.

Stay cool, Daly told him. We don't want to cause trouble.

'Who's going to pay for this?'

'The Irish Republic will pay for this.'

When they got back to Fr. Mathew Park every available Volunteer joined in, and inside twenty minutes the two carts were loaded with weapons.

There was no sign of the rest of F Company arriving at the GPO, but Boss Shields was settling in there, finding his way around.

You, you and you – come with me.

Shields found himself selected as part of a team of Volunteers for a mission ordered by Joe Plunkett. Volunteer Fergus O'Kelly, a university student studying radio, was assigned by Plunkett to set up a radio transmission base in a building on the other side of Sackville Street. O'Kelly selected Marconi radio operator David Burke and electrician Blimey O'Connor.

Lacking any of the specialist skills of the others, Boss Shields was the labouring element on the team.

Blimey, along with Volunteers Liam Daly and Joe

Good, had already improvised primitive telephone communications, re-routing telephone wires throughout the
GPO – allowing James Connolly to keep in touch with a
number of positions in the building.

Fergus O'Kelly's radio group crossed to the block of
buildings between Abbey Street and Eden Quay. On the
corner of Abbey Street was Reis's jewellery shop, above
which was the Irish School of Wireless Telegraphy. The
school had been closed and the radio equipment sealed
since the beginning of the European war. O'Kelly went
upstairs to the caretaker's flat and told her, a Miss
Brown, that she should leave, as there would be fighting
in the vicinity.

O'Kelly broke the seal on the offices and they found
an old 1.5kw ship's transmitter. It was the team's job to
get the radio working and announce to the world the
proclamation of the Irish Republic.

The revolutionary forces were in place.

1st Battalion of the Volunteers, under Ned Daly, took
the Four Courts.

2nd Battalion, under Tom MacDonagh, took Jacob's
biscuit factory. The remainder of that battalion, including many Volunteers from F Company, were still at Fr.
Mathew Park, their orders only now coming through.

3rd Battalion, under Eamon de Valera, took Bolands
flour mills.

4th Battalion, under Eamonn Ceannt, took the South
Dublin Union.

The Citizen Army, under Mike Mallin, took Stephens
Green and City Hall.

The leaders took the GPO as headquarters of the rising.
As well as these primary positions, each command

occupied outposts to extend its reach and to protect the primary positions from attack.

Some Volunteers had the old Mauser rifles, some modern Lee Enfields, revolvers and bayonets. Some had dodgy shotguns.

Some were armed with just pikes – a spear head attached to a long pole. One Volunteer, eighteen-year-old Andy McDonnell, had his first experience of active service at Great Brunswick Street (now Pearse Street). He was ordered to commandeer a tram. He took his six-foot-long pike and stood in the street, the blade of the pike lowered towards an oncoming tram.

Being on the small side, and aware he didn't present the most imposing figure, he was somewhat nervously standing his ground as the tram approached. At the last minute the driver brought the vehicle to a stop. McDonnell ordered the passengers off. And he wondered what he would have done had the tram kept coming. Would he have turned and run? Or would he have charged the tram with his pike?

12

A British soldier lay wounded in Ship Street, perhaps dying. Helena Molony and Jenny Shanahan looked down at him from the roof of City Hall.

'I wonder should we do something for him?' asked Molony.

Nearby, Captain Sean Connolly said, 'No, his own lads will come.'

Down on the street, pacifist Frank Sheehy-Skeffington convinced a passer-by to help him attend the soldier. Before they could get to him, the man's comrades ran out and pulled him to cover.

At rooftop level, the exchange of fire between the British and the Citizen Army continued.

Sean Connolly decided they needed reinforcements and despatched Helena Molony to the GPO to ask James Connolly to send what help he could.

Meanwhile, a detachment of Dublin Fusiliers from the Royal Barracks reached the Castle. They passed through Werburgh Street, cheered by the local population.

From his elevated position on the upper roof, sixteen-year-old Mattie Connolly could see other members of the Citizen Army on other rooftops, exchanging fire with the enemy. His friend Charlie D'Arcy, aged fifteen, had a position on the roof of the Henry & James premises, the tailor's on the other side of the street.

Mattie had been one of those on garrison duty in Liberty Hall in the days before the rising, as had Charlie D'Arcy. As a member of the Citizen Army, Mattie had trained and drilled with the men, and acted as instructor to the boys' section. He had no trouble recognizing the difference between gunshots – the loud roar and echo of the Mauser and the sharp crack of the Lee Enfield.

Word went around – keep your head down: there's a sniper in the clock tower of Dublin Castle.

Mattie could see all the way down Parliament Street, to the Liffey, across the bridge and up Capel Street. He saw a team of Lancers riding up the quays towards the Four Courts, escorting an ammunition wagon. He then heard a volley of shots and saw the Lancers retreating at speed back along the quays, the soldiers bent over the necks of their mounts, sparks flying from the horses' hooves.

His brother Sean came across the rooftop to check on Mattie. He had one sleeve rolled up, a red handkerchief tied to that arm. After a moment Mattie realized it wasn't a red handkerchief. Sean made light of it: 'Look at the blood I'm shedding for Ireland!'

Mattie had a first aid kit and offered to dress the wound. It was just a revolver shot, Sean said – it'll be all right. He returned to the rear of the rooftop.

At Jacob's factory, the rebels told the small number of maintenance workers on duty on the bank holiday to leave, then barricaded doors and windows. Caretaker Thomas Orr refused to go. The building was his responsibility, he said.

You'll be in as much danger as we are, Commandant Tom MacDonagh told him.

I'll take my chances.

I've a request, he added – no smoking in the factory. MacDonagh agreed and gave the order immediately.

Fifteen-year-old Vinny Byrne was among a group detailed to occupy an outpost of Jacob's – two tenement houses in Malpas Street.

Meanwhile, Volunteers were moving upward through the vast building to the two towers that overlooked the area. From there, snipers could see into Bride Street, across Portobello Bridge, Dublin Castle and Ship Street Barracks.

The night watchman, Henry Fitzgerald, had collected his hat and coat and was ready to leave, but the doors and windows were by now blocked. He'd have to stay. He was approached by Major John MacBride.

The major was aged forty-eight and looking ten years older, his glory days fighting the British in South Africa long behind him. His personal life in flitters, MacBride was a drinker. He had had a lunch date that day at the Wicklow Hotel, off Grafton Street. On his way there he met the contingent of Volunteers led by Tom MacDonagh. Realizing that, after all the confusion, Pearse and MacDermott and Clarke had decided to go ahead with the rising, MacBride spontaneously decided to join in. He shortly afterwards turned up in Stephens Green, ready for action.

MacDonagh was delighted to have MacBride's knowledge and experience. He appointed him second in command of the Jacob's garrison. When the contingent marched to the factory they were led by MacDonagh, with his brother John on one side and Major MacBride, in a blue suit, with a walking cane, puffing on a cigar, on the other.

Now, approaching the factory night watchman,

MacBride had a suggestion. He asked Fitzgerald his name, his religion and his address. Then he asked: Would you like to be sworn in as a member of the Irish Volunteers?

The bemused night watchman said no, he'd no interest in that sort of thing. All he wanted was to go home to his wife and children.

MacBride seemed disappointed.

Lieutenant Mick Malone, who was with Eamon de Valera's garrison at Bolands Mills, was ordered to set up outposts to intercept British troops marching into Dublin from the port at Kingstown (now Dun Laoghaire), six miles away. Malone distributed his troops in positions around Northumberland Road, some into the Parochial Hall, more into a large, three-storey house overlooking Mount Street Bridge – Clanwilliam House. Then he brought a company section leader, Seamus Grace, and two young Volunteers, Paddy Rowe and Michael Byrne, to take over a house at 25 Northumberland Road.

At the front door of No. 25, Seamus Grace smashed the Yale lock with the butt of his rifle and they went in. The owners of the house, the Cussen family, were sympathetic to the cause. Knowing what was coming, they had sent their servants away and gone away themselves. The four Volunteers began the work of turning the house into a fortress. They built barricades against the front and back doors and throughout the house set up vessels full of water that would be needed during a siege.

On their way into the city centre from Kingstown, British troops would have to come through south Dublin – almost certainly some of them would have to cross the Grand Canal at Mount Street Bridge. Malone's job was to stop them.

*

At City Hall, the roof slates near young Mattie Connolly were holed and scarred by bullets. He descended to the lower level of the roof, where a junior officer directed him to take a position behind the parapet on the northeast corner. It was safer than the exposed position on the higher level, but with a limited view down Dame Street.

The crack of a sniper's rifle.

Across the street, Charlie D'Arcy took a fatal bullet. Mattie Connolly watched his friend fall into the roof gutter and lie still.

Helena Molony, having delivered a message to James Connolly at the GPO, returned to City Hall. She went back up to the roof, where Captain Sean Connolly and five or six men were still exchanging fire with the British.

It was a bright spring day, the sun hot. Molony joined Kathleen Lynn and Jenny Shanahan, all three crouching. Sean Connolly stood and moved across the roof. The crack of a sniper's rifle. Connolly took a bullet and went down.

Twenty-one-year-old Katie Byrne was the first member of Cumann na mBan into the GPO that day. Her brother Paddy had left the house with his rifle, and she and her sister Alice had heard there was something on. So, they headed into Sackville Street. Alice took off for Liberty Hall and Katie fell in behind a company of marching Volunteers.

What's happening?

The scrap is starting, one of them told her. We're heading for the GPO.

After she saw the Volunteers rush and take the Post Office, Katie made towards a doorway and was stopped from entering. She recognized Mick Staines, captain of her brother's company.

Let me in, she asked.

Go away, he said, or I'll tell Paddy on you.

Volunteers with a handcart were unloading homemade hand grenades, fashioned from empty condensed-milk tins. The grenades were being passed in through a broken window.

Katie Byrne went around the corner to Princes Street, to the first window, and with the help of a Volunteer she climbed on to the sill. She kicked out the glass, jumped inside and fell on to Volunteer Joe Gahan, who was stooped over, working on something.

They both began laughing, and he was pointing at the cuts on her leg and arm from the broken glass. 'What the bloody hell are you doing there?'

She was here, she said, to help the wounded and feed the fighters.

There was an explosion.

'Here's your first case,' Joe said.

Someone had dropped a grenade – one of the home-made batch being passed in through the window. The fuse struck, someone kicked it into a corner, Volunteer Liam Clarke picked it up and it exploded in his face.

Joe Gahan brought a can of cold water and Katie washed Clarke's wound and revealed the extent of his facial injuries – Clarke had lost an eye. He was taken to a field hospital in a room off the main hall.

Katie continued the work of tending to the food and medical needs of the Volunteers. Meanwhile, her sister Alice arrived at the GPO, having got a lift from Liberty Hall in The O'Rahilly's car, which was being used to transport ammunition.

After she served food on the ground floor, Katie went upstairs and found Tom Clarke looking disapprovingly at some kind of makeshift bar, with beer and soft drinks.

Do you know anything about this business?

'No, sir.'

'I want you to destroy all this stuff,' Clarke said, pointing to the beer.

He held one bottle by the neck and tipped it over, pouring the beer down the sink. Then he left.

Katie and one of the Volunteers finished the job, pouring away the contents of one bottle after another.

When he came upstairs, Joe Gahan was outraged. What the hell are you doing that for?

'Orders,' she said, Tom Clarke's orders.

She put some beer in a cup for Joe. He sat in a corner and drank it, asking her to keep an eye out for Clarke.

Alice came upstairs to get a beer for a policeman who was being held prisoner down below. She rescued the last bottle, just as it was being poured away, and brought it down to the captive.

Tom Clarke came back and checked that all the crates were empty. I don't want the men tempted, he said.

At 25 Northumberland Road, after despatching cycle scouts around the area, Lieutenant Mick Malone took a report from one scout who had been watching the comings and goings at Beggars Bush Barracks.

Are you a Volunteer?

No, sir, I'm Fianna.

Malone asked his age and when the boy said sixteen Malone told him he'd have to go home.

I can't accept responsibility for someone of your age, he said.

A British soldier, off duty, strolled down Sackville Street, enjoying the sun, seemingly without a care in the world. After the Great War, the common soldier would be sentimentalized, deemed to be the salt of the earth. In 1916, common soldiers were considered common. There was an unofficial code that meant that soldiers were confined to the west side of Sackville Street, the GPO side. They were not welcome on the east side of the street, home to the Imperial Hotel and Clerys department store. After twilight, it was said, no respectable person – man or woman – would dream of walking on the GPO side of the street, where their ears might be offended by the rough syllables discharged from the mouths of crude and common soldiers.

The soldier approaching the junction with Henry Street was on the proper side of the street, but he appeared baffled. The windows of the GPO were barricaded, the glass broken, armed men on the roof and at every window.

Nearby women called to him to get out of there, run for it, he was in danger. The soldier, still baffled, turned and took his time walking back up the street.

Paddy Berry, who worked as a warder at Mountjoy Jail, came into Sackville Street to see what was going on. Berry had over the years become friendly with a number of nationalist leaders, including Sean MacDermott – who had the previous year served six months in the Joy for sedition.

Berry crossed to the GPO, where a sentry was on duty. Berry recognized him – Vincent Poole of the Citizen Army, a valued customer of Mountjoy, given his eighteen criminal convictions. Berry saluted Poole, who returned the salute.

Fifteen-year-old Frank Saurin from F Company, sent away from Fr. Mathew Park that morning by Frank Henderson, stood in Sackville Street and stared at the dead horses shot from under the Lancers. Behind him, in a shop on the corner of North Earl Street, William

Brennan-Whitmore, the Wexford officer who had become an aide to Joe Plunkett, was setting up an outpost of the GPO. Brennan-Whitmore was still shocked by his discovery of the hidden hand of the IRB behind the rising, but now that the action had started he put all that aside.

Young Frank Saurin crossed the road and approached the GPO. There was a Volunteer officer by the door. Frank assured him he was himself a Volunteer, from F Company, 2nd Battalion. He was here to help.

The officer told the boy to go home.

Mattie Connolly got word that his brother Sean had been wounded again. He tried to get to him, but his section leader pointed his rifle at Mattie and ordered him to get back to his post – probably because moving across the roof had become too dangerous.

On another part of the roof, Dr Kathleen Lynn tended to Sean Connolly. There was blood everywhere. He'd been shot in the shoulder and the bullet had gone through a lung. After an examination, Lynn concluded there was nothing that first aid could do. Helena Molony crouched and said an Act of Contrition into her dying friend's ear.

Reinforcements arrived from the GPO – including John Poole, brother of Vincent. Someone had brought and was passing around a typewritten sheet of paper. Mattie Connolly read it – it told of a general uprising throughout the country. Wexford and Galway were out, a large body of Volunteers was marching on Dublin from Kildare.

Mattie moved carefully up a sloping part of the roof, head down, trying to get to Sean. He could go only so far, bullets zipping past. He got a glimpse of his brother, lying wounded.

Helena Molony looked across the roof and saw the boy crying bitterly.

13

At the GPO, M. W. O'Reilly was setting out his equipment on a large table. A stout, balding, self-confident young man of twenty-six, he looked like he'd be more at home sitting behind a desk in an insurance company. Which is indeed what he did for a living, as assistant superintendent of the Prudential Insurance Company in the Clontarf area.

Having been until recently captain of F Company, O'Reilly had been promoted to deputy adjutant of the Dublin Brigade. One of his roles that day was to oversee the distribution of a variety of small arms, ammunition and an array of edged weapons – daggers, cleavers, butchers' knives, hatchets and bayonets.

Fastidious to a fault, O'Reilly had arrived for battle equipped with a safety razor and shaving kit, so he could look his best when the occasion demanded.

Finally, after all the confusion and false starts, the remnants of 2nd Battalion, Dublin Brigade, were on the move from Fr. Mathew Park. It was between 2 and 3pm. The horse-drawn float was now loaded with arms and munitions.

A curate from Fairview church, Fr Walter McDonnell,

had come into the park earlier. He went into the pavilion and found a quiet place where any Volunteer who needed to could make his Confession. Now, with the Volunteers about to move, there was no time for individual Confessions.

The young priest came out of the pavilion and stood in front of the Volunteers. He'd give them all conditional absolution, he said. Conditional absolution was the Catholic fallback sacrament for times of imminent danger, when Confession wasn't possible – forgiveness for all sins on condition that the receiver of absolution has contrition for his wrongdoing.

The Volunteers knelt on one knee in front of the priest, clasping their rifles with both hands. Fr McDonnell held up a crucifix and spoke of what might come this day.

Looking up, Charlie Saurin was aware of the drama of the moment. The dozens of kneeling Volunteers, the crucifix held aloft, Fr McDonnell's solemn voice.

Think of what the Cross represents, said the priest. Think of your brief mortal life.

Moments later, there wasn't time for thinking. After a frustrating morning, the Volunteers were forming ranks, shouldering their rifles. Charlie Saurin got to his feet and lined up with others of F Company.

With half of the available 2nd Battalion gone to occupy Jacob's factory, what was now moving into action was a mixture of personnel – men from B and E and F Companies, along with some lost souls from 1st Battalion.

Captain Tom Weafer formed the column into three sections. At the front, an advance guard of about two dozen men, under Captain Leo Henderson. At the back, another couple of dozen men made up a rearguard, under Captain Frank Henderson. In the centre, the main party under Weafer himself of about ninety men, protecting the horse-drawn float with the arms and munitions. Around 140 in total.

About a fifth of the column was made up from F Company. Between them and those of its members in Jacob's factory, F Company sent sixty-five members into combat that day. Those quickly organized and sent to Jacob's that Monday morning would find themselves sidelined throughout most of the rising. Those left behind at Fr. Mathew Park, confused and without orders – only now setting off to confront the enemy – would over the next few days find themselves at the heart of the rebellion.

As they left Fr. Mathew Park, marching past the short row of houses in Windsor Villas, Leo Henderson called out a goodbye to his mother, who was standing in the doorway of their home. Frances Henderson's husband had died six years earlier. Of her eight children, the two born first had died. She had long had fears about the nationalist activities of her two eldest sons. A prominent Volunteer officer had called to the Henderson house one evening to see Leo and Mrs Henderson had shut the door in his face.

Now, she stood at her front door and watched her two sons heading off towards the fighting. She seemed calm, resolute – as though preparing herself for whatever was coming.

At Jacob's factory, excitement flared. A detachment of khaki-clad troops was spotted coming down Camden Street, towards the city centre. By the time they got down as far as the junction with Bishop Street the Volunteers were ready. A volley of shots from the factory scattered the soldiers, and they retreated back the way they had come.

The plan for the Jacob's contingent – to intercept soldiers moving from Portobello Barracks to the city centre – was working, so far.

*

Weafer's column of 2nd Battalion Volunteers, with Leo Henderson at the front and Frank Henderson at the back, marched down Philipsburg Avenue, turned right into Fairview Strand, left across the Tolka river at Ballybough Bridge, and on towards the city centre.

There was by now a steady stream of people hurrying away from the city centre, some carrying their belongings, some obviously distressed. They brought news. The rebels have taken over, they've already beaten the British in a couple of battles. Others said the army was beating the rebels out of their hidey-holes.

The Volunteer column could now hear in the distance, faint at first but unmistakeable, the sound of rifle fire and the chatter of machine guns.

A cyclist scout named Joe Bracken came pedalling furiously towards them from the direction of the city centre. He jumped off his bike and handed a note to Leo Henderson. It was from GPO headquarters.

At the GPO, Connolly and Pearse had intelligence coming in from various sources, not all of it reliable. One trustworthy source was a friendly telephone operator, Matt Costello, a member of B Company, 2nd Battalion. Costello listened in to likely calls and picked up information which he passed on to Connolly, using the code name 'Brian Boru'.

The note brought by Joe Bracken told Leo Henderson that a party of British infantry had been using the firing range on the North Bull, at Dollymount. They had left the firing range and were closing up on the column from behind. Leo brought the note to Captain Tom Weafer. The orders were to intercept the British at Fairview and stop their advance towards the city centre.

Weafer ordered the advance guard, under Leo Henderson, back to Annesley Bridge to engage the enemy. He ordered Frank Henderson to take the rearguard back the way they'd come, at the double, and seize a commanding position at Ballybough Bridge and engage the enemy. The main party of the column, under Captain Weafer, would continue on into the city centre with the arms and munitions.

Leo Henderson instructed his section to march at the double. They had to get to Annesley Bridge before the enemy. The detachment turned right on to the narrow Bayview Avenue, past startled residents standing at their front doors. This group included F Company's Charlie Saurin, Seamus Daly, Conway McGinn, Paddy Mahon and Matty Parnell. On reaching the North Strand they turned left and were within sight of Annesley Bridge. A hundred and fifty yards from the bridge, they split in two. Half crossed the street and took up positions in the gardens of houses on North Strand. The other half occupied a corner pub.

Charlie Saurin ran up the stairs of the pub and took up a position at a first-floor window. Others stationed themselves at other windows. Paddy Mahon and Jack McCabe got out on to the roof of a bottling store, overlooking the bridge.

The North Strand area had been fairly busy when the Volunteers reached it, but by now all civilians had vanished, the area was silent.

Almost immediately, four khaki-clad British soldiers, an advance group, came across the wide bridge, two on each footpath. They were carrying their rifles at the trail – single-handed, the weapons held horizontally by their sides.

The soldiers stopped. The lack of normal activity at the junction tipped them off that something was up.

Watching them, Charlie Saurin reckoned they had to see the Volunteers' rifles poking out of the first-floor windows of the corner pub.

Two officers joined the four soldiers and told them to turn left off the bridge, down Wharf Road (now East Wall Road), leading towards the docks. One of the officers gestured and a column of soldiers, about a hundred in all, came on to the bridge in two single files.

To cover the column's move down Wharf Road, an officer posted two men on the bridge with a machine gun. The crew crouched down behind their weapon, in the firing position.

Everyone had fingers on triggers, one touch needed to start the action.

Following Captain Weafer's orders, Frank Henderson's rearguard detachment was retreating at the double towards Ballybough Bridge. Onlookers jeered. Some local women who knew Frank called, 'Look at Henderson running away!'

Henderson knew the area well. He had previously – as a matter of routine – assessed its strategic points, mentally noting the advantages of one building over another. He ordered his men to take over Gilbey's wine shop, at the junction of Ballybough and Fairview Strand, as it commanded views of both Ballybough Bridge and the street leading to Fairview. To take over the building they turned out an old woman and her daughter from the flat upstairs. Both Henderson and Harry Colley were apologetic, but despite the distress of the two women the takeover continued. The Volunteers sandbagged the windows and took up positions.

They heard the nearby sound of gunfire.

*

At Annesley Bridge, the British were firing their machine gun. The Volunteers at the corner pub were firing back.

On the roof of the bottling store at the pub, Volunteer Paddy Mahon took aim at the machine gun and fired. Terrific shooting or lucky shot – no one knew, but the single bullet hit the machine gun and put it out of action. The two gunners abandoned their position and ran with their damaged weapon down Wharf Road.

Leo Henderson ordered those in the pub to follow the departing British. Hurrying down the stairs and into the street, Charlie Saurin fixed a bayonet to his rifle. Baptism of fire, he was thinking. F Company versus the battle-hardened professionals of the British Army, and them fresh from the trenches of European battlefields.

The group of about eight Volunteers crossed the road and ran down Leinster Avenue, parallel with Wharf Road, out of sight of the enemy. Halfway down they crossed through a gap between the houses – a construction site for a new row of homes. They took cover and began shooting at the British soldiers, who broke formation and scattered.

Saurin couldn't tell if the British were dropping because they'd been hit or because they were taking cover.

The Volunteers on the construction site were now supported by Volunteers firing from the back windows of houses on the North Strand Road. The British fired back, using rifles and a machine gun, from half-built houses near a railway viaduct. The exchange continued for a while, then the British withdrew further down Wharf Road.

Private James Boland, shot in the thigh, was taken into a house by four of his comrades. They hid there until the shooting ceased, then the wounded man was taken to hospital.

The Volunteer party was ordered to withdraw from the construction site and return back up Leinster Avenue.

The British climbed an incline to the railway line and began to walk along the tracks.

The shooting over, the locals returned to the streets. By the time Leo Henderson's squad re-formed and got ready to move out, North Strand was teeming with excited people.

Henderson decided to march his men towards the city centre, tracking the progress of the British. In fours, the Volunteers moved down North Strand. At gaps between buildings, they could see the British troops moving parallel, on the railway tracks, heading into the city centre.

When they got to Newcomen Bridge, crossing the Royal Canal, the Volunteers paused. The hump of the bridge, clear of any buildings, left them exposed, and they were told to take cover, as the British might fire. Crouched by the bridge, Charlie Saurin listened while a somewhat ragged young man boasted to him about the lovely new shirt he was wearing, freshly looted.

There was some exchange of fire between the Volunteers and the British soldiers on the railway tracks, but to little effect.

As gunfire sounded across the city, the unarmed Dublin Metropolitan Police were making themselves scarce. One DMP man walked past the Volunteers at Newcomen Bridge, head down.

'Good lads,' he said, as he hurried on his way.

Two Volunteers arrested another policeman and brought him to Seamus Daly.

'What're we going to do with him?'

Daly asked the policeman where he was going. He'd been on duty, the policeman said, and now his shift was over; he was on his way home. He lived down on Bessborough Avenue, two streets away.

Go home, Daly told him, and stay home and don't come out. The policeman thanked him and hurried off.

14

Captain Seamus Kavanagh was in charge of a detail in Stephens Green, near the Cuffe Street gate. He was reporting to Constance Markievicz when he came across his brother Joey and Joey's friend Tommy Keenan. Kavanagh was livid. Tommy was just twelve, Joey not much older. Earlier, he had told them both to go home – they were too young for this.

Tommy Keenan had been upset at being sent away, but eventually the two boys went off.

Now, here they were hiding behind Markievicz.

I told you to go home, Kavanagh said. Why didn't you go home? How did you get back here?

In through the York Street gate, one of them said.

I sent them home earlier, Kavanagh told Markievicz.

She smiled and said it was all right, he could leave them with her. And if their fathers came looking for the boys he was to refer them to her.

The boys were used to deliver despatches.

Leo Henderson's unit was at Newcomen Bridge, headed towards the city centre.

Frank Henderson's unit had taken up positions near Ballybough Bridge. They assembled material for barricades and began to bolster the defences. They did the same at Annesley Bridge – closing off two of the main routes into and out of the north city centre.

The main body of the column, under Tom Weafer, had reached Liberty Hall. There, they unloaded the arms.

Job done, F Company's Harry Colley left Weafer's column and joined with a number of Citizen Army men. They brought a commandeered load of vegetables to the GPO, after which they lined up and were formally inspected by James Connolly.

At around that time, Ernest Jordison was being driven down North Frederick Street and into Sackville Street. He was manager in Ireland of British Petroleum. Earlier, he and some friends had hired a car and driver and had taken a picnic basket on a bank holiday outing to Fairyhouse racecourse.

Word reached the racecourse that the rebels had taken over the General Post Office and had shot soldiers and policemen. As rumours spread through the crowd – heavily dotted with British Army officers – there was an amount of upset, and it became difficult to enjoy the day out. After some time, Jordison and his friends decided to return to Dublin.

On the way back they were stopped by a British Army officer in civilian clothes. He warned them against driving on – for God's sake, don't go into the city or you'll get shot – but they decided to see what the fuss was about.

There were crowds on the pavements in Sackville Street. Among them, they saw children with bats and balls, playing cricket.

Jordison saw the two dead horses near Nelson's Pillar and pools of blood on the ground, where the Lancers had been shot.

There was an overturned tram at the top of North Earl Street, part of a barricade. Civilians rushed about, carrying looted goods.

Men in rebel uniforms crossed the road, pushing hand-carts covered in sacking, towards the GPO. There were sandbags at the Post Office windows, rifles poking out.

With the authorities nowhere in sight, and with the rebels seemingly free to work on their defences, it was indeed possible to conclude that the rebels had taken over the centre of Dublin.

Two of Jordison's friends left the car at that stage and he and his remaining friend, Scott, headed down through Amiens Street and out towards Fairview, in the direction of Jordison's home. At Annesley Bridge they approached the barricade built by members of F Company. There were Volunteers standing at the barricade, others prone on the ground, their rifles aimed. Jordison's driver pulled to a stop.

Where do you live?

The Howth Road, Jordison said.

What's your business?

We're on our way home from Fairyhouse, the races.

One of the Volunteers perked up at the mention of the horseracing. What won the Irish Grand National, he asked Jordison – any chance it was a horse called Civil War?

No, Jordison told him, Civil War was third – the winner was All Sorts.

The Volunteers told Jordison they weren't letting cars through – he'd have to go back.

Jordison and Scott decided to release the hired driver and car and get home as best they could. They were allowed through the barricade on foot and eventually found a jarvey with a horse and sidecar for hire. He agreed to take Jordison to the Howth Road – a distance of three-quarters of a mile – and Scott to Sutton – a distance of six miles – for a fare of 30 shillings. This was at least ten times the going rate.

When they got to Jordison's home the jarvey said he wasn't going any further. This was a serious situation, he said – look at all the people streaming by.

Scott pleaded with the man to honour their deal. The jarvey eventually agreed to take him on to Sutton for an extra £5. Altogether, over forty times the going rate.

Charlie Saurin looked over the parapet of Newcomen Bridge, towards the parallel bridge where the Great Northern rail line crossed the Royal Canal. He saw a smart-looking British soldier on sentry duty – marching briskly to and fro, rifle sloped, oblivious to the Volunteers.

He took aim at the sentry, estimating the range at about two hundred yards. He stared down the length of his rifle at the distant, vulnerable, unaware figure, life and death balanced in the tension of a finger on a trigger.

He relaxed, as the order came to form fours.

Saurin's detachment turned up into Summerhill and down into Great Britain Street (now Parnell Street). When they reached the city centre, Sackville Street had a bank holiday air. No shooting, lots of people about. Some tore British Army recruiting posters from the pillars of the GPO, some stood looking at the dead horses belonging to the Lancers. The looters had moved on to fresh pastures.

Charlie Saurin, marching down Sackville Street in the column just ahead of Seamus Daly, turned around, pointed up to the flags atop the GPO and shouted – his voice alive with excitement: 'Seamus, Seamus, look at our flag up on the Post Office!'

Despite the gunfight at Fairview, it was only now that the reality – and the audacity – of what they had done seemed to dawn on the young Saurin. The days of drilling and training and talking were over. They were standing out in front of an empire and declaring a republic, and there was the proof of it, up there above the Post Office, waving in the wind.

At the sandbagged windows of the GPO, Volunteers waved and cheered to see the men from Fairview arrive. Patrick Pearse wasn't so happy.

Wearing his green slouch hat, and with a sword by his side, he approached Leo Henderson. His expression was grave. Charlie Saurin watched as Pearse spoke, then Henderson saluted and came back to his men. He told them they were going back to Fairview.

After the skirmish with the British at Fairview, Henderson had taken the initiative and resumed the original plan, which was to head into the city centre. Pearse, however, had believed Henderson's men were part of a holding force on the outskirts of the city, and that's where he wanted them.

Having just arrived at the centre of the action, the Volunteers were now marched around Nelson's Pillar and back down North Earl Street.

Passing through side streets, to avoid Amiens Street railway station, where the British had snipers in the tower, the Volunteers paused outside a pub. An off-duty British soldier emerged. He looked around at the armed and oddly dressed people into whose midst he had strolled – some in ill-matching uniforms, some in civvies. The Volunteers paid him no attention. After a few moments he went back into the pub.

There was a shot, a Volunteer collapsed, wounded. Some of the Volunteers had rifles, some had the dodgy American single-barrel shotguns. One Volunteer had taken a blast when a shotgun, left leaning against a wall, fell and discharged. It was a minor wound and the Volunteer was taken away for treatment.

It wasn't the first such accident. Seamus Daly told his comrades that from now on, until they needed to shoot, the shotguns should be unloaded.

The O'Rahilly took some time out from revolutionary activities in the GPO to write a note to his son Niall. 'We are doing grand and are giving the English a run for their money.'

He then spent some time arguing with James Connolly. The rising was under way, there was no more reason, he insisted, to hold Bulmer Hobson – he should be released.

15

By late afternoon on Monday, F Company's available men were spread around both the north and the south side of Dublin. Half were in Jacob's factory and its outposts. Others had taken over Gilbey's wine shop, beside Ballybough Bridge. Some were at Annesley Bridge, under Frank Henderson. Others were on their way back from the city centre, under B Company's captain, Leo Henderson. Still more were scattered around the GPO and other buildings in the centre of Sackville Street.

All the training, the lectures, the relentless drilling, had produced a volunteer army that was as fit, disciplined and enthusiastic as such a body could be. The structure of battalions and companies had given the Volunteers a sense of camaraderie, a familiarity with their comrades' strengths and weaknesses. Such cohesion is part of the strength of any armed body.

Some companies held their structure, after the Sunday cancellation and the Monday mobilization. But ad hoc decisions led to the creation of mixed units of people from various companies and battalions, with mixtures of Volunteers and Citizen Army members. The coherence of 2nd Battalion, and F Company with it, had been sacrificed to the need on Monday morning to get feet on the ground, marching towards Jacob's factory.

Joe Plunkett had said it would take three thousand Volunteers to launch the rising. The MacNeill cancellation drastically reduced the numbers who turned out on Easter Monday. One 3rd Battalion company had turned out 120 men on Sunday, before the manoeuvres were cancelled. On Monday the same company turned out eighteen. That day, perhaps a thousand turned out in Dublin – plus two hundred from the Citizen Army and around 150 from Cumann na mBan. As for the rest of the country – it remained quiet.

At the GPO, the leaders now seemed to see Fairview as a strategic position. Although there had been no plan to set up outposts there, Pearse had now identified the area as a bottleneck through which British soldiers would soon pour, and in which the Volunteers could act as a stopper.

He sent a despatch to Tom Weafer – the positions at Annesley Bridge and Ballybough must be held at all costs.

Sometime after 5pm, James Connolly ordered Sean T. O'Kelly, staff captain to Patrick Pearse, to take twenty or thirty men out to Fairview. He had information – erroneous – that British troops had come from the Bull Wall and were engaging the Volunteers there, so they needed reinforcements to hold their positions.

O'Kelly was taken aback. Although he was a founder member of the Volunteers, he had no experience of military matters. O'Kelly was also a founder member of Sinn Fein. He loved being at the centre of things, and enjoyed the gossip and influence. He was what a later generation would call a networker – fond of intrigue and self-promotion. He was a member of at least two covert outfits, the IRB and the Knights of Columbanus, the secretive band of ultra-Catholic schemers.

Although a member of the Volunteers, he considered himself a 'nominal' captain. He didn't know how to lead troops in the field.

O'Kelly picked out a Volunteer he knew to be experienced – Captain Thomas Craven. He told Craven to assemble a small force at the GPO, then he put himself at the head of it, alongside Craven, and they marched down North Earl Street and off to Fairview.

Among the Volunteers Craven recruited to this mission was Harry Colley, eager to get back to the Fairview area to reunite with F Company.

And Vincent Poole.

Liam Tannam was told there were a couple of odd fellas at one of the windows of the GPO. He ought to go see what they wanted.

The two men at the window wore seamen's clothes.

'I am from Sweden, my friend from Finland. We want to fight. May we come in?'

Why, Tannam asked, would a Swede and a Finn want to fight the British?

'Finland, a small country, Russia eat her up. Sweden, another small country, Russia eat her up, too. Russia with the British, therefore, we against.'

'Can you fight? Do you know how to use a weapon?'

'I can use a rifle. My friend, no. He can use what you shoot the fowl with.'

Tannam told him it was called a shotgun. He decided to admit them, found weapons for them and put them on window duty.

The two men took up their positions. They were shipping out on Thursday, but for the next few days they would fight for the freedom of small nations.

*

Captain Frank Henderson decided that his men needed to take a second vantage point at Ballybough Bridge. He ordered the takeover of Lambe's pub, which would give a field of fire up Richmond Road, towards Drumcondra.

Having arrived back from the GPO with Captain Leo Henderson's group, Charlie Saurin was one of those ordered to take the pub. Inside, locals grumbled at the inconvenience – several complaining they hadn't had time to finish their game of Rings.

Barman John Gavan, however, was excited at the news of the rising. He wanted to be part of it and immediately volunteered to join F Company, and was accepted.

Frank Henderson sent Volunteers to a local butcher, with money to buy meat. The butcher refused to sell, so they took it at gunpoint. A bread-delivery cart arrived and the Volunteers held that up. The driver was friendly enough, and in return for bread he accepted a receipt in the name of the Irish Republic.

Staff Captain Sean T. O'Kelly arrived out at Annesley Bridge at the head of the reinforcements ordered by James Connolly. He spoke with several Volunteers and Citizen Army men, then walked down to Ballybough and met Frank Henderson. He waited around awhile, then sent a message back to the GPO saying there was no activity. Mission accomplished, he and some of the Volunteers returned to the GPO.

Captain Craven ordered the rest of the contingent to occupy the offices of the Wicklow Manure Company, along the banks of the Tolka, just behind Annesley Bridge. Captain Vincent Poole of the Citizen Army was put in charge of that outpost.

Harry Colley was one of those assigned to take up position at the manure company. Two hundred yards away, his fellow members of F Company – Frank Henderson, Charlie Saurin, Oscar Traynor and others – were in place around Ballybough Bridge.

A young Volunteer from Inchicore, John Kenny, arrived at the manure company, having been turned away from the GPO. Vincent Poole accepted him into the Annesley Bridge garrison.

Leaving home that morning, Kenny and his brother had received their mother's blessing: 'Remember that your deaths are ordained by God and not by the English.'

Reaching the GPO, Sean T. O'Kelly reported back to James Connolly and was given another assignment: go up to Cabra Park and release Bulmer Hobson.

When O'Kelly got to Cabra he tried to convince Hobson to support the rising, now that the die was cast. Hobson refused.

Released, he walked alone down into the city centre. On Sackville Street, he stopped across from the GPO. Volunteers stood guard at the Post Office, under the flag of the Republic. On this side of the street he watched looters moving from shop to shop. Sightseers strolled; there were still some high spirits about, it being the evening of the bank holiday.

Hobson remembered a discussion with Pearse in a Dublin restaurant, in which they argued the merits or otherwise of an armed rising. It ended when Pearse stood up from the table and said, 'I can't answer your arguments, but I feel that we must have an insurrection.'

In a similar discussion in another restaurant, James Connolly had said Ireland was a powder keg – all it needed was the strike of a match.

If we must talk in metaphors, Hobson said, Ireland is a wet bog, and the match will fall into a puddle.

Hobson believed armed Volunteers would be needed

to resist the English attempt to impose conscription. This hopeless rising would squander their meagre forces.

Now the thing was under way, and he no longer had a role. He had no doubt that the movement to which he had devoted his life was proceeding inexorably towards failure and humiliation.

Someone raised an alarm at the GPO and Volunteers hurried to their stations, cocking their weapons.

After some moments the order came – stand down, false alarm, and everyone relaxed.

Volunteers who had climbed on to the window barricades jumped down. The Swede and the Finn among them. When the Finn landed, the butt of his shotgun hit the floor, the gun fired and lumps of plaster came down from the ceiling.

Joe Plunkett ran over, demanding to know what was going on. The Finn stared at him.

'Can you not talk, man?'

'No,' the Swede said. 'He has no English.'

The situation was explained to Plunkett.

'Amazing, but obviously that man there is a danger.'

The Finn was transferred to a room at the back of the GPO, making grenades. The Swede went with him. 'Where he go, I go. We together.'

The Finn's first name was Antli. The Volunteers called him Tony.

Up at Stephens Green, Jimmy O'Shea aimed his rifle at a car carrying two British officers towards the Shelbourne Hotel. He fired and saw the hat knocked off one of the officers. The car accelerated out of sight before he could fire a second shot.

O'Shea and Volunteer Jim Fox dug a trench inside the

railings of the park, opposite the top of Dawson Street. From there they could see down the length of Dawson Street and fire at any movement they thought suspicious.

Captain Kit Poole, a brother of Vincent Poole, was busy supervising the dispersal of the Citizen Army men, making sure everyone was dug in, that they had tonight's password and that the shifts for the rest of the night had been arranged.

Jimmy O'Shea was kept busy, shooting at cars trying to exit a garage opposite the Mansion House. About 8.30, a British soldier came down the pavement outside the railings and stopped at O'Shea's trench. With a string of obscenities he cursed the tin soldiers, asking why they wouldn't fight for their king and country. He appeared to be drunk, but O'Shea was suspicious. The trench was camouflaged, yet the soldier came right to it. When O'Shea went up close, there was no smell of drink from him.

Bastard, the soldier said.

O'Shea told him to go away. He now believed the soldier was a spy – playing the drunkard – sent to confirm rebel positions.

Go now, O'Shea told him. Go now and you won't be harmed.

Just then, two women came to the trench with bread and milk.

Whores you have, fighting with you, said the soldier.

O'Shea picked up a shotgun and shot the soldier at close range.

After a couple of minutes, he saw two gents in top hats and frock coats leaving the Shelbourne. He put down the shotgun, picked up his rifle and fired at the ground in front of the two men. They stopped and he called to them to come over. They approached, hands up.

Take the soldier to hospital, he told them. He's a spy.

When one of the men got aggressive, O'Shea raised his rifle to his shoulder. They did as they were told. The one who had become aggressive now addressed O'Shea as 'sir'.

Tom MacDonagh decided to withdraw the various outposts set up around Jacob's factory. Their main effect had been to attract the hostile attention of pro-British crowds, including the wives of men serving in the British Army. These were known as 'separation women', who received weekly allowances as their husbands were off at war in Europe.

As young Vinny Byrne's group withdrew from Malpas Street and approached the factory they were attacked by a jeering crowd. One man was intent on taking a rifle from a Volunteer and ignored calls to back off. Someone shot him.

When Vinny got inside, he was sent to keep watch from a window overlooking Peter's Row. It was there the fifteen-year-old discovered the joys of taking over a biscuit factory – eating as much cocoa, crackers and cream as he could bear.

At City Hall, after hours on the roof, under fire, young Mattie Connolly was relieved from his post and sent downstairs to see Dr Lynn. She examined him, asked how he felt. Mattie said he hadn't had any sleep for three nights running, but otherwise he was fit. Dr Lynn confirmed Sean's death and told him of those others who had been killed – George Geoghegan, Sean O'Reilly – of his sister Kate Barrett's work on the ground floor, nursing the wounded, of the activity in other garrisons around the city. She gave him two tablets and told him to eat, then he should sleep.

Mattie took the tablets with a cup of tea. He was shown upstairs to a small room, where he took off his military equipment and, still in his clothes, lay down on a bed and immediately slept.

British Army reinforcements had arrived at Dublin Castle and were preparing an assault on City Hall.

The O'Rahilly wrote a note for his wife, Nancy. 'All safe here so far. Things going well I believe, in most places. Love and kisses to you and to the boys.'

At Fairview, Harry Colley was feeling sorry for the Dublin day-trippers who had gone to Dollymount to picnic in the bank holiday sun. The trams had been taken out of service. Taxi drivers and jarveys were demanding fares only the well-off could pay. Now, the night was closing in and it was a long, long walk home, particularly for families with children.

A couple of hundred yards away, Lieutenant Oscar Traynor watched a similar stream of tired people shuffle homeward through Ballybough.

Charlie Saurin was upstairs in Lambe's pub, sent there to get some sleep. The beds used by the pub staff when working late were a peculiar shape – deep and box-like. Little coffins, Saurin thought. At first he decided he'd prefer staying awake to lying in one of those, but after a while tiredness overcame his distaste and he crawled into one of the coffins.

Time for bed.

At his home in Drumcondra, Matt Stafford, the old Fenian, had spent the day awaiting orders. A few people had come to his house, other Volunteers out of touch with their officers. No one knew exactly how things stood –

how many Volunteers had come out, how successful or otherwise the day had been. No one had news.

All Matt could do was hold on to the company treasury of £29.17 shillings, which might be needed at any time. And be ready when orders came from Captain Leo Henderson.

At Jacob's, the Volunteers scattered empty tin cans on the road outside, as a makeshift alarm – in case anyone tried a stealthy assault during the night.

In the dimly lit factory, surrounded by vast machinery covered with dust-wraps, the men listened as Commandant Tom MacDonagh told them of the events of the first day of the rising. He spoke of the buildings seized and the British response. He told them of the reinforcements even now marching from outlying districts, and of allied forces landing on various parts of the coast.

He'd had reports, he said, of German submarines forming a cordon around the country – and that would put the clappers on any attempt by the British to use their navy to bring in supplies.

Major MacBride also addressed the men. Shouts of 'Long live the Republic' echoed off the steel floor of the biscuit factory.

At Kelly's gunpowder shop, on Bachelors Walk, Joe Good noticed it had begun to drizzle. That might keep the looters at home. He didn't approve of the smashing and grabbing, but watching it he had begun to wonder what the difference was between the Volunteers 'commandeering' what they needed and the looters taking stuff they could never dream of buying.

There was shooting now, somewhere to the south of his position. Bursts of machine-gun fire.

'The British?' Joe asked Peadar Bracken.

'Must be, I suppose,' Peadar replied. '*We* have no machine guns.'

The walls vibrated with the impact of explosions, and sixteen-year-old Mattie Connolly woke in a dark room at City Hall. His ears stung with the shock of machine guns and rifles firing nearby. Glass breaking, woodwork being smashed, shouts, women screaming.

He heard someone yelling, 'Come in off the roof! Come in off the roof!' Then the same voice shouted, 'Go back onto the roof! Go back onto the roof!'

Mattie rose in the dark, groped for his equipment, buckled it on, found his rifle. 'Who's there?' he shouted.

'Come on quick, they're here!'

He felt his way along a wall until he came to a door, opened it and looked down the corridor. In the glimmer of light from some other room he saw the bayonets and cap badges of British soldiers. He slammed the door shut and stood there, his rifle pointing at the door, ready to fire when it opened.

Outside, the soldiers were talking excitedly, but Mattie couldn't make out what they were saying.

Five minutes passed.

His eyes were accustomed to the darkness now, and he could see a ladder in a corner of the room, leading to a small trapdoor in the ceiling. He went up the ladder and out on to the roof. He moved around, hoping to find some comrades, but there was no one there.

He knew this part of the roof, from earlier. After a minute he found what he must have known was there: the body of his brother. He knelt beside Sean and said a prayer.

Alone up there, the sixteen-year-old moved to the edge

of the roof and peered through the stone balustrade, down on to the street. The blue-tinged light of street-lamps reflected off the wet cobblestones. He could hear a lanyard beating against a flagpole that shook in the wind. The sound of men's voices came up from below, a chain rattling – perhaps an artillery piece being moved.

Mattie took two homemade bombs from his pockets and put them down. He sat on the sloping roof and wondered how his comrades had fared. He didn't know what time it was. After midnight, anyway, he guessed.

There was a sudden bang and a flare shot up from the Castle yard, throwing light on everything on the roof. Mattie quickly lay face down in the valley gutter and stayed still.

After a few seconds the flare burned out.

As he lay there on the rough surface of the roof, Mattie was awash in helplessness. His body was exhausted, his mind battered by the horrors of the past few hours. He fought the fatigue that washed through him, but sank inexorably into sleep. When he opened his eyes, a hand was shaking his shoulder, a voice was telling him, 'Get up!'

He saw a revolver.

The hand holding it, the arm, the khaki jacket with a red cross on a white band.

Are you wounded?

No.

The medic called for an escort for the prisoner.

Mattie Connolly was taken down the stairs by two British soldiers. They passed two others on their way up, carrying an empty stretcher.

Paul Galligan, vice-commandant of the Wexford Brigade, walked past a dead horse on Sackville Street. Back home, the Wexford units had been told they were on their own – their leading officer was staying out of any rising. They had recently lost another senior officer, William Brennan-Whitmore, over the issue of dancing. And now, they didn't know whether or not they were included in the plans for the rising. Galligan had come to Dublin in search of answers, and he'd made his way to the city centre.

Now, he reported to the first outpost he encountered, on the corner of North Earl Street.

Galligan was startled to find that the officer in charge there was Brennan-Whitmore, the very same anti-dancing chap from Wexford. Brennan-Whitmore sent Galligan across the road to the GPO, where he reported to Connolly and Pearse.

Connolly said Galligan should return immediately to Wexford and mobilize the Enniscorthy Battalion. Hold the railway line there, Connolly told him. We're expecting British troops to land at Rosslare. Prevent the enemy from using the railway to get to Dublin.

Connolly sent Galligan to get something to eat. Then, he said, you'll be provided with a good bicycle.

In the canteen, Galligan approached the man in charge of catering, Desmond FitzGerald, and explained that Connolly wanted him to have a feed, as he was off on a long bicycle journey. FitzGerald – who was intent on making the available food last as long as possible – gave him two buns and a cup of tea.

Daylight was breaking as Galligan left the GPO. Don't go through Wicklow, Connolly told him, as Dublin is being surrounded by the British. Take a detour out through the west.

When Galligan got to the Parnell Monument at the north end of Sackville Street he stopped to look back at the two rebel flags flying on top of the GPO. Then, he began his journey of over eighty miles. He cycled up the North Circular Road, north-west out of the city, out through Mulhuddart, then turned down towards the south.

At Maynooth he saw troop trains heading into the city.

Part Five

Gunfire

16

At Stephens Green, the shooting continued through the early hours of Tuesday morning. Bullets rained down from high buildings, out of the darkness. The Cumann na mBan nurses were worried about a young man, Fran O'Brien, who was sinking fast. He'd been shot in the neck and the bullet was still in there. He was in great pain.

Nora O'Daly couldn't even see the patient. If the women lit a lamp to examine the young man they would draw fire. Without light they could do nothing.

Eventually, someone found a potting shed. The nurses brought the patient there, where they could use a lamp and seek to stabilize him. They arranged to get him to hospital, to have the bullet extracted. Civilians volunteered to carry the stretcher.

'God bless the work,' they told one another, the Cumann na mBan nurses and the civilians.

Some of the women lay on the seats of the summerhouse, others lay on the cold ground. As the bullets continued to randomly pepper the park, Nurse Bridie Goff kept up a rattle of comical remarks about the damned snipers and how they were ruining her sleep. Despite the gunfire, Nora O'Daly found herself unable to stifle the laughter. O'Daly had had an aching tooth for over a year, and now she noticed the pain was gone.

Across the road, on the rooftops of the Shelbourne Hotel and the nearby United Services Club, the British Army was installing machine guns.

Two figures appeared out of the darkness. Jimmy O'Shea challenged them and Mike Mallin, commandant of the Stephens Green garrison, gave the password. Mallin was accompanied by his second in command, Constance Markievicz.

There was a complaint, Mallin said. One of the women who had been distributing food had witnessed the shooting of an apparently drunk British soldier, and accused O'Shea of callousness.

He wasn't drunk, O'Shea insisted. He was a spy. The enemy had spies checking out where the trenches were. We'll see, he said – the morning will tell if I'm right.

Liam Daly was woken at 2.30am. He'd fallen asleep exhausted, having spent a couple of hours breaking through a steel-lined door in the Reis building, diagonally across the street from the GPO. While he slept, someone had put a pillow under his head, covered him with a blanket and taken off his collar and tie.

Now there was a pint mug of steaming tea waiting for him, along with a plate of three fried eggs, several sausages and plenty of bread and butter. All he'd had the previous day was a few biscuits, so he dug into the meal.

About an hour later he was high above Sackville Street, on the roof of the Reis building, with Johnny 'Blimey' O'Connor, Boss Shields and the rest of the radio team, struggling to fix in place an aerial through which the news of the Proclamation of the Republic would be broadcast.

It was not yet dawn. The work had to be done in darkness, for fear of snipers.

Blimey O'Connor was at the Abbey Street side of the roof, halfway up a pole. Liam Daly was on the Sackville Street side. Like O'Connor, Daly had quit London and moved to Dublin, rather than be conscripted into the British Army. He was now perched on a ledge, about eight feet above Fergus O'Kelly and Boss Shields.

It took Daly around ten minutes to unbolt a clamp, adjust a pole and bolt the clamp in place again. Dawn was now breaking and Daly took a moment from his labours to enjoy the lovely silhouette of the city rooftops, then he went back to work. A pebble hit the wall beside him, then another and another, and he swore at his comrades below and told them to stop playing around. When a bullet smashed a corner brick he realized these were no pebbles.

Daly quickly finished up and dropped to the roof, imagining what might have happened and feeling faint.

On the other side of the roof, Blimey O'Connor finished his work, with bullets buzzing past him, and slid down the pole.

You dig a small hole under the railway track, Vincent Poole said. Then you put the gelignite in the hole, pile the earth back on top of it, light the fuse and you've three minutes to get away before it blows.

Harry Colley knew nothing about explosives, nor did Harry Boland. The two members of F Company were part of a team of four sent by Vincent Poole to head out over the sloblands (now Fairview Park) to the railway line. Blowing up part of the track would stop the line being used to bring troops into the city centre.

Colley was feeling the pressure of taking orders from

the Citizen Army's Vincent Poole, who made little secret of his lack of regard for the Volunteers.

The previous evening, Colley had been put on sentry duty at a corner at Fairview – where the road split between North Strand and Ballybough. He was to stop and question people coming through the junction. A local man who knew Harry brought him tea and sandwiches at midnight.

About 1.30am Colley got some relief from the boredom, isolation and tiredness when Harry Boland arrived from his home at Marino Crescent, half a mile away. Boland too was separated from F Company. Colley told him Vincent Poole's people had established an HQ at the manure factory beside Annesley Bridge, and Boland headed for there.

By 3am, when he was finally relieved, Colley was exhausted. About fifteen minutes later he was told he had to go back to the Fairview sentry position. He was relieved again at 5.30am, and at 6am he, Harry Boland and two others were sent across the sloblands to blow up the railway line.

They crossed the mudflats, dug the small hole, inserted the gelignite, covered it up, lit the fuse and ran. Hurrying down the embankment – too tired to jump properly – Colley got caught on a barbed-wire fence and his thigh was gashed. The four men were twenty yards from the line when the gelignite went off. It left the railway line intact.

By now Colley and Boland had learned that F Company's officers and some of their men were occupying positions at Ballybough Bridge, a short walk from the manure company. Vincent Poole, however, wanted to hold his force together, as he'd been ordered to do. So, he instructed Colley and Boland to stay at their posts.

There were a number of British Army prisoners being held at the manure works. They had stumbled upon the Fairview outpost and were arrested. Harry Boland decided to take one of them to the GPO.

When Boland left, all Poole's doubts about the commitment of Volunteers were confirmed. You're a soldier, you obey orders, or we don't have an army.

Harry Colley wanted to go home and attend to the barbed-wire wound on his thigh. Poole refused permission.

My house is just three hundred yards away, Colley said. Send an escort with me, if you like.

Poole said no.

Colley waited for a while, then he just walked away, took a shortcut through a laneway and found F Company at Ballybough Bridge.

Frank Henderson enthusiastically greeted him. Oscar Traynor produced a bottle of whiskey, rubbed some into Colley's leg wound, dressed it and sent him home with Paddy Mahon and another comrade to change his clothes. When he got back to Ballybough, Colley finally got to close his eyes and slept.

Meanwhile, Harry Boland made his way back from the GPO, having left the prisoner there. Instead of returning to the manure company offices and Vincent Poole, he rejoined his own unit, F Company, at Ballybough.

James Connolly set up various outposts to protect the GPO. He sent Volunteers across the street to occupy the Imperial Hotel, which was part of the same building as Clerys department store.

A Volunteer hurled a ball of twine from the hotel and it landed close to the pavement outside the GPO. Another Volunteer ran out from the GPO and got the twine, which was then run around a fixture and the ball was thrown back to the Imperial. The ends of the twine were tied and a communications system was in place – notes were sent back and forth in tin cans on the endless loop.

Three couriers left the Stephens Green area – having delivered despatches to various posts, they were on their way by bicycle to report to Pearse at the GPO. Peddling fast down Grafton Street, they came into view of a number of snipers stationed on the roof of Trinity College.

It was light enough now to aim, but the cyclists were moving fast and the angle downward from the rooftop was particularly acute.

Gerald Keogh, aged twenty, from Ranelagh, was slightly ahead of the other two, and more than one of the snipers singled him out. He took four bullets, at least one in the head, and died instantly. His bicycle stayed upright, with Keogh on board, speeding ahead, for about thirty yards, before it swerved and Keogh came off. One of the other cyclists was wounded, the third got away.

It was near morning now, and Mattie Connolly was in an unlit cell in Ship Street Barracks. He had created some interest following his capture, as he was led across Dublin Castle yard.

'That's a young 'un!'

'Yes, the bugler!'

Only then Mattie remembered his bugle was still slung from his neck.

On to the guardroom, where he gave his name and address and was searched.

Could I have my rosary and crucifix back, please?

They gave him back the rosary, but they kept the small brass crucifix. The soldier doing the searching unfolded a small piece of paper he found in Mattie's pocket and read the contents – the lyric of 'A Battle Hymn', written by Constance Markievicz for the Citizen Army.

Who fights for Ireland, God guide his blows home.
Who dies for Ireland, God give him peace.

The soldier looked from the paper to Mattie. His expression made it plain he thought the youngster was mad.

For Mattie Connolly, less than a day into the rising, his war was over. His brother Sean was dead and it would be days before he would learn how the rest of his family had fared. He was taken away to be placed in detention with other captured rebels.

As dawn arrived, fifteen Volunteers woke in Glasnevin Cemetery, having spent most of the night sleeping on grave tops. They had walked the sixteen miles from Maynooth to take part in the rising, wading through the Tolka river to the graveyard, where they arrived at about 2am. Fourteen of them were from the college in Maynooth; the fifteenth was a servant boy at the college who spontaneously decided to join in the rising.

Refreshed, they now marched into Sackville Street and entered the GPO. They were taken to the canteen for a meal – Desmond FitzGerald gave them tea and buns.

After a while the group was welcomed by James Connolly. 'It doesn't matter a damn if we're wiped out now,' he told them. 'We've justified ourselves.'

Tom Harris, from Prosperous, thought to himself: That's a bit rugged.

At Hopkins & Hopkins, overlooking O'Connell Bridge, Volunteers heard murmuring from outside. A group of postmen had gathered there and were discussing whether they should report to work at the GPO. Eventually, they were joined by another postman. He'd been to the GPO and a chap with a bayonet on the end of his rifle had assured him there would be no post to deliver today.

After their meal of tea and buns, several of the Maynooth group were introduced to some members of the Hibernian Rifles – a small nationalist outfit significantly better armed than the Volunteers – who had put themselves at the disposal of James Connolly. Together, they were ordered to cross the Liffey and go to the vicinity of City Hall, to support a Citizen Army unit that was under pressure.

They set out down Abbey Street and across Liffey Street towards the Ha'penny Bridge. The bridge had been there for a hundred years, a private business allowed to charge a toll of one halfpenny per person crossing. A toll taker was there to ensure that no one crossed without paying. That morning, he watched as about thirty men approached, most carrying modern rifles, some carrying shotguns.

He stopped them. A ha'penny each, he said.

History does not record the answer he received as the heavily armed group ignored him and brushed past, but it probably included the words 'you have to be joking'.

17

By daybreak, Tuesday morning, the British Army had their machine guns ready on the rooftops overlooking Stephens Green. They began strafing the park. Bullets sliced through the trees and bushes where Citizen Army men and members of Cumann na mBan crouched, folded up into themselves.

Jimmy O'Shea huddled in the trench facing the top of Dawson Street. He was convinced now beyond doubt that the previous evening the British had sent spies to identify the locations of Citizen Army defences.

Eventually, the machine guns stopped their chatter. The snipers continued firing down into the trenches along by the railings, into the centre of the park, at anything that moved, or anything that might conceal an enemy. There was a scream from a trench near the gate at the top of Grafton Street.

One of those who died in the rain of bullets was sixteen-year-old Jim Fox, who had helped Jimmy O'Shea dig a trench.

Commandant Mike Mallin's whistle repeatedly shrilled as he called his men to withdraw from their positions – the command was to transfer from the park to the Royal College of Surgeons, a robust building on the west side

of the Green. A small band from the Citizen Army –
three men and three women – had taken the college the
previous day.

The Cumann na mBan members ran down the footpath on the west side of the Green, in twos and threes,
towards the safety of the college, bullets ricocheting off
the street.

The rebels barricaded the windows of the college. They
pulled down a large rolled-up screen, used to show slides
during lectures, to divide off a section of the hall where
the women could create a first aid station. Nora O'Daly
and Rosie Hackett set up their equipment.

One good piece of news – Fran O'Brien, the young
man shot in the neck and treated by O'Daly in Stephens
Green, had strengthened. His pulse was improved and
the doctors said he'd be okay.

Over near the Shelbourne Hotel, a small crowd gathered at the corner of Merrion Row. Every now and then
some would venture across to the railings at Stephens
Green, despite the bullets whining overhead. They were
drawn by the sight of a dead man inside the railings,
slumped over his rifle.

Nearby, comrades of Phil Clarke pulled his body into
the cover of the trees and whispered an Act of Contrition
into his ear.

The withdrawal from the park was orderly, done in
groups. It was an hour before it was Jimmy O'Shea's turn
to scramble to safety.

Charlie Saurin had slept for a couple of hours in the
coffin-shaped bed upstairs in Lambe's pub. Then he
was woken and told he had to do sentry duty. He stood
around, with nothing happening, until dawn.

After a substantial breakfast, he had little to do but sit

in the pub. The owner had asked barman John Gavan to keep an eye on the stock, but the Volunteers weren't interested in free drink. Around 8.30am a man came to the pub and said he was a regular and he needed a pint. Gavan confirmed that this was the case.

Go ahead, Saurin told him. As the customer sipped his pint he explained apologetically to Saurin that he needed the drink before he could start his work.

Harry Colley went out around the district with Oscar Traynor to call on Volunteers who hadn't turned out for the scrap. These men had guns and ammunition that would be needed in the days to come.

Bill O'Brien went to a window of the GPO and asked if James Connolly was available. A Volunteer inside went to look for him, while O'Brien, a veteran trade unionist and a friend of Connolly's, stood waiting in front of the Post Office.

Sackville Street was pretty much deserted, quiet, no trouble. Over five hundred yards long, fifty yards across – an expansive street, a fitting place for an impressive building such as the General Post Office. The hundred-year-old building was tall, with a portico, and fronted by six columns. It had recently been refurbished and had re-opened for business just a couple of weeks earlier, dressed in the best of fixtures and fittings.

Immediately to the north, it was flanked by Henry Street, to the south by the cul-de-sac of Princes Street. At the north end of Sackville Street, the Parnell Monument. At the south end of the street, O'Connell Bridge.

There weren't any looters around right now, but they were never too far away. The absence of the police had made the city centre a great attraction for those willing to risk smashing a window. The widespread looting hadn't been a surprise to Bill O'Brien. Give people who have nothing an opportunity to grab something and they would be mad not to. He'd said as much to Connolly before the rising.

'That,' Connolly replied, 'will be one more problem for the British.'

Now, Connolly was walking up along the front of the GPO, underneath the portico. How is it going? O'Brien asked. How's the Citizen Army doing?

They did badly in Stephens Green, Connolly said. Some of them were killed this morning. A machine gun on the roof of the Shelbourne.

They talked about Connolly's daughters for a while. He said nothing about the overall progress of the rising, but his mood seemed low.

Joe Good was sent to the GPO with a message. He brought along a sword he'd found in Kelly's gunpowder shop – a post the Volunteers had taken to calling Kelly's Fort. Good had been on a similar errand the previous day and he knew Michael Collins was in the GPO and was now wearing the stripes that went with being a staff captain. Collins had a history with the Kimmage garrison, where he was respected but not liked. He too often put on a hard-man act, as though his Volunteers might be more disciplined if they were afraid of him.

Joe Good was friendly with Collins, enjoyed teasing him – and had done so the previous day. Now, he presented Collins with the sword he'd found in Kelly's Fort.

It suits your new station in life, he said, deadpan.

Collins stared at Good, wondering if this was a piss-taking gesture. He decided to accept the sword as a peace offering.

*

The outpost at Ballybough Bridge was quiet. Charlie Saurin sat around Lambe's pub, now and then falling asleep in his chair. There would be action only if British troops sought to cross the bridge, heading towards town.

After a while a tall, red-bearded man came to the pub. His name was Byrne. The previous day, his son Eddie had arrived at Fr. Mathew Park and joined the Volunteers, and was now among those at Ballybough Bridge.

Byrne had a long conversation with Saurin, after which he said he wanted to appoint Charlie as guardian of his son Eddie, for the duration of the rising. Charlie agreed he'd take on the job. Eddie was fifteen, Charlie – his guardian – was twenty.

After that, the only diversion at the Ballybough outpost was when someone commandeered a sheep – after a long period in which no one had had anything substantial to eat. The sheep was slaughtered, butchered, cooked and eaten in less than two hours, under the supervision of a cheerful Harry Boland.

Meanwhile, from up the road at Annesley Bridge came the sporadic sound of gunfire, from the manure works.

Vincent Poole had sent another crew across to the railway line on the far side of the sloblands, this time to remove rails, rather than blow up the line. When the British examined the broken rail line, the garrison in the manure works fired on them and an intermittent exchange of gunfire followed.

Among the Citizen Army fighters with Vincent Poole was a man who was known as John Neale. That might not have been his true name, but by the end of the week he would be entrenched in the memories of those who fought alongside him.

*

On the roof of the College of Surgeons the rule was you kept your head down. The gunfire from the Shelbourne Hotel was non-stop, and the British soldiers were good at their job. Jimmy O'Shea was one of those shooting back. He and another member of the Citizen Army were shoulder to shoulder, firing. O'Shea was inserting a new clip in his rifle when the other man tapped him on the arm and said, For God's sake, do something with him.

He pointed back to a space behind them, where Mick Doherty of the Citizen Army, who had just arrived on the roof, was calmly eating a sandwich. O'Shea opened his mouth to shout when a dozen machine-gun bullets hit Doherty, taking off one side of his face.

Fireman Joe Connolly got him down from the roof, through a narrow stairway – exposing himself to enemy fire, risking his life for a man so riddled as to have no chance of surviving. Nora O'Daly gave Doherty first aid, but the wounds were beyond her skills and it was decided to take him to hospital. Opening a side door to allow the stretcher to be lifted out, Citizen Army man Frank Robbins leaned over the wounded man and whispered, 'You're a goner, the Lord have mercy on you.'

18

If it was good for human beings, Frank Sheehy-Skeffington was an activist on its behalf. Full-bearded, usually wearing knickerbockers, looking older than his thirty-eight years, Sheehy-Skeffington was a familiar figure around Dublin. A writer, a journalist and a pacifist, he was also a feminist, agitating for votes for women and equality between the sexes. The Sheehy part of his name came from his wife, Hanna Sheehy.

He was a socialist who resigned from the Citizen Army when it changed from being a purely defensive body and took on a military purpose. He'd gone to jail for agitating against British Army recruitment. He'd been at the Custom House, protesting against recruitment, on the occasion when Vincent Poole was arrested and subsequently convicted of making 'statements prejudicial to the recruitment of His Majesty's forces'.

Sheehy-Skeffington's first encounter with the rising had been shortly after it began the previous day, when he'd tried to help a wounded British soldier beside Dublin Castle. As a pacifist, he didn't support a military rising, but he feared for the lives of the fighters, many of whom he knew. He turned up at the GPO around noon and met Bill O'Brien on the street outside. He asked the trade union leader to let his comrade James Connolly know that a cruiser and two gunboats had arrived and were disembarking British troops at Kingstown.

O'Brien went to a window of the GPO and passed the information on to Diarmuid Lynch, a Volunteer officer.

Sheehy-Skeffington told O'Brien he was worried about the looting. He'd personally appealed to looters to stop their rampaging – it was wrong and it was dangerous. Their response was not encouraging. He was trying to arrange a meeting for that afternoon, to see if anything more organized could be done.

Even in the midst of an historic event, human needs had to be attended to. Sheehy-Skeffington was hungry. He decided to go see a friend, Jennie Wyse Power, who had a shop around in Henry Street – the Irish Farm Produce Company – and who lived above the shop. She'd have something for him to eat.

The shop was closed, but Wyse Power answered his knocking. All she had in the place was tea and an egg, she said.

That would be grand, said Frank.

First, she asked, could he run an errand? Hamilton-Long, the chemist's shop in Sackville Street, was closed, but there'd be someone there and they'd arranged to get in some medicine her sick daughter Maura needed. She asked Frank to fetch it.

Certainly he could do that, Frank said. No bother.

On the second day of the rising, although bullets rained down on Stephens Green and snipers picked off Volunteer couriers, Sackville Street remained safe enough for Bill O'Brien to visit a friend at the rebel HQ, for James Connolly to stroll in front of the GPO, for Frank Sheehy-Skeffington to run an errand close to the centre of the action.

Troop trains were filling up, heading for Dublin, but so far the GPO area was calm, with little hint of what was to come.

At around six o'clock that evening, scouts reported to Captain Frank Henderson that a column of British troops was coming down the Malahide Road, approaching his position in Fairview. Henderson sent the information to James Connolly in the GPO. It seemed as though the twin outposts at Ballybough and Fairview were about to engage with the enemy.

Connolly had further information from other sources. There was another column of British troops arriving at Drumcondra, from Swords. Soon they would be at the far end of Clonliffe Road, forming a pincer movement with the column approaching from the Malahide Road.

Add to this the British troops firing on the Craven/Poole unit at the manure works at Annesley Bridge, and the snipers in the tower at Amiens Street railway station, and the result was that the twin outposts at Fairview were pretty much at the centre of a hive of enemy activity.

The bottleneck that Pearse wanted defended was turning into a vulnerable outpost ripe for annihilation.

Connolly sent a reply to Frank Henderson, ordering him to take command of both the Annesley Bridge and Ballybough units. The entire Fairview/Ballybough garrison was to fall back to the GPO, if possible.

If they didn't succeed in getting to the GPO, Connolly wrote, he was sure they would put up a gallant fight for the freedom of their country.

It was clear to Henderson that Connolly wasn't expecting them to make it.

There were sixty-six men at the Ballybough position, another twenty-five at Annesley Bridge – along with half a dozen khaki-clad British Army prisoners. They formed a column – among them John Gavan, barman from Lambe's pub. Frank Henderson warned the men that they were in for a route march, a fast progress through two miles of dangerous territory, towards the GPO. They found they had more weapons than they had men to use them, which left some of them weighed down with equipment.

Frank Henderson was at the head of the column, flanked on the left by his brother Leo and on the right by Oscar Traynor. The column moved off at a fast pace. Passing the end of Clonliffe Road they could see British troops coming down the long, straight road, with a clear field of fire. Henderson concluded that the British didn't shoot because they saw the khaki of the prisoners.

The pace quickened. Laden with the extra equipment, trying to move speedily yet maintain their order, the column was now somewhat ragged. As well as his rifle, Harry Colley was carrying two homemade bombs in his pockets, and three .45 automatics.

They took side streets where possible, to avoid such potential flashpoints as Amiens Street station. Coming through Summerhill, insults, stones and bottles were thrown at the column by the women whose husbands were off fighting in France.

Further on, a woman who knew Frank Henderson called him over and told him there were Lancers grouped in North Great George's Street. Had the contingent continued on from Summerhill down along Great Britain Street they would have come under fire from the Lancers on their right flank. And the British troops gathered at the Parnell Monument would have taken them on from the front. The result would have been slaughter.

The column turned left into Cumberland Street,

around into Marlborough Street, then up Sackville Place, on the left of Clerys department store. They were now across the street from the GPO.

A newspaper seller nearby was holding a poster that said the Lord Lieutenant had proclaimed martial law.

Frank Henderson sent Oscar Traynor across to the Post Office to find out where Connolly wanted the contingent to go. Traynor came back with orders to send the Fairview contingent across to the GPO. The rebels ran the fifty yards at intervals. The British were in force at each end of Sackville Street. They hadn't opened fire but might do so at any time. The Volunteers at the windows of the GPO cheered the reinforcements.

Harry Boland had custody of the half dozen British troops captured at Fairview, and they had to risk running for the shelter of the GPO along with their captors.

Halfway across to safety, Charlie Saurin ducked just in time to avoid the barbed-wire strung across the street. He made it to Princes Street, skidded on the broken glass where Katie Byrne had smashed a window and came down hard, gashing his right hand.

Just then a ragged burst of firing erupted.

Above Clerys store, at the windows of the Imperial Hotel, Volunteers had seen the khaki figures running towards the GPO and assumed the building was under attack. They began firing on the running figures and F Company's Liam McGinley received minor wounds.

With no idea who was doing the firing, several of the Fairview men began shooting back. Charlie Saurin squeezed off a round in the general direction of the Imperial Hotel, ejected the shell, loaded another round and fired again.

James Connolly, waiting in the doorway of the GPO to greet the Fairview men, ran out on to the pavement, waving his arms at the Imperial and shouting an order to cease fire.

The O'Rahilly shook his head. 'A good hundred rounds of ammunition wasted.'

Inside the GPO, Charlie Saurin was taken to have his hand bandaged. He missed the speech of welcome delivered to the Fairview contingent by Patrick Pearse.

Pearse climbed on to a large table to address them. By getting out successfully from the encircling British forces at Fairview, he said, they had performed a great deed. By rising against their enemies, they had lifted the stain that had rested on Dublin's fair name since the rebel leader Robert Emmet's execution in 1803 had been carried out without protest from Dublin citizens.

Charlie Saurin, his hand bandaged, fortified by a slice of rich cake provided by a member of Cumann na mBan, rejoined the Fairview group. He saw a heap of saddles and swords on the floor, taken from the fallen horses of the Lancers. On a wooden structure above an entrance, a Volunteer in a top hat and frock coat was strutting and posing for the amusement of his comrades. A member of Cumann na mBan was sitting behind a typewriter. Joe Plunkett, his throat bandaged, stood taking it all in.

James Connolly began deploying the Fairview forces. He ordered about a dozen of the men to go back across the road to reinforce the Volunteers at the Imperial Hotel, and he assigned Frank and Leo Henderson to take a couple of dozen men to prepare defences in Henry Street. He told Oscar Traynor to take the remainder of the men, including those from the Citizen Army – about two dozen in total – into the Metropole Hotel, on the block of Sackville Street immediately to the south of the GPO. This block consisted of the Metropole, Eason's newsagent and Manfield

& Sons boot shop, on the corner of Abbey Street.

Approaches to the GPO would now be defended by positions to the south – the Metropole block; and to the north-west – the Henry Street block. And across the road, outposts included the Imperial, the buildings between the Liffey and Abbey Street – from Hopkins & Hopkins through the Dublin Bread Company building to the Reis building. In addition, Brennan-Whitmore had set up an outpost at the junction with North Earl Street.

All the outposts had orders to bore through the walls, to provide safe and hidden access along the length of each block.

As was also standard operating procedure, all available vessels were to be assembled and filled with water, in case supplies were cut off. Where possible, loopholes were knocked through under windows, to give the rebels a safer vantage position from which to fire at the enemy.

Charlie Saurin and Harry Boland were among those assigned to the Metropole. Harry Colley and Seamus Daly were among those sent across the road to the Imperial.

Oscar Traynor approached Connolly. He said he didn't feel comfortable with the assignment. He was a lieutenant. He was being given command of Citizen Army men, among them Vincent Poole, a Citizen Army captain.

Connolly had a habit of ignoring rank and appointing whomever he thought best for the job.

'Is it not sufficient that I give you the command of this unit?'

'It is, sir,' Traynor said, 'but I want to be assured that if I'm in command I'll be obeyed by all, including the officer senior to me in rank.'

Poole bristled: 'Did I say that I wouldn't obey you?'

I just need to have that clear, Traynor said. He accepted Poole's assurance.

19

At 25 Northumberland Road, Lieutenant Mick Malone watched a British Army unit march past. They were a volunteer unit known as the GRs, and they were returning to Beggars Bush Barracks from drill. Mostly older men, the GR was short for Georgius Rex, denoting the King George insignia they wore. They were known in Dublin as the Gorgeous Wrecks.

The unit was armed with rifles and Malone and his colleague Seamus Grace fired at them. The GRs, without ammunition, were unable to fire back. They took several casualties and hurried away.

Grace had fifty rounds for his Lee Enfield rifle and two hundred for his automatic pistol. Mick Malone had a Mauser C96 – a relatively sophisticated weapon, a semi-automatic with a long barrel and a magazine that held ten rounds. He had hundreds of rounds.

Malone had spent much time moving between the outposts around the area. Up the road, the Parochial Hall was held by four men. Further up, at Mount Street Bridge, there were seven men in Clanwilliam House. There were four more Volunteers in a builders' yard at Clanwilliam Place.

Now, at No. 25, the bullets fired by a British sniper

in a house across the street were coming uncomfortably close.

Malone brought Seamus Grace to the top floor.

You take the room on the right, I'll take the one on the left.

Grace crept to the window and raised his head. A bullet took his cap off.

'Are you all right?'

'Yes.' Grace had seen the sniper's position. 'He's in the right-hand top window.'

Lieutenant Malone fired several times and the sniper went down, dragging the window blinds along with him.

Around the corner at Beggars Bush Barracks, a young British soldier approached Captain Gerrard of the Royal Artillery – home on leave from the Dardanelles, and called in to defend the poorly staffed barracks.

'I beg your pardon, sir, I've just shot two girls.'

'What on earth did you do that for?'

'I thought they were rebels. I was told they were dressed in all classes of attire.'

The soldier pointed towards the street where this had happened, about two hundred yards away. From the way the girls were lying, Gerrard had no doubt they were dead.

Harry Boland was entering the vestibule of the Metropole Hotel when Captain Vincent Poole approached him. He said he was charging Boland with desertion.

Oscar Traynor wanted to know what this was about. Poole explained how Boland was under orders at the manure works in Fairview. Yet he'd taken a prisoner to the GPO and hadn't returned. A clear case of desertion.

How, said Traynor, could Boland possibly be a deserter

if he was standing right here, under Traynor's orders, next door to the headquarters of the revolution?

Poole and Boland began to argue.

Boland had in fact disobeyed orders, had without permission abandoned his post to bring a prisoner to the GPO, and hadn't returned to his post.

Boland said that he'd been with Poole's unit because he couldn't find F Company, but as soon as he did he switched back to his own unit. During this row, Poole raised the butt of his rifle and Traynor had to intervene.

You're under my orders, he told Poole. 'And my orders to you now are to go upstairs and ensure that all persons occupying rooms in this hotel have left.'

Poole followed orders.

The Metropole was a fairly swanky affair. It was advertised as having 'electric light throughout', as well as an 'American elevator' and 'telephones in all rooms'. Charlie Saurin was sent to the top floor, to prepare defences. There, he found a long, wide corridor that connected all the rooms that looked out on to Sackville Street. All the doors were closed, except to one room – from which a young woman ran in tears. She disappeared down the corridor.

Some of the volunteers began shouldering the closed doors of the rooms. Young Eddie Byrne, whose father had asked Saurin to look after him, was poised to smash a lock open with the butt of his shotgun – Saurin stopped him. The muzzle of the gun was pointing at the young man's head.

Among Saurin's unit of seven was a dark, foreign-looking young man with what might have been a Cockney accent – he'd been part of the contingent at the manure works at Annesley Bridge. He gave his name as John Neale. He may have been from London, or from Norwich.

Or from elsewhere. He owned a modern German service rifle, which he kept in good condition, and he knew how to use it.

Neale had once been a hotel pageboy and knew the routine. No need to break down doors – he suggested to Saurin that the hotel manager would have a master key. Saurin left Neale in charge while he went in search of the manager.

Late afternoon, Fergus O'Kelly's detail finally got the radio transmitter at the Reis building working. In Morse code, the message went out over and over again: 'Irish Republic declared in Dublin today'.

The range of the equipment was about three hundred miles. There was no hope of the signal travelling to other countries – certainly not to America, where supporters of the IRB waited to spread the word. The hope was that the dots and dashes would be picked up by ships at sea, that the radio operators would decode the message and pass it on.

Returning from a visit to Glasthule, James Neil, a junior employee of the National Library, decided to avoid Sackville Street – it was too dangerous. He took the Ha'penny Bridge across to the north side, where he lived, and at some point startled a looter, who drew a pistol and shot him.

He was taken to nearby Jervis Street Hospital with a wound that left him paralysed from the waist down. He would linger for two weeks before his injuries killed him.

Walking to his home in Rathmines that evening, Frank Sheehy-Skeffington was arrested crossing Portobello

Bridge and taken into Portobello Barracks. He had attracted attention because he'd been giving out anti-looting leaflets, calling for concerned citizens to come together and urge the looters to stop. For this, he was being followed by a small crowd, who seemed to think him something of a comic figure.

The soldiers searched his pockets and found nothing incriminating.

Do you support Sinn Fein?

Sheehy-Skeffington said he supported the aim of a separate Ireland. Aware that Sinn Fein was the catch-all label applied to nationalists, he made it clear he opposed militarism. He was a pacifist.

The overall response of the authorities to the rising was calm. After all, this was a flea bite delivered by a tiny amateur army. While the ranks of the rebels swelled during the week to about sixteen hundred, the British forces numbered about twenty thousand.

It was first necessary to assess the strength and where-abouts of the enemy. Then, the task would be to cordon off each rebel garrison and to block routes of communication and escape. All the while, troops had to be assembled and transported from down the country, from the north and from England.

In the meantime, martial law had been proclaimed; there was a curfew. The military had the authority to question and search anyone who came under its scrutiny. It was inevitable that some of the innocent – such as Sheehy-Skeffington – would be swept up temporarily, as the authorities prepared their response.

Frank and Leo Henderson got the job of setting up barricades halfway down Henry Street, one on each side of the junction with Moore Street. The Volunteers took huge bales of material from a tailor's shop, thick enough to absorb any bullet. They rolled a bale into place, went back to get another. As soon as their backs were turned the looters had a go at nicking the first bale. The Volunteers fired shots over their heads. These looters seemed experienced enough to know they wouldn't be shot, so they paid no attention.

Fix your bayonets, Henderson told his men – but don't stab anyone. The sight of the bayonets was enough to convince the looters to go elsewhere.

Far tougher was the job of boring through the walls from the GPO down through Henry Street, past Moore Street and towards Arnott's department store. Frank and his men tunnelled from one end, Leo from the other. Their work was made easier by four brothers named Ring – Joe, Leo, Pat and Tim – and a friend of theirs, James Hunter. They were all carpenters and construction workers, strong and used to consistent, tough manual work.

Bill O'Brien, James Connolly's trade union comrade, found himself drawn into the city centre that Tuesday evening. He watched a young man smashing the window of McDowell's jeweller's shop. The man climbed in and began grabbing fistfuls of watches and chains, then threw them to the crowd outside.

Further up the street, Willie Findlater, head of the grocery chain, sat on a chair outside his shop with a blunderbuss – an ancient and primitive form of shotgun – in his lap, ready to blow away anyone who tried to steal his groceries.

Some youngsters looted Lawrence's sports shop, brought armfuls of fireworks out on to the street and set them off. The evening sky over Sackville Street fizzed and crackled with explosions, sparks shooting and smoke drifting. Volunteers on the roof of the GPO watched nervously as Catherine wheels spun across the sky. Their homemade bombs were lying exposed on the roof – the sooner this gaiety ended the better. The Volunteers fired several shots over the heads of the looters, some of whom scattered. Others went back into the shop and set fire to it.

Near Mount Street Bridge, the Volunteers waited patiently at the Parochial Hall. Sooner or later, they expected, the enemy would come in force and things would get hot and heavy. In the meantime, they were taking it easy.

On duty at a front window, Volunteers William Christian and Pat Doyle perked up as a young British soldier in khaki came along the street, went in the front gate of a house on the other side of Northumberland Road and approached the front door.

Pat Doyle tracked him from the moment he appeared, looking down the barrel of his rifle, finger on the trigger.

The young soldier knocked on the front door. Then he turned and faced Christian and Doyle, obviously aware of their presence. Very carefully, he held his hands away from his sides, showing he was unarmed.

The two thought about it for a moment. They agreed they couldn't shoot an unarmed man.

The door opened and the soldier went inside. Given the risk, it must have been a very important visit.

Another long day, another day without communication from his officers. Matt Stafford still waited at home, taking care of the company treasury, pending orders from Leo Henderson. What he couldn't know was that Leo had decided, for compassionate reasons, to leave the old Fenian out of the fight. There was no doubt about Stafford's commitment, but he had visibly struggled to keep up during drills. A man on his last legs had no place in such an enterprise. Rather than formally stand him down, Henderson decided to quietly overlook the old man, simply not to mobilize him.

Matt Stafford doggedly awaited the call to duty, assuming it might still happen at any minute.

In the Metropole Hotel, Charlie Saurin stationed his men in the rooms overlooking Sackville Street. They broke the large oval windows and barricaded each opening high enough for protection. As darkness came, Saurin put sentries in rooms at each end of the corridor and told the others to get some sleep.

Saurin got into conversation with the Citizen Army man who called himself John Neale. The man's shoes and socks had been destroyed by contact with the sulphuric acid in the manure works at Fairview. He'd found a good pair of boots in one of the hotel rooms, and a pair of women's stockings that he pulled up to his knees. He looked odd, but that didn't seem to worry him.

He was a socialist, he said. He had come to Ireland to side with the Citizen Army in its troubles.

One of the Volunteers later remembered hearing Neale speak, in 1913, at Hyde Park Corner, in London, in support of the Industrial Workers of the World – a union of socialists, anarchists and radical trade unionists.

For Neale, as for many such socialists, nationality wasn't what defined him. Nationality was an accident of birth – to a radical like Neale, a belief in what is right and what is wrong cannot depend on which side of a border we are born. He saw himself as having more in common with the workers of Ireland than he had with the wealthy of his own country – so he put himself at the disposal of the Citizen Army. He could support a national demand for freedom against the right of an imperial power to deny that freedom – so he put himself at the disposal of the rising.

At one stage, Neale decided he didn't approve of Nelson's Pillar, in the centre of Sackville Street. It was erected on the initiative of the businessmen who controlled Dublin's municipal government, the Corporation, and it was financed by merchants and bankers, in memory of the hero of the Battle of Trafalgar. The 120-foot-high pillar, topped by a statue of Admiral Nelson, was in the exact centre of Sackville Street, at the junctions of Henry Street and North Earl Street (where the Spire is today).

John Neale began sniping at the statue, trying to hit Admiral Nelson's nose. Eventually, an order came from James Connolly to cut that out.

After cycling from first light, and all through the day, Paul Galligan – despatched by James Connolly to rouse the Volunteers of Enniscorthy – arrived in Carlow as darkness fell. He had cycled fifty-seven miles when he took his first break, found a hotel and got some much-needed sleep.

In what was becoming his daily custom, The O'Rahilly wrote a note to each of his four children. He wrote another to his wife: 'We are still to the good . . . probably it will be only in ten years' time that the value of our little fight will become known.'

Frank Sheehy-Skeffington was taken out of his cell and had his hands tied behind his back. British Army officer

Captain Bowen Colthurst said aloud a prayer: 'O Lord God, if it shall please Thee to take away the life of this man, forgive him for Our Lord Jesus Christ's sake.'

Colthurst then declared Sheehy-Skeffington a hostage and took him out with a patrol of about forty soldiers. His mission was to raid a shop at the top of Camden Street. Should the patrol be fired on, he said, the soldiers were to shoot Sheehy-Skeffington.

This made no sense at all, but none of the many soldiers – including officers – who knew about it intervened. Colthurst was an experienced officer, with a strong personality, blooded on the fields of France. His judgement of the powers conferred on him by the declaration of martial law was not to be contested.

On the way to Camden Street, Colthurst took a rifle from one of his men and fired into the air several times. Some other soldiers did likewise. This seemed to be the army's way of ensuring that people stayed away from their windows while the troops were passing.

On Rathmines Road the patrol came across three teenage boys, JJ Coade, Laurence Byrne and a boy named Keogh. The boys had been to a Sodality meeting in the nearby Catholic church.

Colthurst asked, Don't you know there's a curfew?

Coade said they didn't know.

'Bash him,' Colthurst said, and a soldier gave JJ Coade the butt of his rifle in the face.

Young Keogh got on to his bicycle and left. Coade and Byrne began to walk away.

A commercial traveller named Hughes happened along, with a friend, and Colthurst pointed a revolver at him. Hughes put his hands up and said, 'Not with anybody' – indicating that whatever was going on he wasn't involved.

Colthurst pointed the gun at Hughes's friend and Hughes said, 'He's with me.'

Colthurst turned to Coade and Byrne, now about twelve yards away, and shot Coade dead.

The patrol continued.

The soldiers raided a shop on Camden Street owned by a local politician, Alderman James Kelly, a Justice of the Peace. Colthurst suspected the shopkeeper of being a subversive, which he was not.

Kelly had left the shop momentarily, leaving behind his friend Patrick MacIntyre. MacIntyre was a journalist who campaigned on behalf of employers against militant trade unionism. There was another journalist, Thomas Dickson, in the shop. He had taken refuge there when he heard the approaching troops shooting in the air. Dickson edited a paper called *The Eye Opener*. He seems to have been a journalist in a loose sense – there were some who accused him of blackmail by threatening to print scurrilous material about individuals.

The soldiers first threw a bomb into the shop. After it exploded they went inside. 'Hands up,' Colthurst said.

A stunned MacIntyre explained that he was the editor of *The Searchlight*.

'Another rebel paper,' one of the soldiers said.

'No,' said MacIntyre, 'a loyal paper.'

Alderman Kelly approached his shop, saw what was happening and hid.

'Remember,' Colthurst told the civilians, 'I could shoot you like dogs. Martial law is proclaimed.'

Colthurst arrested MacIntyre and Dickson. When the patrol returned to Portobello Barracks both journalists were locked up for the night.

Sheehy-Skeffington was locked up separately from MacIntyre and Dickson, as the authorities acknowledged what they referred to as 'his superior social status'. Had he known about this discrimination he would certainly have agitated against it.

At 25 Northumberland Road, as midnight approached, Lieutenant Mick Malone was considering the reality of his circumstances. He was quite aware of what was likely to happen over the next few hours.

He took Seamus Grace aside. Grace was a member of the IRB, Malone was not. But Malone was a natural leader – calm, always thinking things through, making an impression not with rhetoric or rank but with action.

The way things had gone, he said – the confusion caused by MacNeill cancelling the manoeuvres on Sunday, the loss of the guns down in Kerry, the overwhelming odds – we're going to take a hiding.

There were four of them at No. 25: Malone, Seamus Grace, Paddy Rowe and Michael Byrne. The latter two were lads, neither of them yet sixteen.

The two boys, if they stay, they're going to get killed. Do you agree we send them away?

Grace said he did.

Malone called Rowe and Byrne. I've got despatch work for you, he said. There were two letters to be delivered – one to Malone's mother, the other to Grace's.

The boys knew this was a ruse and protested.

'It's orders, boys – you must go.'

And they'd have to leave their rifles behind.

At around 2.30am, on a landing, Rowe and Byrne were given the despatches. And under no circumstances come back, Malone told them.

The boys went up through a skylight and across the rooftops.

Malone seemed grey and haggard. He hadn't slept

since Sunday, and he'd had little sleep in the previous week, preparing for the rising. Seamus Grace took command and told Malone to get some rest.

As his lieutenant slept, Grace set booby traps in the hall and on the stairs, just in case, then he sat on watch. He hadn't got any more sleep than Malone over the past few days. Eventually, he too fell asleep.

In Henry Street, the Henderson brothers and their comrades continued working through the night, boring through walls, to secure the defensive positions behind the GPO. On the far side of Sackville Street, Clerys department store was barricaded and Volunteers, including Harry Colley, were tunnelling all the way towards North Earl Street.

At the top of North Earl Street, Brennan-Whitmore's garrison commanded the eastern approach to the main street.

The Metropole garrison, including Saurin, Traynor, Boland and Vincent Poole, had already bored through Eason's and Manfield & Sons, giving complete access along the block, from the GPO to Abbey Street.

Anyone seeking to take the GPO would come under a hail of defensive fire, not just from the building itself but from its secure outposts – the Metropole, the Imperial, the Hibernian Bank on the corner of Lower Abbey Street – and from the units controlling the Kelly's Fort and Hopkins & Hopkins outposts at the south end of Sackville Street.

The insurrection was two days old. Even if you didn't believe the stories about the risings down the country and the thousands fighting their way towards Dublin, you knew the past two days had been well spent in preparation for the fight to come.

Few believed there was a chance of outright victory. But, by creating such stout defences, achieved with back-breaking work, the rising's leadership had ensured that the enemy would pay a high price to take back the rebels' iconic headquarters in the heart of the city. This wouldn't be a skirmish easily dismissed by history

It didn't seem to occur to anyone that the British Army had no intention of taking back the GPO.

Part Six

Shellfire

20

In the early hours of Wednesday morning, 26 April, the third day of the rising, six men slipped out a side gate of Trinity College, carrying pickaxes, crowbars and spades. Some of them were reserve officers in the British Army, some were civilian volunteers, all wore civilian dress. They turned the corner into Tara Street, from which they could see the two-storey Liberty Hall, and began working to break up the road surface.

There had been sustained fighting at the South Dublin Union, the Mendicity Institute and elsewhere, but in the heart of the city the British had been preparing a response, assembling troops and putting cordons in place. They mounted machine guns at strategic points. The previous day, they had moved artillery pieces into Trinity College. Now, two 18-pounders were brought from Trinity into Tara Street.

Firing an 18-pounder gun produces a violent recoil. Unless the gun is somehow fixed in place, the operators would have to cope with almost two tons of machinery bouncing around every time it was fired. To avoid this, there was a spade-shaped piece of metal called a trail, which jutted down behind the weapon. When used in the countryside, the recoil from the first shell that was fired normally drove the trail into the earth, stabilizing the gun.

The streets of Dublin were lined with cobblestones. The trail would simply skid along them. The six men from Trinity were assigned to remove some cobblestones, exposing soft ground that the trail could pierce. They began digging.

Residents of Tara Street emerged, asking what was going on. It's the gas, they were told. There's some sort of a blockage, Trinity College isn't getting the gas. We're here to fix it.

It was a hard job. The cobblestones were six by four inches, up to seven inches in depth, set close together in tar. Just getting the tools into the gap between the cobblestones was difficult. After labouring for half an hour they had dug up one cobblestone, and already one of the crowbars had broken. They worked on.

For some years the Castle authorities, the police and the organized league of employers had developed a hatred of Liberty Hall and the defiance it symbolized – even more so since the building had been used as the centre of planning for the rising. The artillery teams were tasked with levelling the union offices.

The 18-pounders fired almost simultaneously, the noise shattering every window pane in Tara Street. Machine guns opened up from Trinity and from the tower of Tara Street fire station. Liberty Hall was instantly wreathed in dust and smoke.

The building was empty. Given the level of surveillance, the authorities had to know that the empty union hall had no value as a military target – the bombardment was revenge for the insubordination of the previous few years.

The gunboat *Helga* came up the Liffey and joined in.

For an hour it showered shells inland from a 12-pounder. Because of the terrain, including the railway bridge curving past the union hall, the *Helga* couldn't fire directly at the building; instead, it adopted the technique of 'dropping fire' – lobbing shells into the air, above the obstacles, hopefully to drop on its target.

The artillery bombardment and the constant rattle of machine guns poured an immense amount of lethal firepower into a crowded urban area. The *Irish Times* reported that this 'caused intense excitement in the district, where there is a large population of the poorer class of residents'.

As a synonym for rampant terror and the slaughter of the innocent, 'intense excitement' somewhat understated the matter.

Shortly after dawn on Wednesday there was sporadic Volunteer activity in Galway. The cry of Volunteer Padraig Thornton typified the reaction of many to the news that Dublin was out, and the leaders wanted the country to rise: 'What's the use against the army, without guns?'

Between five and six hundred Volunteers came forward, with rifles available for perhaps a tenth of that number. Some got hold of revolvers or shotguns, others could rely only on hayforks.

At Carnmore, outside Galway City, some Volunteers came under attack from the police. One of the policemen, Constable Patrick Whelan, knew several of the rebels by sight. A determined district inspector pushed Whelan up on to a wall, to observe and confront the rebels, and held him up by the collar of his tunic.

From his vantage point, Whelan shouted at the rebels, 'Surrender, boys, I know ye all.' They shot him dead.

*

At Portobello Barracks, at about 10.20am, Captain Bowen Colthurst told a sergeant to bring the three prisoners out into the yard behind the guardhouse.

I'm going to shoot them, he said. I think it's the right thing to do.

Colthurst ordered seven soldiers into the yard and told them to load their rifles. He was not alone in believing that, under martial law, the military had the right to shoot anyone, for anything, at any time.

Sergeant Aldridge brought out Frank Sheehy-Skeffington, Thomas Dickson and Patrick MacIntyre. Colthurst told them to go to the far end of the yard.

When the prisoners did so, with no idea what was going on, Colthurst gave the order to fire and the three men fell dead or dying. Some of the soldiers missed the men, whether through nerves or choice, and their bullets smashed into the wall behind.

One of the officers saw Frank Sheehy-Skeffington's leg twitch. He hurried to ask another officer what to do.

Shoot again.

Four soldiers stood over Sheehy-Skeffington and fired a volley into him.

The Volunteers at Kelly's Fort watched a group of British soldiers beginning work on the other side of O'Connell Bridge – three hundred yards away, at the junction with D'Olier Street. The soldiers were calmly stripping off their jackets and working with tools to lift the cobble-stones, preparing the ground for an artillery assault.

The Volunteers began firing at the soldiers.

In return, Kelly's Fort was peppered with rifle fire, machine-gun bullets and tracers. There were troops in the buildings on the other side of the Liffey, letting loose.

Peadar Bracken had the only rifle, and he scored a couple of hits on the soldiers preparing the artillery position – the others had shotguns, useless at that range.

Joe Good was coming down the stairs when the first shell hit Kelly's Fort and made the whole building shake.

From a window on the top floor of the Metropole Hotel, Charlie Saurin watched his friend Boss Shields, Blimey O'Connor and the rest of the radio team leave the Reis building and run across Sackville Street, towards the GPO.

The leader of the team, Fergus O'Kelly, had received an order to withdraw. And, he was told, pass the same order to the Volunteers in nearby positions, including the DBC building – a tall building with an outsize dome on top. O'Kelly passed on the word, and although there was some dissent about leaving the positions, orders were orders.

The team crossed the street under fire, one at a time, moving fast. All made it safely to the GPO. There, O'Kelly reported to James Connolly, saying he'd received an order to abandon the Reis building.

'I know,' Connolly said. He had ordered the evacuation of the dome on top of the DBC, knowing it would attract the attention of the British artillery. The message, passed from one Volunteer to another, became garbled, and the whole block had been evacuated.

'Now,' Connolly said, 'you can go back to Reis's.'

O'Kelly had no idea what was going on, but again he followed orders. On the team's way back across Sackville Street, the gunfire was more intense. Two of the men were wounded and had to be stretchered away by Volunteer medics.

From his position at the Metropole Hotel, Charlie

Saurin could also see a party of men and women grouped at a window of Wynn's Hotel, near the top of Abbey Street – as though in a box at the theatre, enjoying the spectacle.

At street level, the casual behaviour seen around Sackville Street in the first two days of the rising was no more. The looters had moved to safer areas. Rifle fire had over those days caused a number of civilian deaths and injuries from stray bullets. Now, with machine guns constantly spraying great numbers of bullets great distances, the chances of being hit had vastly increased.

At the corner of Bachelors Walk and Liffey Street, there were shots from somewhere. A woman and a man fell dead. People scattered – no one knew who was responsible.

A blind man, moving down Sackville Street towards O'Connell Bridge, took a bullet and went down. He lay there wounded, almost a piece of bait to entice another target into the open.

Henry Olds, a Red Cross member, was working in George's Street when he got word of the blind man's plight. He got down to the bridge quickly, went directly to the wounded man and began treating the wound. Olds took a bullet in his own shoulder. He finished the work and got the blind man to safety.

The Volunteers in Hopkins & Hopkins were convinced the shooting of the blind man and the Red Cross man was the work of a sniper in McBirney's department store, on Aston Quay. Henry Olds thought he was himself the victim of a stray shot.

Oscar Traynor took James Connolly to inspect the defences prepared at the Metropole Hotel block – stretching from Prince's Street to Middle Abbey Street. They discussed the need for a barricade across Middle Abbey

Street. As Connolly spoke, Traynor decided he'd better draw his attention to the bullets smacking the pavement around them. Perhaps, he suggested, it might be better to move indoors.

A shell hit a building on the other side of Abbey Street. The two went back inside.

At about that time, in Galway, a public meeting took place at the town hall, organized by some of the town's leading citizens and presided over by the chairman of the Urban Council, Martin McDonough.

A Committee of Public Safety was formed. The meeting noted the public shock and outrage at the rising, at this time when 'Irish troops have done so much to shed glory on the arms of the Empire'. The meeting called on the authorities and the people of Galway to 'co-operate to crush by every possible means the efforts of the disaffected fanatics and mischief-makers'.

Machine guns at Trinity College were strafing Sackville Street from the south end. Machine guns at the Parnell Monument were strafing Sackville Street from the north end.

There were machine guns in the tower of Amiens Street station, from which the gunners could see up Talbot Street, about five hundred yards, to Nelson's Pillar, in the centre of Sackville Street.

From the opposite direction, at Capel Street, machine gunners had another straight five-hundred-yard vista, all the way up through Henry Street to Nelson's Pillar.

The stone admiral was at the exact centre of four fields of fire: from Amiens Street, Capel Street and both ends of Sackville Street.

The machine guns were sweeping the streets with

bullets, whether or not there were visible targets. The aim seemed to be to immobilize the rebels by making the streets unusable.

There were snipers at Trinity College and elsewhere. And anything living that entered those fields of fire was a trigger-touch away from death.

On the top floor of the Metropole Hotel, the English socialist John Neale periodically sat out on a parapet, using field glasses to keep track of enemy movements. He seemed to have no fear, and a total lack of confidence in the marksmanship of the British Army.

Apart from keeping track of the enemy and shooting at them, Neale sometimes cooked for the others. At one stage he found himself looking for a good knife to cut some meat. Charlie Saurin gave him his sheath knife and Neale began cooking.

Just then, Oscar Traynor called Saurin into the hotel manager's office and gave him a despatch for Pearse. If you can't find him in the GPO, bring it back.

In the GPO, there was no sign of Pearse, or of any of the other leaders. Upstairs, Saurin found three British officers, prisoners, sitting down to a good meal, while a Volunteer stood guard with a shotgun. Rank-and-file British prisoners were working in the kitchen.

In a room looking out on to Sackville Street he found Boss Shields and Harry Coyle from F Company. No one knew where Pearse or any of the other leaders were – perhaps at a meeting. Saurin had a chat with a priest from the Pro-Cathedral, who had come to hear confessions and stayed, and there was still no word of Pearse, so he went back to the Metropole, where John Neale was about to serve up a fine meal.

The rebels in the GPO continued to suffer the austere eating regime imposed by Desmond FitzGerald, still doling out food a few crumbs at a time – seeking to make the rations last into a second week.

Meanwhile, fires were starting.

The *Helga* was shelling Volunteer positions at Ringsend. The 18-pounders at Tara Street were now firing shells into the buildings along Eden Quay. Artillery in Trinity College pounded Bachelors Walk.

A shell aimed at the GPO exploded in the offices of the *Freeman's Journal*, a newspaper that backed John Redmond and his Parliamentary Party. The Volunteers in the Sackville Street area cheered at this own goal.

Pearse, Connolly and the others believed that their carefully chosen buildings could be defended for days, perhaps a week or two, as the British threw waves of infantry at them. Eventually, inevitably, as enemy attrition wore down the rebel's defences, they would be overcome. Some might, at best, escape to the countryside to carry on the fight a while longer.

It didn't seem to have occurred to them that the British would decide to lay waste to the city centre, that the generals would simply burn down the heart of a place they held in no great regard.

Burning the enemy's city is the smart thing to do. It gives them a choice – come out with your hands up, or die in the flames.

Much better, from the British point of view, than fighting from building to building, taking casualties and wasting soldiers whose blood could more usefully be spilt in the trenches of France.

There are consequences to this, particularly for the people who live in the city, but that was not a consideration, given that to the generals this was a foreign place.

As the big guns pounded the buildings and the machine

guns decontaminated the streets, thousands of troops were throwing cordons around the occupied positions. The rebels were being locked in, communications cut off and lines of retreat destroyed.

Inside the glass dome on the roof of Arnott's department store, in Henry Street, Volunteer Domhnall O Buachalla was scanning the shops on the other side of the river, through a good pair of binoculars. The sniper in McBirney's department store had become a deadly nuisance. A shot intended for a Volunteer at Hopkins & Hopkins had killed a civilian. The sniper had also shot dead a young woman outside the jeweller's.

All the windows on the top floor of McBirney's were closed, except one. As O Buachalla watched, a waitress in uniform carried a tray across the room. What was a waitress doing up there, with the shop closed because of the fighting?

Fifty-year-old O Buachalla was one of the group of Volunteers who had walked from Maynooth to Dublin. Just before the rising, he had bought a Lee Enfield rifle. He had it ready now.

Using the binoculars, he took in every inch he could see of the dim room at the top of McBirney's. Eventually, he made out the form of a soldier, stooped and holding a rifle.

O Buachalla's first shot hit the wall above the window. The second and third shots went through the window. There was no further shooting from McBirney's.

The garrison at the Mendicity Institute, on the south side of the Liffey quays, was surrendering. The men had been sent there on Monday by James Connolly to delay the dispersal of British troops for a few hours. The garrison held out for two days before being overrun, at great cost to the British.

Volunteer Richard Balfe was seriously wounded. He had temporarily lost the use of all limbs, but was conscious. He'd been left behind by his surrendering comrades, who apparently thought him dead.

When a British officer and a Dublin Fusilier entered this part of the building, Balfe managed to manoeuvre himself into a sitting position. The British officer had an automatic pistol, the Fusilier a fixed bayonet. The two began to discuss whether to shoot the rebel or run him through.

A Royal Army Medical Corps officer came in and saw what was happening. He quickly claimed Balfe as his prisoner. There's been enough of this dirty work, he said.

Working on the Henry Street defences, Frank Henderson was approached by James Connolly. A party of British troops had taken over a house on a corner of Liffey Street. From there they could control access along Middle Abbey Street. Connolly told Henderson to select eight or ten of the best men from 2nd Battalion. Connolly would lead them down to Liffey Street, to dislodge the British outpost.

Henderson selected Patrick Shortis from his own F Company and several men from other 2nd Battalion companies, and Connolly set off.

At Mount Street Bridge, the garrison continued to wait for any sign of newly landed British troops approaching from Kingstown. The four Volunteers in the builders' yard at Clanwilliam Place noticed a British sergeant – a scout – way off to their left, approaching a barricade at Grand Canal Street Bridge. Part of their job was to attack reinforcements coming from the barracks at Beggars Bush. Two of the men, Seamus Doyle and Bob Cooper, fired at the sergeant and watched him jump slightly, drop to the ground and lie still.

At noon, at Clanwilliam House, Tom Walsh was keeping watch at a back window when he caught a glimpse of khaki. A soldier, running from Percy Lane along Percy Place and up the steps of a house. Walsh aimed carefully and squeezed the trigger of his Howth Mauser.

It was the first time he'd ever fired that rifle – or any rifle.

He regained consciousness some time later, with no idea how long he'd been out. The butt of the rifle had hit him on the chin, the bullet had taken a lump of granite out of the windowsill. He had no idea what happened to the British soldier.

In the tension of the moment Walsh had forgotten all the lectures about the correct way to hold a weapon. He'd forgotten that the kick from a Howth rifle made it almost as lethal for those behind the gun as in front.

Around the same time, two members of Cumann na mBan arrived at 25 Northumberland Road, carrying a despatch which they put through the letterbox. It told Lieutenant Mick Malone that hundreds of British troops had landed at Kingstown.

The reinforcements had begun their march towards the city, in three columns. One column of five hundred soldiers was coming their way, and would soon be passing No. 25 and crossing over Mount Street Bridge.

There were seventeen Volunteers waiting. Malone and Grace at No. 25, seven more at Clanwilliam House, four at the Parochial Hall, four more in the builders' yard at Clanwilliam Place. They were a mixed group – from the cool, committed Mick Malone to Tom Walsh, the teenage amateur soldier who knocked himself out when he fired his first shot.

Over the next few hours, these seventeen men would leave hundreds of British troops dead or wounded in the streets around Mount Street Bridge.

21

For almost twenty-four hours, the improvised radio station at the Reis building on Sackville Street had been broadcasting its message in Morse code:

> *Irish Republic declared in Dublin today, Irish troops have captured the city and are in full possession. Enemy cannot move in city. The whole country rising.*

That block of Sackville Street was now coming under intense sniper fire. The artillery threw both explosive and incendiary shells into the area. At some stage, the radio broadcast was updated:

> *British troops have been repulsed with great slaughter in the attempt to take the Irish position. The people are wildly enthusiastic for the new government.*

The second broadcast was as inaccurate as the first. Probably the messages were prepared by Joe Plunkett before the rising. It was what the leaders expected to happen – a British infantry assault on secured rebel positions, significant enemy losses and patriotic enthusiasm among the people.

Instead, the GPO and its outposts were cordoned off, machine guns harassed the rebels and artillery was destroying their positions. The rising was confined to Dublin and the people were more frightened and confused than patriotic.

The shelling had started fires. The Reis building took a pounding and orders again came to abandon it, and bring the radio equipment across to the GPO.

Easier said than done.

Boss Shields, Blimey O'Connor and their comrades dismantled the radio equipment. They struggled to get it down the narrow stairs. Then came the hard part – getting the equipment across Sackville Street, under fire.

At Clanwilliam House, overlooking Mount Street Bridge, some of the Volunteers remembered the lectures on protecting a position – break the window glass to ensure that gunfire and explosions don't create a blizzard of flying glass splinters. It was a standard procedure – break the glass, sandbag the windows, put water aside for when you need it for drinking or to fight fires. Tom and Jim Walsh mentioned this to George Reynolds, who was in charge of the Volunteer unit.

No, Reynolds said. When he'd taken over the house from its owners he'd assured them that he'd hand it back in the same condition he got it. No breaking glass, no damaging the furniture.

So, they raised the bottom sash of the windows to allow them to shoot at the enemy without damaging the glass.

The approaching troops, the Sherwood Foresters, were newly recruited, freshly trained. They had been destined for France until the rising saw them diverted to Dublin.

Some of them – disembarked at Kingstown, marching towards Dublin – didn't know what country they were in. A few were heard to shout 'Bonjour!' to people on the pavements. It might have been black humour – it's possible some of them thought they were in France.

The British Army knew there were rebels in the vicinity. The GRs had been fired on, the British sniper and Mick Malone had exchanged fire. Yet the brass marched their troops straight up Northumberland Road.

Again and again, Boss Shields and the other members of the radio team crossed between the Reis building and the GPO, hauling heavy equipment, under intense fire. They carried the lighter pieces individually, bullets hitting the ground around them as they ran. They got a horse-dray to carry some of the heavier pieces.

During one trip, they used a table. They turned it upside down, with the equipment in the middle, covered by a white tablecloth. Six of them carried it. As they came out into the line of fire they were amazed to find the shooting tapering off. All the way to the GPO, they shuffled as quickly as they could, and not a shot was fired at them.

Afterwards, they could only conclude that the enemy assumed they were moving a badly wounded or dead man across the road and behaved decently.

Finally, the flames made it impossible to go back inside the Reis building to fetch what equipment was left. James Connolly called off the effort to relocate the radio.

With the radio team defunct, Boss Shields moved to the Hibernian Bank, where Captain Tom Weafer – the officer who had led the movement of the arms and ammunition from Fr. Mathew Park to the city centre on Monday – was in charge.

*

Malone and Grace had barricaded the entrances of
No. 25. They had agreed on where each of them would
fight. They had prepared a room on the top floor, a last
resort to which they could fall back and make a final
stand. There, they left a Lee Enfield rifle and two Howth
Mausers, all loaded, all with bayonets fixed.

They briefly discussed moving to another location –
Malone may have thought that since the British knew
they were there the likelihood was they'd avoid and
cordon off the area.

Now, in the third-floor bathroom, at around 11am,
Malone looked out the window and called out to Grace:
'Look, Seamus.'

Hundreds of British soldiers were marching along
Northumberland Road towards No. 25.

Malone and Grace commanded the junction of
Northumberland and Haddington Roads. Once the
column of troops went past No. 25 it was extremely
vulnerable. One hundred yards further up Northumberland Road, the British column's left flank was open
to attack from the men in the Parochial Hall. At the
same time, fifty yards beyond the Hall, the seven men
in Clanwilliam House, on the far side of Mount Street
Bridge, had a clear field of fire back down the length
of Northumberland Road. The four Volunteers at the
builders' yard could pick off the enemy as they scattered
to avoid what was coming.

The troops were entering a small, tight urban valley.
Although they vastly outnumbered the rebels, the pos-
itioning of the rebels gave them a massive advantage.

As the column moved past No. 25, Malone began
shooting from a third-floor window. He was an excellent
shot with the Mauser automatic, but in these conditions

he didn't have to be. The troops were in a column, in a relatively narrow street.

Seamus Grace was shooting from a window on the floor below.

A hundred and fifty yards further up Northumberland Road, the Volunteers at Clanwilliam House began firing back down along the street, towards the advancing troops.

Unseasoned cannon fodder, until this week destined to bleed for the Empire in the fields and trenches of France, the troops responded blindly to this urban ambush. They threw themselves down, they crawled to the nearest wall and tried to make themselves small, they hid behind trees, behind the steps of houses, in the gutter by the side of the road. Since they didn't know where the firing was coming from, the cover they achieved was too often imaginary.

Some made it to Warrington Place and crouched behind a wall. It was the wrong side of the wall, leaving them open to gunfire from the four Volunteers in the builders' yard.

Soldiers began shooting at houses they imagined the firing might be coming from.

From Clanwilliam House, Tom Walsh and his six comrades blazed away. You hit one soldier in the roadside gutter and the man behind him crawls forward, passing him out, and you shoot him, too. Then the next one comes forward. From behind his rifle, it seemed to Walsh like a giant khaki-coloured human caterpillar was inching its way towards him.

Fire at the one in front, you hit him or – if you missed – you hit someone crawling forward behind him.

Soldiers who shied away in the face of fire from Clanwilliam House and tried to run back, risked being cut down by bullets from the Parochial Hall.

Some of the soldiers eventually made it as far forward as Mount Street Bridge, where they threw themselves into cover. Officers appeared and ordered the men to charge Clanwilliam House – 'Up and at them, lads!' And the men stood up and ran over the crest of the bridge into the relentless gunfire.

The dead and wounded littered the bridge.

Eventually, the doomed advances on secure positions stopped, and the British settled for long-range firing.

At the height of the battle, nurses arrived from the nearby Sir Patrick Dun's Hospital. They and some local clergymen forced a ceasefire, simply by walking out on to Mount Street Bridge. Two nurses, Loo Nolan and Kathleen Pierce, stepped out on to the bridge and approached the wounded, and the firing withered and stopped. A priest from Haddington Road church, Fr Wall, arrived on his bicycle. Visibly frightened, he left it leaning against a railing and began comforting the wounded.

The nurses used quilts as stretchers to remove the dead and wounded. Both sides withheld fire.

A man in a white coat moved from one wounded man to another, rendering what emergency aid he could. He was Charles Hachette Hyland, a dentist who lived on nearby Percy Place.

When they had done their work, the nurses left, the clergymen left, and the dentist left. And the battle began again. All of them would, in the course of the hours the battle raged, again and again intervene to aid the wounded.

Further along Northumberland Road, Anna O'Rahilly, The O'Rahilly's sister, watched the battle from a window. After a while, neighbours told the soldiers that Sinn Feiners lived in the O'Rahilly house and the soldiers began shooting at it.

Around the corner at 103 Haddington Road, Maggie Veale, wearing a green jumper, peeped through the curtains at her bedroom window. A British soldier saw the movement, the binoculars, the green outfit, and raked the window with machine-gun fire. The thirteen-year-old fell, mortally wounded.

Inside Clanwilliam House, Volunteer Pat Doyle kept up a non-stop chatter as he fired his rifle. 'Isn't this a great day for Ireland?' When the chatter stopped they knew he was dead. Shot through the head.

They stopped firing for some moments. Tom Walsh and his brother Jim and Dick Murphy said a prayer for Pat. Some time later, sitting in a chair and firing his rifle, Dick went down, shredded by bullets.

By now, the British troops had taken control of every house and vantage point overlooking No. 25, and the officers had organized a by-the-book assault. On command, the soldiers discharged sustained volleys of suppressing fire at the windows of No. 25, while attacking teams charged the house with grenades.

Three soldiers were assigned to each window. At the sound of a whistle, they used their rifles – rapid fire, about ten shots each.

Inside No. 25, Seamus Grace shook with fear. He crouched in cover as a relentless storm of lead swept the room. The air around him alive with bullets, any one of which might instantly end his life, he felt fear overwhelm him.

And when there was a moment's relief from the chatter of the guns he popped up, aimed towards the enemy and began firing again. And the fear was gone.

Shooting back, even though it meant breaking cover and making a target of himself, dispelled the fear he felt when all he could do was cower.

Upstairs, Mick Malone was calmly aiming at the advancing soldiers and firing. The attack faltered.

Their work done, the four Volunteers in the builders' yard at Clanwilliam Place withdrew to the garrison HQ at Bolands Mills. There, Fr McMahon from Westland Row parish was hearing Confessions in the back of a bread van.

Some of the Volunteers complained that Fr McMahon, while hearing Confession, tried to convince them to desert. An officer told the priest if he wanted to continue hearing Confessions he would have to cut that out. He agreed to do so.

At Northumberland Road, the soldiers were hungry. Locals offered them cakes and sandwiches, but officers – perhaps wary of spies – ordered the soldiers not to accept. The manager of the Blackrock branch of Findlater's grocery, Billy Vaughan, began rolling apples and oranges along the street towards the young soldiers, who gratefully ate them.

Captain Bowen Colthurst arrested a rebel. Dick O'Carroll, an official of the Bricklayers' Union and a Dublin City councillor, climbed off his motorcycle and surrendered, with his hands in the air.

Colthurst shot him in the chest and left him lying in the road.

Inside the Hibernian Bank, Volunteers crouched at sandbagged windows and responded to the incessant sniper firing. On a small balcony at one of the windows, jutting out over the pavement, Jack Stafford – son of the old Fenian, Matt Stafford – crouched, head down. At irregular intervals he popped up, quickly took aim and fired down towards Westmoreland Street and Trinity, then crouched again. He kept this up until a bullet shattered the stock of his rifle.

Captain Tom Weafer, coming down from the second floor of the bank, turned on a landing and walked past a window. Somewhere up in Westmoreland Street a sniper saw movement and squeezed a trigger. Weafer took a bullet in the back, crumpled and fell. He appeared to have been shot in a lung.

As his life ebbed, Cumann na mBan nurse Leslie Price said an Act of Contrition in his ear. His shocked comrades gathered around him, knelt and said prayers.

Off to one side, Boss Shields stood silently. Boss was Church of Ireland, from a home that was extraordinarily broad-minded for that time. His German mother, Fanny Sophia, described herself in the 1911 census as 'agnostic'. Boss's older sister Madeline described her religion as 'spiritualist'.

Boss waited respectfully as the other Volunteers carried out their religious duties to the dying man.

After a long break, sometime after 7pm, the soldiers were coming again at 25 Northumberland Road, front and back, rifles blazing away, grenades flung at the house. The plan of making for the top floor, where Mick Malone and Seamus Grace had prepared for a last stand, wasn't going to work out.

Go down, take a position at the hall door, Malone told Seamus Grace.

In the hall, Grace could hear movement in a room to the left, someone turning the door handle. He fired through the door and heard footsteps running away.

Troops out in the back yard.

Smashing glass in the back door.

Coming through.

Troops in the house.

Grace barely had time to finish loading a fresh clip into his automatic pistol, then he was firing again – the soldiers retreating, regrouping, beginning a new rush, and Grace was backing away, still firing, being driven down the back stairs towards the kitchen.

The clatter of Mick Malone running down the stairs at the front of the house.

'All right, Seamus, I'm coming!'

Soldiers coming in the front door.

The enemy appearing at the top of the kitchen stairs, Seamus Grace kneeling and firing at them.

'Get him! Get him!'

A rifle volley, and Mick Malone was dead.

Grace ran to a small cellar window, saw an officer leading some men up the steps, shot at him, saw him go down.

Grace's pistol jammed. He turned on a tap, ran cold water on the gun. Through a gap in the shutters he could see khaki and he fired, again and again.

A soldier threw a bomb down the stairs and it exploded by the kitchen door. Another bomb came through a window and Grace scrambled for cover behind a stove. He was still alive after it exploded.

In desperation, Grace ran down a basement corridor. He and Malone had used a heavy iron garden seat to barricade an outside door. Now, he tugged at it, strained to get it out of the way. It moved, he pulled the bolts on the door, someone firing at him from inside the house, and he returned fire as he went out the back and over a garden wall.

*

At the Parochial Hall, Joe Clarke was muttering, 'Oh my God, oh my God,' over and over and his comrades thought he'd been hit. He was wrestling with his Martini rifle and the dud ammunition he'd been given.

Pat Doyle had a Mauser C96, like Mick Malone's. He'd had a hundred rounds when this started and he was running out. Here too the firing from outside was relentless and the troops were throwing grenades.

The four men decided it was time to leave, to try to make it to the garrison at Bolands Mills.

They left the Parochial Hall by the back way, into Percy Place, where they were immediately captured by a British patrol.

They were taken into a house, where an officer ordered that a rope be found to bind their hands – they were going to be shot, he said.

The officer went away. After a while, when the soldiers hadn't found any rope and there was no sign of the officer coming back, someone else gave orders that the prisoners were to be taken away into custody. As they were marched out into Percy Place, they saw that Clanwilliam House was on fire.

Still the rumours continued. There were thousands of Volunteers marching up the Naas Road. Then it was the Germans who were said to be marching up the Naas Road – one of the priests from Inchicore had seen them. All around the country, it was said, the people were rising in response to the events in Dublin. The Germans were massing in Dublin Bay. And the Pope had sent the rising his blessing.

One basis for the German rumour was that Sir Roger Casement had been in Germany, trying to recruit a regiment from among the Irish members of the British Army held prisoner there to come to Ireland and join the rising. He had little success and was captured days before the rising.

Captain Frank Henderson took a break from organizing the defences in Henry Street. The commander of F Company was a solid, matter-of-fact man. He leaned towards a practical rather than a romantic nationalism. He had no illusions about the Irish Volunteers. Many were disciplined as well as enthusiastic and were therefore reliable. Those with good intentions and a weak sense of discipline just made up the numbers, but you didn't call on them if you could do without.

His attitude to the rumours of impending reinforcements and imminent victory was similarly down to earth. Some people need such rumours to bolster their spirits. If the rumours were true, well and good. But a practical man had to check these things out.

Henderson went up to the roof of the GPO. It was risky, with snipers at work, but the roof had a terrific view of Dublin Bay. And Henderson could see that the bay was clear of any ships – there was no German fleet on its way.

And if that was the case, there was no reason to trust any other rumours – whether about friends from abroad or the rest of the country awakening. They were on their own.

At Clanwilliam House, a red settee by a window, hit repeatedly by tracer bullets, was on fire. Jim Walsh found a soda bottle and sprayed the flames. He then used the soda to slake his thirst. He offered the bottle to his brother Tom and a bullet shattered it.

Bullets smacked into ceilings and walls, plaster fell on the grand piano, bits of a chandelier came down.

Crawling upstairs, they found the stairs were mostly shot away. There were fires raging at various places around the house. Ammunition was running out; mostly what was left was handgun ammo.

It was time to go.

George Reynolds stood at the window. Leaning forward for one last shot, he took a bullet and died. The four men left alive headed for the back door, leaving three dead comrades behind.

The British Army lost 234 dead and wounded in the area around Mount Street Bridge.

The industrial area at Barrow Street, near Bolands Mills, was overrun with cats. There was a cats' home in the street, but the fighting was rough around Bolands Mills, too dangerous for the cats' home carers to come near the place. Since there was no one to feed them, the cats were released to fend for themselves.

The rising had paralysed the city – no reliable transport, no deliveries, whole areas cordoned off by the military, barricades everywhere, shops closed and few food deliveries to those that were open. The city was hungry. The fruit and vegetable markets were closed, much food was spoiled. Some Dubliners went outside the city by bicycle, seeking farmers who would sell milk, meat and eggs.

Johnson, Mooney & O'Brien, the bakers, worked overtime to meet demand. They sold at the normal price and limited purchases to two loaves per customer, to prevent profiteering.

The Richmond Hospital used black tape on a white sheet to write 'Richmond Hospital Supplies' and put it over a horse and cart, on which a doctor and two students safely made an expedition to the south side of the river for food.

On Tuesday the gas to the Rotunda Hospital had been cut off. Now, on Wednesday, the electricity went. As evening arrived, the medics were working in the dark.

Most hospitals had an intake of civilians wounded as they travelled about trying to find food for their families. As the week went on, the hospitals were dealing with dozens of dead, hundreds of wounded. Staff were stretched to the limit, working night and day without a break, without even time for a change of clothes.

At the Richmond, Cumann na mBan nurse Eilis Ni Riain, accompanying a patient on a stretcher, felt a hand on her shoulder. Assuming she was about to be arrested, she turned to find Sir Thomas Myles, one of Ireland's leading surgeons, with a superb reputation as both a physician and a teacher. He was also a knight of the realm and a lieutenant-colonel in the Royal Army Medical Corps. And he was Honorary Surgeon in Ireland to His Majesty the King.

Myles, a supporter of the Irish Protestant Home Rule Association, had used his yacht to import guns for the Volunteers at Kilcoole in 1914. He quietly congratulated Ni Riain on the nursing work of Cumann na mBan.

At the College of Surgeons, Nora O'Daly and the other Cumann na mBan members were exhausted from dealing with the wounded. The accidental discharge of a shotgun came close to wounding O'Daly. A young man named Keogh was hit and had to have his wrist stitched without anaesthetic.

Late that evening the nurses were visited by a sympathetic doctor from outside. When he discovered it was Nora's third night without sleep he insisted she take an injection. She eventually agreed, and the doctor gave her a shot of opium. She slept peacefully.

22

Late Wednesday evening, nearing the end of his epic bicycle journey, a saddle-sore Paul Galligan was close to Enniscorthy when he met a Volunteer at work, delivering bread. I can't go into town in case I'm picked up, Galligan told him. Fetch the officers, I've got orders from James Connolly.

The Enniscorthy Volunteers had been isolated, confused by the MacNeill cancellation. On Monday they heard that the whole country was rising, and – just as reliably – they'd been told that only the Citizen Army was out.

The officers met Galligan outside the town and he explained what was happening in Dublin, and what Connolly wanted the Enniscorthy company to do. At 2am on Thursday morning, 27 April, the fourth day of the rising, the Enniscorthy Volunteers were mobilized.

It was four in the morning when Nora O'Daly was woken from her opium-tinged sleep. Casualties had been brought in. Among them twenty-three-year-old Margaret Skinnider, a member of the Citizen Army. Born of Irish parents, Skinnider had come from Glasgow to take part in the rising. She served as a sniper on the roof of the College of Surgeons.

Skinnider, Bill Partridge and Fred Ryan had been on a mission to set fire to enemy outposts near the Russell Hotel, from which the college had repeatedly come under attack. They were surprised by a firing party. Fred Ryan, aged seventeen, was shot dead, Skinnider was severely wounded. When Partridge returned to the college, he and Constance Markievicz went out and found Skinnider. Partridge carried her back to the college while Markievicz kept up a blaze of covering fire.

Nora O'Daly, Rosie Hackett and the other nurses went to work.

When Seamus Grace went over a garden wall at the back of 25 Northumberland Road he was wearing a Volunteer uniform. That limited his movements in daylight – anywhere he went, he was identifiable as a rebel. He decided to make his way to the garrison at Bolands Mills. He got to Mount Street Bridge, but that was crawling with troops. Clanwilliam House was burning.

During the night he came across British patrols and had pistol-versus-rifle duels with them. As dawn arrived on Thursday, he climbed over a wall and found a safe place to lie down. He would spend the day there and move around at night.

The four men who escaped from Clanwilliam House got food and changes of clothes from family members. They spent the night in a nearby coach factory, then split up, the Walsh brothers finding refuge at a convalescent home in Drumcondra run by Sister Angelus and her nuns.

It was just after dawn when Charles Hachette Hyland, the dentist who the previous day had tended the wounded at Mount Street Bridge, opened the back gate of his home at Percy Place. The battle of Mount Street Bridge was

over, but he could still hear shooting in the area. There
was no doubt there would be further need for the skills of
anyone with medical knowledge. As he stood at the gate
a single bullet killed him.

It was probably a stray shot. Or a British soldier or a
rebel saw movement, feared an enemy move and reacted.
Charles Hachette Hyland, son of the manager of the
Gaiety Theatre, was twenty-nine.

A man appeared from somewhere and stood in front
of the GPO, demanding to be allowed in. Those inside
shouted at him to go away.

'I'm a bloody Dublin Fusilier. I don't give a damn about
anyone.'

Again, the Volunteers shouted at him to go away.

To Harry Colley, watching from the Imperial Hotel, he
seemed off his head.

The man lurched away from the building. 'I'm a
Dublin Fusilier,' he shouted, 'and I want to die like
a Dublin Fusilier.'

He was now near the centre of the street. Down at
O'Connell Bridge, soldiers opened up with a machine
gun and the man crumpled over.

Two Volunteers with Red Cross armbands tried to get
out to him, but were driven back by machine-gun fire.
After a while, a Volunteer appeared on the street, carrying a white flag. The British soldiers didn't fire. He went
out to the dead man, knelt and said a brief prayer, then
got off the street.

The twine-and-tin-can mechanism for sending messages
between the GPO and the Imperial Hotel had been shot
out of existence by British snipers. Instead, Volunteers
dashed back and forth, as needed.

Nineteen-year-old Noel Lemass, who had come into

the city centre along with Frank Henderson's rearguard column on Tuesday, almost made it to the Imperial with despatches when a bullet smashed one foot and sent him sprawling and helpless. Two Volunteers ran from the hotel and dragged him to safety.

The O'Rahilly was writing to his wife. 'There is no doubt at all I did the right thing.'

Thursday would be dominated by artillery.

Sometime after noon, a shell hit a building at the top of Lower Abbey Street, yards from Sackville Street. This one shell, more than any other, would eventually have a devastating effect on the centre of the city.

The fire it caused destroyed a reserve printing office that belonged to the *Irish Times*. The flames moved on to the Hibernian Bank, on the corner of Lower Abbey Street and Sackville Street. It was hurriedly evacuated. Boss Shields, Jack Stafford, the Cumann na mBan nurses and the rest of the contingent decided to try to make it across the street to the GPO. Captain Tom Weafer's body was lost to the inferno.

The fire spread to a barricade at the top of Lower Abbey Street, which included large rolls of newsprint taken from the printing office. The flames moved along the barricade towards the Reis building and Wynn's Hotel, on the far side of the street. That block had already taken a pounding.

From the top floor of the Metropole Hotel, Charlie Saurin noticed that the spectators at the window of Wynn's Hotel were gone, now that the flames were spreading and the hotel itself had become part of the spectacle.

The fire was by this time eating its way both north and

southwards along the east side of Sackville Street. It was also moving down both sides of Lower Abbey Street – from the Hibernian Bank and from Wynn's Hotel – towards Marlborough Street.

All the while, as the shells continued to fall, the Volunteers and the Citizen Army readied themselves for what was considered the inevitable infantry attack. Arms and ammunition at the ready, bombs lined up for igniting and throwing.

There was little sign, however, that the British were in a hurry to send in troops. Instead, they continued to use machine guns and snipers to pin down the enemy, and artillery shells to pound them into oblivion.

The carnage at Mount Street Bridge, during which the army threw waves of vulnerable infantry at well-armed positions, with predictable consequences, was an example of the old military way. For the heart of the rebellion, technology would do the job. And the tactics of the IRB leaders made it easy.

Lieutenant Michael Boland of the Volunteers had fought with the British Army against the Boers. Now he was in the GPO, fighting the British. This was, he thought, 'a mad business'. They should have taken to the hills like the Boers. He summed up the rebels' position: 'Shut in here with our leaders, and the flags over our heads to tell the enemy where to find us, when they want us.'

Like most soldiers in most wars, his criticism was balanced by a resigned commitment to duty. 'We're here now and we'll just have to stick it.'

23

When word circulated, about a hundred Volunteers responded to the call in Enniscorthy, with another hundred
or so turning up over the next couple of days, along with
the local Cumann na mBan.

They had twenty rifles between them, with a hundred
rounds per rifle. After that, you took what you could get
– the odd revolver or shotgun, or a pike from the cache
prepared and hidden over the previous months.

They set up headquarters in the Athenaeum Theatre,
ran up the tricolour, surrounded and cut off the police
barracks, put guards on the banks, took the keys of
all the pubs, put out scouts, set up outposts, contacted
Volunteers in other Wexford towns and villages, and
within hours were in control of their town.

The shelling of Dublin city centre continued through
Thursday. Unable to do their job, the Dublin Fire Brigade
watched helplessly as the flames spread.

Around 7.30pm, the outsize DBC building collapsed
into Sackville Street – a terrible noise, a vast mass of
falling bricks and debris, the impact shaking the whole
street. Colossal clouds of dust and smoke rose into the
sky.

Watching from the Imperial Hotel, F Company's Seamus Daly saw the broken building only as material that would, when the flames died down, have the makings of a fine barricade.

Having consumed the Hibernian Bank, flames continued moving north along the block. Hoyte's, a chemist's premises equipped with barrels of turpentine and methylated spirits, caught fire and the whole building went up. Barrels of chemicals exploded, some of them landing on the roof of the Imperial Hotel.

The immense conflagration at Hoyte's took the fire to the end of that block, with just the narrow lane of Sackville Place separating it from the block dominated by Clerys department store and the Imperial Hotel.

The flames crept along the barricade at the top of Sackville Place – the barricade through which Frank Henderson and his F Company comrades had passed when they arrived in the city centre on Tuesday evening. The fire soon reached the building on the other side of the lane and began to crawl up the window frame. Clerys and the Imperial Hotel would be next.

The British artillery was taking its time about finding the range of the GPO, and its efforts were spraying shells far and wide. Guns in the garden of the Rotunda Hospital were lobbing shells over buildings to drop into the Sackville Street area. Some hit the roof of the Imperial. A water tank attached to a side wall, under the roof, took a direct hit and shattered. The water fell straight down into an annex where a number of Volunteers were resting – it hit them like a wave and washed them along the floor.

Besides drenching the Volunteers, the direct hit on the water tank had deprived the Imperial garrison of water to fight fires.

A shell hit the roof of the Metropole Hotel. In the room

directly below, Charlie Saurin and another Volunteer were sent sprawling. The ceiling came down in a shower of debris. Bricks clattered down the chimney. Fumes filled the room.

Saurin and his comrade moved on hands and knees towards the door. As they reached the corridor, Oscar Traynor appeared at the top of the stairs, hurrying to check the damage. Another shell hit the roof directly over the corridor. Traynor staggered from the effects of the explosion and a crack opened in the wall behind him.

Bullets came through the windows and through the damaged walls. Saurin heard a bullet pass his ear and fancied he could feel his hair flutter as it travelled past. He moved into another room, where two Citizen Army men were sitting beneath the window, a range of bombs beside them, ready to ignite the fuses when the British infantry attacked and throw the explosives down to the street. They were part of a half dozen reinforcements – tough, laconic individuals – who had arrived at the Metropole that morning.

As Saurin entered the room another shell hit the roof just above him. When the debris settled and the smoke cleared, the two men were still sitting beneath the window, smoking their pipes, continuing their conversation.

Further along the corridor, a chimney collapsed into the room below.

Oscar Traynor decided it was time to move everyone down a couple of floors. They left only John Neale, the English socialist, upstairs to keep watch for fires.

At his home in Drumcondra, Matt Stafford got down his rifle and his double-barrel shotgun. He pulled on his bandolier and made his way around to Jones's Road. He was hailed from across the street by an acquaintance named Burke. Burke asked Matt where he was going. Matt told him he was off to join the lads down at the mills.

That would be a mistake, Burke said. He told Matt he was about to walk, visibly armed, into a building that had been taken over by British troops. At best he'd be arrested; he might even be shot out of hand.

Matt Stafford went home.

Paddy Mahon of F Company, who at Annesley Bridge on Monday had put a machine gun out of action with a single shot, was proving to be an expert sniper. From a window of the Imperial Hotel, he took patient aim at British snipers in Westmoreland Street. Again and again he put them out of action, whether wounded or killed.

A British gun crew at the Parnell Monument hauled an 18-pounder around until it was pointing at the GPO. It took six men to operate the gun, with another four to keep a supply of shells coming – providing a range of targets.

The Imperial Hotel snipers began to shoot at the gun crew from a range of about 550 yards. As crew members dropped, wounded or worse, reinforcements took their place.

Eventually, the 18-pounder blasted off a shell. Standing free on the cobblestones, without the stability of having the trail embedded in the earth, the gun spun around and the shell hit a nearby building. This was occupied by British troops, who assumed they were under fire from rebel artillery – unaware that the rebels had none. They hurriedly left the building. The snipers at the Imperial Hotel now had an abundance of new targets.

At the other end of Sackville Street, the incessant shelling set alight Kelly's Fort and Hopkins & Hopkins, on the junctions with Bachelors Walk and Eden Quay. Joe Good and his comrades began to withdraw to the Metropole Hotel and the GPO.

Paddy Shortis of F Company survived unscathed the mission to dislodge British soldiers from Liffey Street. James Connolly wasn't so lucky. On his way back to the GPO a ricochet shattered an ankle. Connolly already had a minor arm wound, but the ankle injury left him in severe pain. He crawled through William's Lane, the long, narrow alley between Abbey Street and Prince's Street, to make his way back to the GPO, every movement agonizing. Only when he got to the end of the alley was he discovered by someone from the GPO. His men came with a stretcher.

Dr John Doyle gave Connolly an anaesthetic. He operated, with the help of a British Army prisoner named O'Mahony from the Indian Medical Service. They stopped the bleeding and tried to treat the broken bones – but the ankle was too much of a mess.

Connolly's continuing pain limited his ability to lead. Pearse seemed subdued. Joe Plunkett, odd as ever, with his sword and his jewelled fingers, moved among the rebels, encouraging them with quiet words. It was widely believed he'd left his deathbed to take part in the rising. Eccentric or not, his steadfastness won him increasing admiration among the rank and file.

At Marlborough Street, close to the Pro-Cathedral, members of the 3rd Royal Irish Regiment arrived to construct a barbed-wire barricade across the street. They'd just finished the job when, from down the street, an elderly man advanced towards them. He moved in a kind of hopping motion, from side to side. He was wearing a heavy overcoat and had a cap pulled down low over his forehead. He carried a rook rifle, a single-shot weapon, small calibre, short range – a rifle usually used for shooting crows and rabbits.

He fired towards the troops, reloaded and kept on coming. They shouted at him to stop; some took aim.

The man continued to advance, dodging from side to side, taking no notice of their warnings. Almost at the barricade, he fired again.

Three of the soldiers fired back. One bullet took him in the forehead, another in the throat. The third severed two of his fingers. The elderly man dropped the rook rifle and fell across the barbed wire, legs on one side, head and shoulders on the other – his blood flowing.

His severed fingers were found to be connected to his hand only by the wool of his glove.

No one knew who he was, whether he was drunk or angry. There was a roll of banknotes in one of his pockets.

The O'Rahilly received a note from his son Aodogan. 'Dear Daddy . . . I heart [*sic*] from Nell and Anna that the Volunteers are winning. I don't suppose they will ever get the GPO for as long as you are in command.'

On guard duty at the Prince's Street entrance to the GPO along with Volunteer John McGallogly, Joe Good was approached by a man who said he wanted to join the rebels. Joe held him at gunpoint while John went to find an officer. 'You can trust me,' the man said. 'You have no need to be afraid.'

Joe considered this, then said, 'While I'm at this end of the gun you're the one to be afraid.'

The man was eventually told to go home. Joe was sent

up on to the roof to repair the telephone wires he had helped install – now damaged by shellfire. With snipers about, he kept flat, crawling from one position to another.

The Imperial Hotel and Clerys garrison was under the command of Frank Thornton. As the building burned around them, Thornton's unit prepared to leave. Even had the water tank not been destroyed, there was no fighting this volume of fire.

The holes bored in the walls between the Imperial and the buildings alongside would allow the garrison to move safely to North Earl Street, where they would link up with the garrison occupying the corner there, under Brennan-Whitmore. From there, according to the plan, they would break out to the country and continue the fight.

First, the Cumann na mBan members left – along the block through the bored holes, across North Earl Street and eventually to the presbytery of the Pro-Cathedral in Marlborough Street, where they found safety.

The Volunteers prepared to leave the Imperial Hotel in two groups. Frank Thornton would lead one, F Company's Seamus Daly would lead the other.

With Thornton's group, Harry Colley went through the bored holes, towards the Pro-Cathedral. He and another Volunteer had already been refused permission by Frank Thornton to break into the Gresham Hotel, further up Sackville Street, take it over and make a stand. Or to crawl across Sackville Street to join the garrison in the GPO. They were, Thornton insisted, going to break out to the north of Dublin.

It was dawning on Harry Colley that what was happening didn't make sense.

The officers leading the supposed breakout to the

countryside were Brennan-Whitmore and Thornton. Brennan-Whitmore was from Wexford, with no knowledge at all of Dublin geography. He wanted to make it to Fairview, to get some space behind him into which he could retreat and from which he could manoeuvre his forces and renew attacks on the enemy.

To Brennan-Whitmore, Fairview and North Strand were just names – he had to depend on others to tell him how to get there; he had no idea where they were in relation to anywhere else – and he had no knowledge of the number and disposal of British forces in that area.

The other man in command of the proposed escape to the countryside, Frank Thornton, was born in Drogheda and had lived in Liverpool from the age of twenty, where he had become involved in nationalist politics. He had no knowledge at all of Dublin.

Harry Colley knew that he and his F Company comrades had been forced to withdraw from Fairview on Tuesday evening, two days previously, because they were about to be surrounded. There were now more British troops in Dublin than ever. Fairview, he knew, wasn't likely to be the place of safety Brennan-Whitmore seemed to imagine it to be.

Having reached the Pro-Cathedral, Colley went down the lane behind the church, then on to Findlater's Place, around to the right and up Gloucester Street (now Sean MacDermott Street). He had become separated from Brennan-Whitmore. He had no notion of where he was going, but at least he wasn't on a mission to find some imaginary sanctuary in Fairview.

24

Seamus Daly's unit was the last to leave the Imperial Hotel.

'Is this the end, Seamus?' Paddy Mahon asked.

'Well, as far as this building is concerned, it is the end.'

'I think we ought to stick it out to the finish.'

We're going, Daly said.

There was no doubt that Mahon would follow orders. First, though, he called on the remaining men to sing 'A Soldier's Song'. And they did, with great emotion.

> Soldiers are we, whose lives are pledged to Ireland;
> Some have come from a land beyond the wave.
> Sworn to be free, no more our ancient sire-land
> Shall shelter the despot or the slave.

Though written nine years earlier, the song had become popular among nationalists over the previous couple of years. In later generations – for whom the song would be the national anthem – the words would become hackneyed reflections of an outdated nationalism. For the rebels in the Imperial Hotel, the words were an accurate description of the feelings of young men for whom freedom had a precise, if limited, meaning – living in a country without foreign domination. A freedom to be won through putting their lives in hazard.

They sang the words and meant every one of them.

Then it was time to go.

The large plate-glass windows of Clerys department store were running molten across the pavement and into the gutter.

Seamus Daly's unit followed the same route as the others who left the Imperial – through the bored holes, across North Earl Street, through that block and along the lane at the back of the church. There, a machine gun opened up and Daly's men crouched against a wall as bullets hit the pavement beside them.

A dozen men came running back down the lane – some of Thornton's group, which by now had broken up, its members dispersed as they ran to cover, scattered by machine-gun fire.

They'd come across a barricade, they said. Several of their comrades had been shot.

Daly led them all, his own men and the refugees from Thornton's group, over a wall and into the garden of the Pro-Cathedral presbytery. There, one of Thornton's men said a priest had been talking to them, asking them to lay down their arms. He'd offered to negotiate surrender with the British.

Daly told them Thornton might have broken through. He might be relying on us to follow on, he said. I'm for pushing on. What do you think?

Some went with him, some didn't.

*

The unit led by Brennan-Whitmore came under machine-gun fire. Brennan-Whitmore took a glancing bullet wound to the inside of his right knee. Noel Lemass, having been shot dashing from the GPO to the Imperial Hotel with despatches, had a much more serious injury to one foot, and was unable to walk.

They hurriedly broke into the basement of one of the tenement houses. There they rested and bandaged their wounds.

No one knew exactly where they were. Railway Street, or Gloucester Street, perhaps some other tenement street. The British were all around, and many of the tenants were wives of soldiers fighting for the British in France – and so could be expected to be hostile.

Two Volunteers wounded, seven more exhausted by sleepless nights and non-stop enemy fire, all crammed into the filthy tenement basement room. They could only wait for daylight.

In the crowded room, Noel Lemass, in pain from his foot wound, was given the ramshackle bed. Brennan-Whitmore slept underneath it. He told the others not to let him sleep for more than an hour. Then, he drew his automatic pistol and slipped off the safety catch. Above him, Lemass was groaning.

The tenement fleas went to work. Swarms of them. They worked their way under the bandage on Brennan-Whitmore's knee. His exhaustion was such that he didn't care. Let them have their way – he fell asleep.

Under machine-gun fire, Harry Colley and some other desperate stray Volunteers forced their way into houses on Gloucester Street.

Everything was confusion, there was no plan, no pattern to follow. Volunteers took refuge where they could. Colley found himself with just one comrade, a man named Flanagan. They tried looking for the others, with no luck.

They were, Colley knew, running out of options.

Seamus Daly and his few remaining men ended up in a tenement flat. The man who lived there was sympathetic but frightened.

'The orders the soldiers gave us are that anyone who looks out a window here will be shot.'

Like the other Volunteers, Daly had been driven off the street by machine-gun fire. And like them, his unit had been broken up by panic, fear and the need to rush to the nearest cover. There were just four of them in this tenement.

Where exactly this house was, Daly wasn't sure.

He crept to the window and looked out. Spread across the wide street, and as far along Gloucester Street as he could see – army tents, a field kitchen, troops and more troops. An entire encampment.

We can do nothing here, Daly thought.

It's over.

In the GPO, Patrick Pearse was addressing the army of the Republic. They had, he said, 'redeemed Dublin from shame and made her name splendid among the names of cities'. He said they deserved to win the fight. And 'win it you will, though you may win it in death'.

Joe Good, on defence duty at one of the windows, strained to hear Pearse's words. They had established the Republic, he said, and by their actions the government of the Republic had won a place at the 'peace table' when the Great War was over and the nations were sorting out the future.

Someone had come up with the notion that if a

rebellion held out for a week it earned the rebels the right to international recognition and a place in whatever negotiations followed the Great War.

Joe Good didn't reckon that was very likely.

Seamus Daly convinced the other Volunteers with him that there was nothing to do but surrender. They'd done what they could; the forces against them outside were overwhelming. One of their comrades, Harry Manning, was wounded.

Outside, the tramp of boots – hundreds more soldiers arriving, with fixed bayonets.

While they were trying to work out how to surrender without being mown down, the door was kicked open and British soldiers shouted at them to come out with their hands up.

In the tenement basement, Brennan-Whitmore woke suddenly to the sound of shouting, looked up, saw British soldiers at the open door, a lieutenant in front, someone screaming, 'Hands up!'

Instinctively he raised his automatic and fired at the officer.

He slid from under the flea-ridden bed and got to his feet.

The Volunteers had their hands up. Their rifles were stockpiled several feet away.

The excitable lieutenant shouted at them, 'Who fired that shot?'

No one said anything. The lieutenant held up his sleeve, showing a bullet hole.

'Who fired that shot?'

Brennan-Whitmore had already slid the automatic under a pile of rags.

If they didn't tell him, the excitable lieutenant said, he'd have them all shot.

With much shouting and threatening, the prisoners were taken out on to the street, where locals screamed abuse and called on the soldiers to shoot them.

Just then, a British Army captain came strolling casually down the street.

When no one owned up to the shooting, the excitable lieutenant ordered that the rebels be brought to the other side of the street and stood in a single line to be shot. Some of the local women cheered when they heard the order.

Convinced the excitable lieutenant would carry out the killings, Brennan-Whitmore decided to own up to firing.

The captain, with an air of nonchalance about him, came level with the troops. The lieutenant, still excited, held up his bullet-drilled sleeve. He told his senior officer what had happened and that he was about to shoot the rebels responsible.

The captain's air of indifference didn't alter as he turned to an NCO and said, 'March the prisoners to the Custom House, sergeant.'

On seeing that two of the prisoners were wounded, he ordered some of the soldiers to sling their rifles and help them.

The O'Rahilly was writing his daily note to his wife. 'Darling Nancy, we are still going strong with hardly a regrettable incident.'

If they stayed here in the tenement they'd be found. If they were found, Harry Colley believed, they'd be put up against a wall and shot.

If they went out on to the street with their rifles and

made a run for it, there was at least some chance of getting through.

Colley and Flanagan agreed that was best.

They left the tenement. They saw a barricade further up the street, soldiers crouched behind it.

Colley in front, Flanagan behind, they began to run towards the barricade, zig-zagging, rifles at the ready. The shooting began immediately and bullets were in the air all around them.

Behind the barricade the soldiers fired and fired again and saw the bullets hit home, but the two rebels kept coming. The one in front had his bayonet fixed and reached the barricade quickly. He was coming over the top, his bayonet poised to plunge.

The soldier he was coming for lunged with his own bayonet and drove it into the rebel's thigh, but the rebel was already weakening, the gunshot wounds finally taking effect. He fell on to the barricade, lay still and moaned.

The second rebel had gone down somewhere, and now there were more of them running up the street. The rebel on the barricade had stopped moaning. The soldier rested his rifle across the body, steadied himself and began shooting again.

When the rebels stopped coming, the soldier took the body by the back of the neck and pulled it forward across the barricade. The body tumbled over and down, the head catching on the back of a chair, and Harry Colley landed upright, bloody and silent.

From the Metropole Hotel, Oscar Traynor watched the fire take over the whole of Clerys and the Imperial Hotel, fifty yards across the street. Sheets of flame shot out into the middle of Sackville Street. Charlie Saurin and another

Volunteer went from floor to floor of the Metropole, cutting down curtains and blinds – so intense was the heat from the Imperial, it might set them alight.

In the GPO, the sandbags at the windows – some of them filled with coal – got so hot that Volunteers had to douse them with water. Despite that, every now and then one of them burst into flames.

In the small hours of the morning, the sudden sound of horses' hooves, galloping.

Rebels sprang to their posts, adrenaline rising: the long-expected attack was here. One Volunteer swung a billycan bomb round his head, holding it by the handle, preparing to unleash it at the enemy charge. The handle broke, the bomb flew across the room.

It didn't explode. Oscar Traynor saw three bombs thrown towards the horses, none of which exploded.

Volunteers were shooting at the horses, but there was no cavalry charge. The horses had been released from some city-centre stable threatened by fire. As they galloped through the city some were shot in Abbey Street, some on Moore Lane, one in Prince's Street – others ran clear.

At the barricade on Gloucester Street, working by flash-light, a corporal of the Royal Army Medical Corps leaned over Harry Colley. 'Take him gently, boys, he appears to be very badly hurt.' The only bullet Colley felt was the one that hit his ankle; the other wounds happened without him noticing.

He was transferred to an ambulance, where his comrade Flanagan was already strapped down, along with two other wounded men.

Over the previous couple of days, Volunteers had

claimed that ambulances were being used to transport military and Castle officials around the city. They warned the British that ambulances had to stop for inspection or they'd be fired on.

As the ambulance carrying Colley and Flanagan motored down the quays, there were shouts for it to stop, but the driver kept going. The Volunteers opened fire. Flanagan was hit in the shoulder, as was an orderly, and the driver was shot through a lung.

After two hours lying in the shot-up ambulance, Colley woke up in the Castle Hospital, where a doctor told him: 'I don't wish to appear brutal, but I think you should know that you're dying.' Making up in powers of prognosis what he lacked in compassion, the doctor added: 'You haven't got half an hour to live. Make your peace with God and prepare to meet Him.'

Part Seven

Hellfire

25

The flames from the great fire that was destroying the centre of Dublin were visible from various points around the capital. Arriving by boat in Dublin Bay at 2am on Friday, General Sir John Maxwell had a clear view of the blaze. Maxwell was arriving to take charge of the final assault on the rebel positions.

'If necessary, I shall not hesitate to destroy all buildings within any area occupied by the rebels.'

For the military, the aim was to kill the leadership of the rising, or force them to surrender. Wipe out the leaders and a demoralized insurrection would collapse.

To achieve this end, the artillery set out to level most of Sackville Street and much of Abbey Street and Henry Street. If the rebels didn't die from explosive shells they would die in the burning buildings. Maxwell was threatening to expand that tactic to any part of Dublin harbouring rebels.

In Drumcondra, north of the city centre, near Binns Bridge, Matt Stafford, the old Fenian, was on a rooftop, behind a chimney. He had his shotgun and a rifle, his bandolier of ammunition.

There's no record of how he got there, but he later

said he worked together with a man he called 'English' Murphy. The two of them began sniping at British troops.

By his own Fenian code, Matt Stafford was bound to do what he could to assist the rebellion. Cut off from 2nd Battalion, no word from Captain Leo Henderson, this sniping role was all that was available to him. And he hated it. It was nothing to be proud of, he believed, hiding behind a chimneystack and shooting men who had no notion they were in the line of fire.

Isolated, but feeling duty-bound, that was the only role available to him and he fulfilled it as best he could.

He fired again, and again, and again, and he watched the enemy drop.

Frank Henderson went up on to the roof of the GPO with his rifle. The enemy snipers had been busier than ever this morning, and it was dangerous to allow them to dominate the streets unchallenged. He spent several hours, with a number of other Volunteers, exchanging fire with British snipers.

The snipers Henderson was trying to dislodge were also being taken on from street level. Three men in particular were having a devastating effect. Vincent Poole, Harry Boland and Volunteer Tom Leahy had settled into Manfield & Sons shoe shop on the corner of Sackville Street and Middle Abbey Street. As they traded shots with the enemy, Poole kept the others amused with tales of his adventures in the British Army fighting the Boers.

Apart from his entertainment value, Poole gave the others advice born of experience. He was an excellent shot and had an impressive ability to identify the position from which enemy fire was coming. Again and again he located and picked off British snipers on the far side of Sackville Street.

The British were building a barricade in Lower Abbey Street. If they were successful, they would have cover from which they could advance on Sackville Street and perhaps launch an assault on the GPO. To discourage this, Poole, Boland and Leahy kept up a continuous rate of fire – so relentless that their rifles grew too hot to hold. Having no oil to cool them, Poole got hold of some tins of sardines and suggested they use the oil from those, and it worked.

From time to time, they withheld fire to allow the Red Cross to remove the wounded soldiers from Abbey Street.

Oscar Traynor, like most officers and many of the rank and file, seemed not to sleep. Day and night he passed back and forth between the Metropole, Eason's and Manfield & Sons, crawling through the linking holes in the walls, covered in dust, constantly moving, checking, informing, encouraging, at times joining his men in shooting matches with the enemy. At one point he shouted, 'Thank God – I can die happy now, I've just shot one.'

The shooting continued for hours. Eventually, Frank Henderson and the other snipers left the roof of the GPO, under heavy artillery fire. An incendiary shell landed on the roof and began to burn down through the building.

Paddy Shortis from F Company was on guard at a window in the GPO. A Cumann na mBan nurse asked him if he was all right and he said he was, but he'd appreciate it if she'd say the Rosary with him. The two began to pray. Five years earlier, when he was eighteen, Shortis had studied for the priesthood at All Hallows.

Some other Cumann na mBan nurses came and joined them. Volunteers passing by either joined in or bared their heads momentarily as they passed. Most Volunteers carried rosary beads in their pockets, some wore them around their necks.

At the Castle Hospital, Harry Colley was anointed by a priest. A nurse told him he was dying. She prayed for him and he silently followed her prayers. The way he felt, it was like his life's blood was draining away.

On the south side of the city, there was some sniping from and at Jacob's factory, but the British mostly ignored the garrison. A large section of the Volunteer force, including over half of F Company, had occupied the factory throughout the week – but had very little engagement with the enemy.

Major John MacBride was frustrated by the lack of activity and urged Tom MacDonagh to organize forays out to areas where other garrisons needed support. MacDonagh stuck to the original plan – take the factory and wait for the enemy to attack.

One group was sent out on bicycles to give support to the garrison at Bolands Mills. It couldn't get through the army cordons and returned to the factory under sniper fire, with one Volunteer wounded and dying.

The British were content to cordon off the factory and leave it alone. Plenty of time for mopping up, once the GPO was destroyed.

Volunteer Tom Harris, from Prosperous, looked up at the ceiling of the GPO, where he saw a small dark circle, about the circumference of a teacup. It was getting bigger. The fire begun by that incendiary shell on the roof had made its way down through the building, and was beginning to burn through the final barrier.

By midday on Friday there was no doubt that the GPO

was finished. Patrick Pearse ordered the Cumann na mBan members to gather and leave, taking with them the wounded to Jervis Street Hospital. The women protested, insisting they must stay. 'You told us we were all equal!'

Pearse became flustered as the women argued their case. Sean MacDermott appeared to cancel Pearse's order, but Pearse insisted. Most of the women left under a Red Cross flag, accompanied by Dr John Doyle and Desmond FitzGerald, but a handful of those most experienced in first aid stayed on. Among those who remained was Winifred Carney, James Connolly's aide. She continued to type his orders, her Webley revolver next to her typewriter.

As the women left, Tom Clarke approached one of them. 'If you see my wife,' he said, 'tell her the men fought . . .' He turned away, unable to continue.

The O'Rahilly had earlier formed a group to remove explosives and homemade bombs from upstairs and bring them to the ground floor – moving them from the path of the advancing flames. Now, the explosives had to be brought to the basement.

The flames now came down through a lift shaft. Firefighters could at best keep them from spreading widely on each floor, but they couldn't prevent the fire's downward progress.

More and more Volunteers were withdrawn from defence duties to combat the flames. Most of The O'Rahilly's time, along with Michael Collins', was now taken up with firefighting. The pressure in the hoses was pitifully inadequate.

Standing next to Volunteer Joe Reilly – from London – both of them fighting the fires, Collins found his trousers alight. Reilly turned his hose on Collins, who was drenched from head to foot and not at all grateful.

As it became clear that the GPO was running out

of time, there was talk among the officers of breaking through to the countryside, perhaps taking to the hills along with Volunteer units in Wicklow, Wexford and Carlow.

Vincent Poole's knowledge of the sewer system under the streets was considered – perhaps that would provide a way to bypass the surrounding enemy – but damage caused by the persistent shelling had blocked many of the sewer tunnels.

Someone came up with a notion – not quite a plan – about making a run for the Williams & Woods factory, a tough, granite building in Great Britain Street. It meant travelling through enemy-held territory: across Henry Street, down Moore Street, around to the left, then down Great Britain Street to Williams & Woods. From there, the new headquarters of the rising, it might be possible to link up with Ned Daly's garrison in the Four Courts, which was engaged in a furious battle with the enemy.

Such a journey would be steeped in blood.

First there was the gamble of crossing Henry Street, avoiding the fire from the machine guns chattering from down the far end of the street. Then, the much more troublesome obstacle of the British barricade at the far end of Moore Street. It was a formidable obstruction, constructed from railway sleepers, butchers' blocks from nearby shops, crates and barrels.

Behind it, the soldiers, their rifles and two machine guns.

For some of the rebels, the Williams & Woods factory became an idealized goal – as though making it that far would bring a change of fortunes. For others, it was an unlikely goal. But, with the GPO in flames around them, it was at least a goal.

*

The Cumann na mBan nurses and the wounded reached Jervis Street Hospital safely and were allowed entry by the military. Dr John Doyle and Desmond FitzGerald were refused admission. 'No, you're going out to where you came from, to be shot or burned out.'

As the men left, a captain addressed his troops. The Red Cross protection was to be respected until they reached cover.

There was a British sniper on a rooftop in Henry Street, and he'd picked off some Volunteers who had left the GPO by the Henry Street door. Patrick Pearse sent Volunteer James Kavanagh to a room beside the exit and asked him to keep an eye on the rooftops and try to get the sniper.

Kavanagh put a few shots where he thought the sniper might be, then waited, poised to shoot again should the gunman pop up.

By six o'clock, most of the rebels were being brought together, posts abandoned, awaiting orders to leave the GPO.

Emotions were raw. For five days the building had been the heart of the rising. To leave it, with only the haziest notion of what might come next, was to concede that the republic it symbolized was a fragile, faltering thing.

Tom Clarke, waving his automatic pistol, said he'd never leave the GPO alive. 'You can all go and leave me here. I'll go down with the building.'

Sean MacDermott quieted him, convinced him that there was no gain in surrendering to the flames. The fight would go on.

The decision made, a sense of calm descended. There was no scramble to leave – orders were given, units readied themselves.

Someone began singing 'A Soldier's Song' and many joined in.

> Our camp fires now are burning low
> See in the east a silvery glow
> Out yonder waits the Saxon foe
> So chant a soldier's song.

Small groups lined up at the Henry Street exit, prepared for their dash across the street. One small, sharp-featured sixteen-year-old boy, known as Moggy Murtagh, from Cecil Avenue in Clontarf, was a Fianna scout attached to F Company. He had served in the DBC building until it was burned down and had since been stationed in the GPO. Now, carrying a large crucifix across his shoulder, he calmly strolled across the street to Henry Place, as though immune to bullets.

In order to clear the way for the advance towards Williams & Woods, The O'Rahilly had agreed to lead a group of about thirty men up Moore Street to overcome the British barricade at the other end of the street. He began assembling men for the mission.

Sparks were coming down through the lift shaft, embers flying, flames leaping, burning timbers falling – and someone realized the explosives banished to the basement were directly underneath where the Volunteers were gathering to leave the GPO. Some men were sent down to shift the explosives to another part of the basement.

Joe Good could see that some of the British prisoners, who were being brought along with the Volunteers, were paralysed with fear. He suggested to The O'Rahilly that maybe it would be best if they let the prisoners take their chances.

The O'Rahilly thought the suggestion was that they should use the prisoners to draw fire from the enemy. For a moment, he looked as though he was about to strike Good. Then he saw the point and apologized. The prisoners were told they could go.

The O'Rahilly led his unit out, staying close to the buildings, moving down Henry Street to prepare for the charge. Bayonets fixed, the group included Eamonn Dore, John Reynolds, Charles Steinmayer, Paddy Murray, John Kenny – the young man who had served at the manure company with Vincent Poole – and Paddy Shortis from F Company.

It was getting dark now, making it harder for the British gunners to identify targets.

Within minutes, the main body of Volunteers had begun the GPO evacuation – in small groups, dashing the fifty feet across Henry Street, under fire, to Henry Place, an L-shaped lane that led to Moore Street. British machine guns, down at the other end of Henry Street, sprayed the street with bullets.

No one had informed the Metropole garrison that the GPO would soon be abandoned. They had been ordered to hold their position until told otherwise. At the last minute, Sean MacDermott remembered. Frank Henderson offered to order the withdrawal. As he went into the blazing hotel to contact Oscar Traynor's unit, he marvelled that anyone could be alive in such a hellhole.

At the Castle Hospital, Harry Colley woke from a deep sleep. A doctor was leaning over him, asking him how he felt.

I'm all right now, Colley said.

He was still alive, and something had changed. He didn't know anything about medicine, but he knew that the feeling he'd had earlier in the hospital, of his life's blood draining away, was gone. He knew now that he'd live.

When they got to the junction with Moore Street, The O'Rahilly split his men into two files, one on each side of the street. He himself was on the left side. They advanced slowly, moving perhaps half of the 240-yard length of Moore Street without incident. The O'Rahilly finally raised his pistol and yelled, 'Charge!'

Paddy Murray was within seconds lying on the pavement, badly wounded. After running thirty yards, John Kenny was cut down, rose and carried on, and was hit again, his leg shattered by bullets. Others were still running, some were on the ground, some were scattering towards cover – the charge was immediately broken up by the intensity of the machine-gun fire.

The O'Rahilly made it up Moore Street to within fifty yards of the barricade. He crouched in a doorway. Paddy Shortis was in cover nearby.

In shops and lanes and nooks and crannies the length of the street, Volunteers squatted, waited, didn't dare move. It was impossible to go on, it was impossible to go back. Out there was nothing but blood, pain and death.

From his hiding place, The O'Rahilly could hear soldiers calling to the machine gunners, telling them the rebel officer was in a doorway to their right.

Before they could resume shooting, The O'Rahilly jumped out of the doorway and ran – the machine gun firing now – heading for the safety of Sackville Lane, on the other side of the street.

26

Led by Frank Henderson, the Metropole contingent – including Charlie Saurin, Vincent Poole, Oscar Traynor and John Neale – retreated from the hotel and reached the GPO safely. They joined the other rebels gathering to leave the building via the Henry Street exit.

Flames crackled, glass shattered, debris fell from the ceiling of the main hall of the GPO, there was smoke everywhere. And all the time the sound of machine-gun, rifle and artillery fire. As Peadar Bracken headed towards the door a man walking in front of him was shot dead. Bullets came in through the flames and smoke at the windows.

Perhaps it was a bullet coming through the flames, perhaps a piece of shrapnel – whatever it was, it pierced an ammunition pouch on Volunteer Andy Furlong's chest. The revolver ammunition inside exploded.

Furlong took several bullets in his right thigh and collapsed. Another Volunteer went down, rolling on the ground in agony. Charlie Saurin was so startled by the explosion that he never felt the bullet that hit his right hand.

Beside him, John Neale said, 'Can't you stand away and let a fellow lie down?' The lower part of Neale's body had been torn by Furlong's exploding ammunition – he was so severely wounded that it was obvious to Saurin there was no coming back from this.

Oscar Traynor asked Neale how badly he was hurt.

'I'm dying, comrade.' He was calm, quiet, holding himself together. They found some mail sacks for him to lie on.

There was panic in the Moore Street lanes.

Sixty-five yards in from Henry Street, Henry Place took a sharp left turn. Thirty yards down from the turn there was a three-storey building, the ground floor whitewashed. Countless tiny puffs of smoke were erupting from the building. Volunteers scrambled to find cover where there was none.

The sound of firing was non-stop.

A couple of men went down.

Some Volunteers were trying to break in the door to the house, using the butts of their rifles. In the scramble, safety catches had been shaken off and when the butts hit the door the rifles fired, hitting those standing behind. Harry Coyle of F Company died this way.

Tom Clarke shot at the lock on another building, trying to find a place where the men could find cover. It didn't work.

The injured James Connolly was left lying on his back in the lane, alone and shouting orders.

Volunteer Sean McLoughlin was screaming at whoever was inside the whitewashed house, 'You're firing on your own men!'

A Volunteer took a bullet in the chest and went down, falling across the handles of Connolly's stretcher. Connolly panicked, trying to get off the stretcher – he was sure that it was Joe Plunkett who had been shot and wanted to get him into cover. Just then, Plunkett came walking calmly up the lane.

Joe Good decided this problem needed a hand grenade. One grenade in the window of the whitewashed building and the shooting would stop, the panic would end, the advance could continue.

It was their own men in there, their own men they would kill – but that's not what mattered, Joe decided. The panic centred around the whitewashed building was creating chaos and putting everything at risk. It had to be stopped.

He went back down the lane asking Volunteers if any-one had a grenade. No one had. One Volunteer pointed back towards the GPO. It was full of abandoned grenades and bombs.

At the home of Frank Sheehy-Skeffington, a large number of British soldiers, headed by Captain Bowen Colthurst, were searching the house. They heaped books and pam-phlets on to a sheet and took them away.

They had arrived at 7pm and over a period of three hours, as they took the place apart, they terrified Hanna Sheehy-Skeffington, her seven-year-old son and her maid.

Bowen Colthurst had already procured a copy of the forged Castle Document. He attached to it a note claiming to have found it in Frank Sheehy-Skeffington's pocket. Now, the dead man's books and pamphlets would be examined to see if there was anything within them that could be used to justify the murders of the three journalists.

Charlie Saurin held his rifle in his left hand as blood streamed from the bullet wound in his right palm. The GPO's first aid post had gone with the Cumann na mBan nurses.

M. W. O'Reilly was tending a wounded man and called to Charlie to help carry a stretcher – Saurin showed him his bloody hand and moved to take his turn at the exit into Henry Street. On his turn, he ran across the street into Henry Place, bullets hitting the ground like hailstones. He ran up the lane and rounded the corner to where the panicked Volunteers were still clustered.

Someone shouted a command to fix bayonets. There was to be a charge on the whitewashed house. Saurin fixed his sword bayonet to the top of his Martini-Henry rifle and prepared to join the charge.

Oscar Traynor and Liam Cullen from F Company were first in the door, with others crowding in after them. The house was empty.

The shooting, however, continued.

Liam Cullen went into a front room, took a bullet in the thigh and went down.

Facing the whitewashed house there was a long lane – Moore Lane, almost parallel to Moore Street and stretching right up to the Rotunda Hospital in Great Britain Street. From two-thirds of the way up the lane, a British machine gun was strafing all in front of it, the bullets peppering the whitewashed house, the white dust rising from each bullet, giving the impression that the firing was coming from inside the house.

Men had been shot, some accidentally at the hands of their own comrades, in a pointless assault on an empty house.

Patrick Pearse and his brother Willie, along with Frank Henderson, George Plunkett, M. W. O'Reilly and about ten others, were standing just inside the Henry Street exit from the GPO. The firing from the bottom of Henry Street was intense.

I'm going back, Pearse said, to make sure there's no one left behind. He spent a while moving from room to room, finding them all empty – then he remembered James Kavanagh, ordered to try to shoot the British sniper on the rooftops above Henry Street.

Pearse found an exhausted Kavanagh asleep. 'I was nearly forgetting you – they're all gone.'

Kavanagh hurried to the side door, while Pearse had one last quick look around. When Pearse came back to the door – his face swollen with heat and smeared with soot and dust – all but a handful of the remaining GPO garrison had run into Henry Place.

Frank Henderson, M. W. O'Reilly, George Plunkett, Willie Pearse, James Kavanagh and finally Patrick Pearse left the GPO. They ran across Henry Street, bullets clipping the ground around their feet, and into the lanes that led to Moore Street.

There were now between two and three hundred rebels in the narrow lanes. Artillery shells were still landing throughout the area. The crackling noises and the drifting smoke from the many burning buildings overlay everything.

Worst of all, the air was alive with bullets from the British machine guns.

The rebels couldn't go forward on to Moore Street, or turn right into Moore Lane, without being mown down. British snipers picked off occasional targets.

Some rebels clambered over walls, into yards.

Waving his revolver, Tom Clarke urged the men to run past the entrance to Moore Lane.

'One more rally for Ireland!'

Volunteer John Twamley got past safely; a Volunteer behind him took a bullet in the calf and went down.

Twamley reached out and pulled him out of the line of fire.

A Volunteer with a shotgun rested against a wall and put the gun down, butt first. The gun went off and he took the blast in the throat.

Tom Leahy stumbled and fell. Patrick Pearse and Vincent Poole pulled him to his feet.

Michael Collins located a van somewhere and organized a detail to push it across the entrance to Moore Lane. The move worked – the van sheltered the Volunteers from view, and from the deadly machine-gun fire, as they ran past the entrance to the lane.

Moore Street was a market area, but it was also residential. Citizens had suffered days of gunfire, shortage of food, hour after hour of artillery shells landing nearby, and were too afraid to leave. Now, there were armed men all over the place, frantically seeking cover.

John Twamley kicked open the door at the end of Henry Place and found a terrified old couple inside. It's all right, he told them, we won't harm you. The pair ran off and locked themselves into the basement.

At the back of one house, a Volunteer couldn't open a door. He either tried to shoot the lock or smash the glass panel and accidentally discharged his rifle. Either way, the bullet went through the door, through a lung of the man who lived there, Thomas McKane, and killed his fifteen-year-old daughter Brigid, standing behind him.

Sean MacDermott was enraged, demanding to know who had fired that shot. The girl's distraught mother said she knew it was an accident.

The rebels now had access to Cogan's grocery shop, at the junction of Henry Place and Moore Street. Inside, John Twamley was barricading the back-room window against snipers. Pearse came into the shop, then James Connolly was carried in on a stretcher.

A couple of Cumann na mBan women began cooking a large ham.

Oscar Traynor stood at the entrance to Cogan's, directing the men into the shop and up to the first floor. 'Arthur Shields is gone upstairs,' he told Charlie Saurin.

The front room upstairs was dark. It had two windows, but it was night outside and the windows were covered. The room was very crowded. Volunteers huddled together in the dark. It took Saurin some moments to find Boss Shields, hunkered down near a window, rifle in his hand.

From outside, the sound of the British machine guns – bullets scoring along the brickwork of the buildings. The crack of the rebels' rifles, the flames roaring from the GPO and other buildings nearby.

Many in the room were asleep, all were worn out. Most had been awake day and night over the previous few days.

A Volunteer complained to an older man, who was sitting with his back to the wall, his hands clasped around his knees. You took my place, he said, you took my place.

Charlie Saurin recognized the older man as Tom Clarke. He leaned over and put his hand on the Volunteer's leg and gently told him who he was quarrelling with. The man stopped complaining. He clung to Saurin's hand.

The air was alive with raw nerves and mortal fear.

Across the road from Cogan's shop, a British soldier was lying in the street, badly wounded. He repeatedly called for help. He was one of the prisoners released from the GPO.

George Plunkett took a water bottle from another

Volunteer and ran across the street, knelt beside the soldier and gave him a drink. In the darkness, the machine gunners most likely couldn't see much of what was happening. Their persistent firing was randomly disruptive. But anyone on the street was putting themselves in danger.

Plunkett carried the soldier to safety. Then he went out on to the street again and brought back the soldier's rifle. Even at this stage of things, good weapons couldn't be allowed to go to waste. Someone could use the rifle against the comrades of the man Plunkett helped.

At the far end of Moore Street, in Sackville Lane, forty yards from the British barricade, The O'Rahilly was preparing to die. He'd made it to the lane, badly wounded, a number of bullets hitting him diagonally from left hip to right shoulder.

Committed to the last to doing what he saw as the proper thing, he wrote a final note to his wife. He found his son Aodogan's letter in a pocket, folded over, a hole through it from one of the bullets that hit him. He wrote on the back of this, in pencil:

> *Written after I was shot –*
> *Darling Nancy, I was shot leading a rush up Moore Street took refuge in a doorway.*
>
> *While I was there I heard the men pointing out where I was & I made a bolt for the lane I am in now.*
>
> *I got more [than] one bullet I think.*
>
> *Tons and tons of love dearie to you & to the boys & to Nell & Anna. It was a good fight anyhow.*
>
> *Please deliver this to Nannie O'Rahilly, 40 Herbert Park, Dublin.*
>
> *Good bye Darling.*

Later, there would be claims that the British withheld medical help, to ensure The O'Rahilly died. Given that they tended the wounds of others, including rebels more senior than The O'Rahilly, the evidence for this is so terribly weak as to be dismissible.

He fought as he thought best. Alone, as his comrades further down Moore Street struggled to find a way out of the encircling enemy, The O'Rahilly lay back and died from his wounds.

A British officer later found the note and ensured it was delivered to Nancy.

27

After working day and night all week, the rebels were close to the limit. Some hadn't slept since Tuesday night, some even further back.

Frank Henderson oversaw the construction of a barricade, level with Cogan's grocery shop, to divert attention from the tunnelling work. Volunteers, including Harry Boland and Vincent Poole, engaged the enemy, giving the impression that the rebels were digging in at this end of Moore Street.

As Henderson watched, something heavy crashed to the ground beside the barricade. He later found out it was an unexploded incendiary shell.

Nearby, Seosamh Mac Suibhne from E Company, 4th Battalion, totally exhausted, lay down near the barricade. Despite himself, in the midst of battle, he couldn't help falling fast asleep.

Frank Henderson went in search of food and drink for his men. Entering a house at the end of Henry Place he simply collapsed. He woke at some stage, in darkness. Able to do no more than recognize that he was lying on a floor, he sank back into exhaustion. He wouldn't wake until daybreak.

*

Above Cogan's grocery store, Leo Henderson leaned into the darkened room. 'Is Mr Clarke here?'

Tom Clarke identified himself and Leo said, 'Mr Clarke, I have a bed for you.' Clarke stood, carefully stepped over the men, most of them sleeping, and left the room.

A few minutes later Leo Henderson returned. 'Is there anyone here knows me?'

'I do,' Charlie Saurin said. Henderson put him in charge of those in the room.

Saurin suggested that anyone not on guard at a window should unload their weapons – to prevent accidents. It was the bloody American shotguns that worried him. He went around the room, getting anyone awake to unload.

Then he gave Boss Shields the little automatic pistol that Paddy Shortis had given him when they shared a meal at M. W. O'Reilly's house on Monday.

Saurin decided he'd better do something about the bullet wound in his right palm. With mock solemnity, he formally handed over his powers, as commander of the darkened room, to Boss Shields. Then he went downstairs in search of first aid.

There was a light on in the kitchen at the back of the building. The wounded James Connolly was lying on the floor, on a mattress, sleeping fitfully. A man in civilian clothes, Dr Jim Ryan, dabbed iodine on Saurin's wound. James Connolly's aide, Winifred Carney, dressed it and Julia Grenan, a nurse, got Saurin a ham sandwich and a mug of tea. It's Friday, he remarked, as he wolfed down the food. Catholics were forbidden meat on Fridays. Not to worry, Grenan said, a priest had had one of her ham sandwiches at the GPO.

Across the room, Moggy Murtagh, the boy carrying the large crucifix, was getting to his feet.

'I think,' he said, 'I'll stroll over and see what's happening at the GPO.'

Sandwich finished, Saurin returned to the room upstairs, where Boss Shields formally passed back to him the command of the room. Then Boss went down to get something to eat.

Along Moore Street, a now-routine job was under way: boring through walls to give the Volunteers safe and stealthy passage towards the British barricade at the top of the street. The more space became available, the more the Volunteers would be able to spread out in the crowded buildings.

Oscar Traynor organized and took part in the heavy work, along with Vincent Poole, Harry Boland, Tom Leahy and several others.

In one house, an old man told Oscar Traynor there was a Volunteer lying outside. Traynor opened the front door and found John Kenny, one of The O'Rahilly's unit, lying wounded on the pavement. The machine guns were chattering. Traynor urged Kenny to crawl towards the door, but he couldn't – Traynor reached out and pulled him to safety.

The Volunteers carrying James Connolly had the toughest job, passing the stretcher through holes in the wall that were roughly hacked, intended for use by able-bodied adults. Hearing Joe Good's Cockney accent, Connolly remarked ruefully, 'Heavy load, chum.'

At times, they had to lift Connolly through in a blanket. It was agonizing for the wounded man. Eventually, the leaders decided to stop at Plunkett's butcher shop, No. 16.

Almost midnight, Friday, Guinness's brewery.

The British knew they had the leadership of the

rebellion trapped in Moore Street, under persistent machine-gun and shell fire. The end was certain, probably in hours, not days. But they had no notion of what the rebels might be planning. There had been a bloody battle that day in Ashbourne, north of the city, with heavy losses on the British side. And savage fighting was continuing in North King Street. The garrison at the Four Courts was holding out, as was that at the South Dublin Union. Jacob's factory remained isolated, fighting continued at Bolands Mills. And there was hardly a flutter outside Dublin.

There had to be precautions, in case the rebels took new positions and changed the focus of the rebellion.

Lieutenant Algernon Lucas, from the King Edward Horse, arrived at Guinness's brewery. He was assigned to relieve another officer who was in charge of a small number of soldiers from the Royal Dublin Fusiliers – sent to hold the brewery in case the rebels belatedly tried to take it.

At thirty-seven, a veteran of the battles in France, Lieutenant Lucas was an experienced soldier. He was admitted to the brewery by William Rice, a Guinness worker. Lucas and Rice made contact with Captain Charles McNamara, who formally handed over command of the brewery's small forces. 'This is the officer who is to relieve me for the night,' he told the soldiers.

The lieutenant set about assessing potential problems.

On the third floor of the brewery, one of the soldiers – Company Quartermaster Sergeant Robert Flood – became suspicious. Flood had been present when Captain McNamara passed command to Lucas, but little things the lieutenant did and said convinced Flood that Lucas, and his accomplice Rice, were rebels come to infiltrate the brewery.

For instance, he opened a window, although McNamara had given orders that windows weren't to be opened.

Sergeant Flood decided he had to do something about this. Arresting Lucas and Rice was out of the question – Flood's unit was small and he couldn't spare the men to guard prisoners. He ordered the five soldiers under him to shoot Lucas.

A shocked Lieutenant Lucas argued and pleaded but Flood was unyielding. He was expecting rebel infiltrators – and here they were. They had to be dealt with before the rebels outside attacked the brewery.

With all hope gone, the lieutenant asked to be allowed to pray and the sergeant told him to go ahead. Lucas knelt, and as he prayed his eyes filled with tears. When he had finished he rose and stood by a window. He explained that he was crying not for himself but for his wife and child.

Lucas, a graduate of Cambridge, had emigrated to Montreal where he established a school. He then worked on the stock market and made a lot of money. When the war started, he returned to England and enlisted. He fought in France, was wounded in action and invalided home. He was then sent to serve in Ireland.

Present and fire, Flood said, and his men fired. Lucas fell dead. William Rice, the Guinness worker standing beside him, was untouched.

Flood decided that some of his men hadn't fired. He insisted that this rebel too was to be shot, and the soldiers followed orders. The fusillade didn't kill Rice, so one of the soldiers shot him again.

Some time afterwards, on the floor below, Sergeant Flood and his men found another lieutenant from the King Edward Horse, Basil Worsley Worswick. With the lieutenant was another Guinness worker, Cecil Dockeray, who had admitted him to the brewery.

Sergeant Flood had these two men shot dead, too, on the grounds that they were rebels.

Lieutenant Worsley Worswick, aged thirty-five, was – like Lieutenant Lucas – a veteran of the war in France.

Rice and Dockeray were long-time Guinness employees who had nothing to do with rebel activities.

While Tom Clarke slept separately, Pearse, Plunkett, Connolly and MacDermott spent the night in the same room – at 16 Moore Street, Plunkett's butcher's shop. A few feet away from Connolly was the British soldier that George Plunkett had rescued from the street. He was badly wounded in the groin, and sometimes in his delirium he called out, 'Jim Connolly, Jim Connolly', over and over. Pearse sat beside him and spoke with him for a while.

The room smelled of chloroform and cordite.

Joe Good was helping out a Red Cross man, making the wounded as comfortable as possible. He remembered one man, apparently dying, who had been carried from the GPO and left on the top storey of one of the Moore Street houses. He brought the Red Cross man with him and they found John Neale lying on the floor. Together they trussed his stomach in an attempt to compress the wounds.

Good went into an adjoining room, where two Volunteer officers were sleeping on a mattress. He disturbed them, took the mattress and brought it out to put under Neale.

Good visited the dying man several times. Neale was always cold. Good had no blankets to give him. Neale always asked, 'How are things going, Comrade?'

There was no cheerful news, Good told him.

Neale answered that it's always darkest before the dawn.

*

Through the night, as the machine guns continued firing, few if any of the rebels returned fire – most were catching what sleep they could. Several of the strongest continued gouging a route, with sledgehammers and crowbars, through the shops and houses, towards the far end of Moore Street.

Oscar Traynor came across the old man who had earlier told him there was a wounded Volunteer lying outside. The man, his daughter and her children were preparing to move. All of them were terrified. They'd leave the house under a flag of truce, the old man said. That was preferable to staying here. He had a white bedsheet.

Traynor argued it was safer inside, at least until daylight. He asked the young woman to try to persuade her father to change his mind.

Moving from house to house, in near total darkness, there was a lot of stumbling. James Kavanagh lit a match and found he'd tripped over one of the Liverpool lads, shot through the hip.

Passing through a house, ambulance man Volunteer Seamus Donegan came across a young girl lying on the floor. In the darkness, Donegan felt the girl's face, seeking a wound he might treat. His fingers found her mouth, her teeth. He struck a match and was startled to find it wasn't her mouth, but a large head wound. The girl was past help.

Sometime during the night, there was an explosion loud enough to shake buildings in Moore Street and to waken even some of the exhausted Volunteers. At the GPO, the fire had at last found the explosives in the basement.

Seosamh Mac Suibhne, who had fallen asleep from exhaustion, came awake and looked around. He was in some kind of barn. It didn't make sense. He stood and looked around and found he was on the second floor of a stable. This made less sense.

Mac Suibhne had fallen asleep outdoors, close to the Moore Street barricade where Harry Boland was sniping at the British. He didn't understand, and never would, how he'd ended up indoors, on an upper floor.

As dawn arrived on Saturday, 29th, the sixth day of the rising, the work of boring through the Moore Street walls was still continuing. Charlie Saurin and his comrades were roused and told to go downstairs and make their way through the knocked-through walls.

The aim was to get a clear passage all the way up to Sackville Lane, which was within yards of the British barricade at the far end of Moore Street. Someone had commandeered food, and the Volunteers were told to carry it with them.

Charlie Saurin was handed a large uncooked ham which had an S-hook attached at the top. Carrying the ham and his rifle, with one hand wounded, made climbing from room to room awkward. It wasn't just a series of holes at ground level. The floors weren't at the same height. It meant the journey was staggered. Side to side, up and down – on and on, house after house, most of them occupied by terrified civilians.

The march seemed never-ending, a procession of weary men, all armed, many of them toting a substantial cargo of food, all the time the sound of machine guns adding a deadly perspective to the journey.

In a grocer's shop, Sean MacDermott found a couple of eggs. He cracked them open and swallowed them.

Sometimes the men lagged behind and were urged to hurry. At other times they caught up with those knocking holes in the walls and sat around, waiting. Then, there was the fear, each time the breakthrough was made in a wall, that there might be British soldiers on the other side, ready to toss grenades through.

Finally, they reached Hanlon's fish shop, Nos 20–21 Moore Street.

The hundreds of survivors of the GPO garrison were now strung out along about two-thirds the length of the east side of Moore Street.

The rising's leaders continued to assess their prospects. A young officer, Sean McLoughlin, had come up with a new plan for breaking out of the Moore Street area and getting to the Williams & Woods factory. Like all ideas on how to proceed, it came up against the obstacle of the British barricade at the top of the street.

McLoughlin's proposal was to advance through the bored holes as far as Sackville Lane, then to emerge from the lane and charge the barricade, with covering fire from the Moore Street buildings. To give this operation the best chance of success, there would have to be a diversion.

After a week of tumult and a night of broken sleep, tired, unwashed and unshaven, Pearse, Connolly, Plunkett, MacDermott and Clarke talked it through. Pearse needed something to write on, so he took a picture from the wall, tore the back off it and used that to make a sketch of the Moore Street area.

The whole thing, they knew, would be costly in lives, but there weren't a lot of choices.

Hanlon's fish shop had a large floor space, with frontage usually open to the street. With the shop closed, the front was covered by wooden shutters. As the Volunteers gathered inside, machine-gun bullets chipped pieces out of the wood.

Charlie Saurin checked the ham he was carrying. It was covered in dust and mortar. The smell of the fish shop made the thought of food revolting. He used the S-hook to hang the ham from a ledge and walked away from it.

At the far end of Moore Street, behind the machine-gun barricade, British soldiers were being equipped with tools for smashing locks and breaking through doors. The plan was to send several storming parties out to work their way systematically down the street, flushing out the rebels.

Seamus Grace, still hiding in the area of Mount Street Bridge, woke that morning in the garden shed at the back of Haddington Road in which he had found refuge after another night of exchanging fire with troops. When they found him, the troops smashed the glass of the shed and shouted, 'Hands up.' It was all over.

M. W. O'Reilly rose from sleep and washed. He took his shaving materials from his kit bag, shaved, had his breakfast and was ready to meet whatever the day might bring.

He made his way down through the Moore Street houses until he reached No. 16, Plunkett's butcher's shop. There, in a first-storey room at the back, Pearse, Clarke, Connolly, MacDermott and Plunkett finished discussing their options.

They decided to implement Sean McLoughlin's plan to charge the enemy barricade and rush for Williams & Woods. The plan, they agreed, would need a bayonet charge, sustained rifle fire to give the charge cover, and a diversion to distract the British. They issued orders to select men for the charge, the covering fire and the diversion.

*

At Hanlon's fish shop, an officer began picking Volunteers for a special mission. Among the seven he chose were Charlie Saurin and Boss Shields. He led them through Hanlon's, out a back door and through a yard, past piles of fish bones, to an empty barn-like structure behind the shop. There, he ordered them to climb a stepladder into a small loft. There was a hole in the floor of the loft, through which to climb, and an opening out on to Moore Lane. The loft was used to haul deliveries up from the lane, and to take them in through the opening for storing.

Don't look out, they were told.

There was an enemy machine gun in Moore Lane, the one that had peppered the whitewashed house in Henry Place the previous evening. It was firing and there were bullet marks around the edges of the loft opening on to the lane. None of the seven was in too much of a hurry to look out. They sat, backs to the walls, in the small, overcrowded loft.

Eventually, a young officer with curly red hair climbed into the loft. He was followed by Patrick Pearse. 'This is the place, sir,' the young officer said.

Pearse deliberately stared each man in the face, in turn, as though assessing what, after the rigours of the week, they might still be capable of. He might have been imprinting their faces on his memory. Then he stood at the opening into Moore Lane, leaned out in view of the enemy machine gunners and looked up the lane.

Satisfied, he turned and left the loft without a word.

The waiting continued.

Charlie and Boss climbed down the ladder to stretch their legs. They found that by standing on the bottom step of the ladder, they could see through a crack in a door that gave them a view of the machine-gun emplacement in Moore Lane. Boss had acquired a good pair of binoculars. They took turns looking at the enemy. Mostly, all they saw of the soldiers was a peaked cap here and there. But there was no missing the muzzles of the machine gun and several rifles poking out from behind cover.

Near the machine gun there were three dead horses. They must have been among those released from the city-centre stable, careering wildly down the lane, shot dead by British troops confused by the noise and the movement, just as the rebels were in the GPO.

After a while, when the junior officers were informed of the leaders' plan for the breakout, the seven Volunteers in the loft were given the details of their special mission. They would, on a given command, jump out through the opening of the loft, down into Moore Lane. They would fire a volley towards the machine gun, then they would charge the enemy's position.

Their mission, they were told, was a diversion – to distract the British while the real attack force carried out a surprise bayonet charge on the barricade in Moore Street.

Charlie Saurin contemplated this news, and the prospects for success.

He imagined the Volunteers in Moore Street charging the machine guns, bayonets fixed, carrying all before them, sweeping on down Great Britain Street and into the Williams & Woods factory.

Or perhaps not.

Whichever way he thought it through, the outcome always included seven corpses lying in Moore Lane.

Saurin realized that he, Boss and the others were to be given what used to be called 'the place of honour' in the coming battle.

*

In a yard behind Moore Street, George Plunkett was assembling the men who would charge the Moore Street barricade.

'All men with bayonets proceed to the front.'

For many Volunteers, the response to an order was automatic – you did it, you didn't think about it. Harry Boland was one of those, and he was among the men moving to the front of the crowd. Oscar Traynor, too, readied himself for the attack, and James Kavanagh. Blimey O'Connor fixed his bayonet to his rifle, Peadar Bracken too.

All we can do, Boland said to his companions, is our best. Not much hope that any of us will come through it.

Volunteer Feargus De Burca had a dread of bayonet charges. He imagined himself at the other end of the action – a lengthy piece of steel being run through his chest or his stomach, leaving an irreparable trail of damage. He could imagine the ferocity of an enemy trying to fight off that fate. The previous evening, during the panic around the whitewashed house, he was one of those who had to fix bayonets and charge what they believed was a dangerous position. He didn't like it then and he didn't like it now.

He'd been in the GPO most of the week, on duty on the roof. Despite having endured days under fire, his nerve was now wavering. In the exhausted throng, with no one paying him any attention, he realized it would be easy to slip the bayonet off his rifle and get rid of it.

He was tempted, and he held on to the thought. Then he rebuked himself for cowardice and made his way to the front of the crowd to join in the impossible charge. Fear of letting himself and his comrades down won out over fear of pain and death.

Men with magazine rifles, who could produce a decent rate of fire, were stationed at the upper windows of several Moore Street buildings, to target the British barricade and provide suppressing fire when the charge began.

At the last moment, the Volunteers were told to stand down – to be ready to resume the attack at any time. Some, including Oscar Traynor, lay down in exhaustion and instantly fell into sleep. Others sat and talked.

From nearby came a tremendous crashing sound – the roof of the GPO was collapsing.

A long time passed, during which Charlie Saurin and Boss Shields scrounged some food. Hunger had overcome the revulsion caused by the smell of the fish shop. The way things were going, it might well be their last meal.

There doesn't appear to have been any discussion about evading what was certain to be a fatal mission. They were in serious circumstances, things had developed in a certain way – and that was the way it would be.

They went back to using Boss's binoculars to observe the British machine-gun emplacement at the end of Moore Lane. Gradually they realized something had changed.

They could see the enemy soldiers were relaxed. Then a young child appeared, a girl, approaching the soldiers fearfully. Charlie and Boss concluded she had been sent out by her family to ask the soldiers if it was okay for the family to use the lane to leave the area.

The child became upset when she saw the dead horses. The soldiers tried to calm her, to help her make her way through their position, to show her there was nothing to be afraid of.

Gradually – and no one seemed sure where the information came from – the word went around among the rebels that negotiations with the enemy had started.

28

Awake now, Oscar Traynor was looking across Moore Street. He could see the old man he'd pleaded with last night, advising him to stay indoors. The old man had ventured out, to seek a way to safety for his daughter and grandchildren. His corpse lay on top of the white sheet he had hoped would save them.

He wasn't the only one. Here and there, the corpses of elderly men lay on the pavements of Moore Street, sprawled on or grasping white bedsheets.

It's probable that most of the civilians lying on the pavements died not from deliberately aimed shots but from random bullets sprayed in the darkness by machine gunners ordered to strafe the streets. To venture out into those streets was foolish, but to stay inside a war zone, with shells falling and bullets clattering into walls and ripping through windows, was for many intolerable. They did what they believed they ought to do to save their families, and they perished.

There is evidence of Patrick Pearse being affected by such sights.

It's possible he was also thinking of his visit to the loft overlooking Moore Lane, where he had made himself look into the faces of Charlie Saurin, Boss Shields and the five other men who were about to be sent, on his orders, to a futile death.

The leaders had entered into the rising ready for a straight fight – soldiers against soldiers, with defeat inevitable, given the odds. They believed defeat would be followed by the execution of those who signed the Proclamation of the Republic, and they were prepared for that.

They were not prepared for a persistent artillery barrage and machine-gun strafing in a confined and populated area – with consequent slaughter of civilians. They hadn't counted on this level of civilian bloodshed.

Another factor was the desperation from which the escape plan was born – a bayonet charge in Moore Street, a diversion in Moore Lane, within an area completely dominated by massively superior forces.

And the prize, in the unlikely event of success, was the Williams & Woods factory. It was close to the British cordon line, and there was a hope that the enemy would cease shelling because of the proximity of their own men.

Even if the plan worked, it would be at the cost of the shredding of the rebel forces, as they sought to overcome the machine guns, rifles and bayonets of the enemy. The lives of large numbers of Volunteers would be senelessly sacrificed.

On top of that, continuing the insurrection would result in ever more civilian deaths.

The leaders of the rebellion counted on their own lives being taken, but it was clear that any greater slaughter was pointless.

They talked and eventually Pearse drew up the surrender document: 'In order to prevent the further slaughter of Dublin citizens and in the hope of saving the lives of our followers now surrounded and hopelessly out-numbered . . .'

*

Does anyone have shaving gear?

Yes, indeed, came the response from the well-shaven M. W. O'Reilly. He passed over his safety razor and kit to Patrick Pearse. When Pearse was finished shaving he passed the kit to his brother Willie. James Connolly sat up in his bed and used the razor, with Winifred Carney holding a mirror for him. Then Sean MacDermott and Joe Plunkett.

Someone pointed out to Plunkett that somewhere along the way he'd lost one of his spurs. He took the other one off and kicked it under James Connolly's bed.

Sean MacDermott went to bring word to the men – it was over; they would seek terms of surrender.

Some of those who had faced imminent death in the bayonet charges may have been relieved. For others, this was a bitter end. Oscar Traynor raged at MacDermott: 'Is this what we were brought out for? To go into English dungeons for the rest of our lives?'

MacDermott held up a piece of paper. 'No – we're surrendering as prisoners of war.'

Officers went along Moore Street, through the ranks, advising everyone to ditch anything that might conceivably be considered loot. Anyone caught with loot might well be shot out of hand by the British.

One elderly Volunteer confessed to stealing a cheap comb he'd picked up to give to his wife. Another, in someone's house, had hidden an expensive watch inside a grandfather clock – hoping to come back later and collect it. It was his own watch, but he'd risk being shot if some British officer didn't believe him and declared the watch to be loot.

At the last minute, Charlie Saurin remembered

he'd taken a copy of R. D. Blackmore's romance novel *Lorna Doone* from a room in the Metropole. He hadn't finished reading it. They couldn't consider that loot, could they?

Boss Shields thought it reckless to take a chance. 'Leave it there,' he said. 'I'll buy you a copy afterwards.'

They had no idea when afterwards might be, or what form it might take.

Inside the shops in Moore Street, there was dissent in the ranks. Some of the rebels believed they would be shot after they surrendered. Better to die fighting. Many among the Kimmage company, mostly Irish 'refugees' from England, believed they would be shot as deserters.

Tom Clarke addressed them. Only he and the other leaders would be shot, he said. The lead they had given the people, in showing it was possible to stand up to the Empire, meant that 'Ireland's future is now assured'.

The men listened respectfully and weren't convinced.

Michael Collins addressed them. The signatories to the Proclamation would be shot – yes. But to fight on meant that *all* the leaders would be shot, and nothing lasting would be achieved.

Listening to his friend, Joe Good reckoned Mick was thinking of the junior officers. The reorganization, when all this was over, would depend on the junior officers. To reject the ceasefire, to carry on a pointless fight, would mean that the next leadership layer would be wiped out. In battle or in executions.

Still, the dissent simmered. Joe Plunkett, obviously seriously ill, was listened to with respect, but he didn't change any minds, either.

Sean MacDermott, leaning on his stick, asked the men what they wanted. He listened as they listed the reasons

for continuing the fight. Then he said: Take a long look
at the dead civilians lying out there.

Imagine how many more of them there'll be if this con-
tinues.

The civilians around here, they're the very poorest, and
they'll be butchered with us. The soldiers, he said, are
going wild, killing civilians without restraint.

'You've all seen what happened to the Post Office.'
The British will do the same to the rest of our beautiful
city.

'The thing that you must do, all of you, is to *survive*.'

He used the word over and over again. *Survive*.

'We who will be shot will die happy – knowing that
there're still plenty of you around to finish the job.'

The dissent in Moore Street ended.

Joe Good paid one last visit to John Neale, in the top-
floor room in Moore Street. They talked a bit, and they
agreed they'd meet again when all this was over.

Outside, Good found Joe Plunkett standing in the
centre of Moore Street, holding a white flag. Plunkett
told him to go to the British barricade and tell an officer
the Volunteers would be bringing out the wounded and
leaving them on the pavement, to be brought to hospital.
And among them there would be British wounded.

In the course of two visits to the barricade, Good saw
the body of The O'Rahilly, in Sackville Lane. He thought
of taking a memento for the family – a button or the like
– but there wasn't time.

The rebels lined up in Moore Street, around them the
dead and the wounded. Liam Cullen, his thigh bandaged,
sitting with his back against a wall. Kevin O'Carroll
of the Citizen Army, waking up in Hanlon's fish shop
to find it was all over. He'd been unconscious since the

previous evening, when he'd been shot in the chest during the chaos in Henry Place.

A dead British soldier, huddled in a doorway, his head resting on the step. Nearby, a civilian, his head torn open by shrapnel. Two dead Volunteers at the corner of a lane, their rifles lying beside them.

And, close to where The O'Rahilly died, Joe Good found the body of a Volunteer – Paddy Shortis of F Company. He'd been sprayed by the same machine gun that did for The O'Rahilly.

Paddy's eyes were open and staring. Little tufts of underclothing poked out from several bullet holes, making him look like a small, ragged scarecrow. Joe Good knew and liked Paddy – both had come from England to fight. Joe covered his comrade's face and said a short prayer.

Paddy Shortis, aged twenty-three, was one of the four men who had eaten together at M. W. O'Reilly's house at lunchtime on Monday during the confusion at Fr. Mathew Park, while Tom Weafer went into the city centre to get orders from James Connolly. Of the four, Shortis and Harry Coyle were dead, Charlie Saurin was wounded in the GPO and Seamus Daly was captured in Gloucester Street.

Wherever they surrendered, the rebel forces were intent on displaying the characteristics of soldiers. They formed up in columns, their weapons shouldered, their movements precise – and they were not herded by captors: they marched to the orders of their own officers. All the months of drilling counted now, to preserve their discipline, their pride and their identity as soldiers of a republic.

At Moore Street, the column marched around into

Henry Street and on into Sackville Street, past the still-blazing buildings. The smell of burning was everywhere.

Already, the British medics were removing the wounded from Moore Street, British and Irish alike, and taking them to the Castle Hospital.

The surrendering rebels could see that one of their flags was still atop the GPO, albeit on a flagpole now bent out over the street. They marched up towards the Parnell Monument, the leaders grouped together at the rear, other ranks taking the lead.

There, surrounded by what seemed to be thousands of British troops, they maintained their formation and came to a halt. As instructed by their officers, they grounded their weapons and moved three steps back. They stood, backs to the Gresham Hotel, as British officers took their names.

Boss Shields watched a soldier pick up and casually pocket the small automatic that had passed unfired from Shortis to Saurin to Shields.

Frank Henderson was standing beside Joe Plunkett, who was next to Tom Clarke and Sean MacDermott. Plunkett chatted with his comrades until he was ordered to step forward. An officer searched his pockets and made insulting remarks. Plunkett behaved as though the man didn't exist. When ordered to stand back in line, he continued his conversation exactly where he'd left off.

General Lowe, officer commanding the British troops, passed down the ranks. He stopped opposite Charlie Saurin, stooped and picked up Saurin's belt, from which dangled the empty sheath of the knife he had carried.

'Who's the owner of this thing?'

'I am,' Saurin said.

'Where's the knife belonging to this?' He obviously believed Saurin had the knife concealed.

Saurin remembered John Neale cooking in the Metropole, Saurin handing him the sheath knife to cut meat.

He said to Lowe, 'I gave it to another man.'

'Can you show me this man?'

'The man is dead now.'

Lowe took Saurin's word. He dropped the belt and moved on.

Some time around then or shortly afterwards, John Neale, carried on a stretcher by British soldiers, did indeed die as he was being taken into the Castle Hospital.

29

Many didn't want to believe it could end this way. On being told of the surrender, some raged that the sacrifice of their comrades would be wasted. Others were angry at being ordered to surrender before they had had a chance to confront the enemy. The week had seen terribly bloody fighting in some areas – the South Dublin Union, Mount Street Bridge, Ashbourne, the Mendicity Institute, North King Street – while garrisons such as Jacob's hardly fired a shot in anger.

The surrender process began after midday on Saturday, and it was Sunday before the last outposts formally surrendered. Nurse Elizabeth O'Farrell, of Cumann na mBan, had a lengthy, dangerous task, from approaching the British in the first place to bringing word of the surrender to various commandants, assuring them that these were the orders of the rising's leaders.

At the College of Surgeons, Mike Mallin called a conference of officers. Some of them proposed taking to the hills. A majority was in favour, but Mallin said that James Connolly had endorsed the surrender document signed by Pearse, and that was enough for him.

A British officer approached the College of Surgeons under a white flag.

Fireman Joe Connolly of the Citizen Army was distraught, sobbing. His brother Sean had been killed on the roof of Dublin Castle, and his younger brother Mattie had been captured. Now, he'd been ordered to surrender.

As the British officer entered by York Street gate, Connolly took out an automatic pistol and made to shoot him – but those around overpowered him.

At the Four Courts, more shouts of dissent.

Ned Daly said he agreed with the dissenters, but these were Pearse's orders and soldiers obey lawful orders.

At Jacob's factory, when the men were paraded and Tom MacDonagh told them of the surrender order, the air was full of shouting: 'Fight it out!' 'Fight it out!' 'We will fight it out!' A Franciscan priest pleaded with the men to lay down their arms before there was a massacre.

Major John MacBride stood silent.

As the reality of the defeat became inescapable, some of the men began smashing their rifles on the steel floor. Many wept. It was a consolation that they would be treated as prisoners of war, not criminals, but after a week of frustration, isolated in the biscuit factory, cordoned off and ignored by the enemy, the humiliation of surrender was hard to take.

As the parade ended, Captain Tom Hunter broke down in tears.

Major MacBride, grim and terse, said to a group of men: 'Some of you may live to fight again and, if you do, take the open country for it and avoid a death trap like this.'

The original hundred who had come out in Enniscorthy had been joined by another hundred, and then plenty more. Cumann na mBan had mobilized, the Volunteers had organized a police force, patrolled the town – and waited. They were desperately short of rifles, but that turned out not to matter. There was no reason to fire them. And there was no attempt to route enemy troops through Wexford.

The British put a local retired army officer in charge, Lieutenant Colonel French, and sent him hundreds of troops and some artillery. French was a reasonable man who didn't want to destroy a local town, or slaughter his neighbours. He organized negotiations with the Volunteers. When they were told that Pearse had surrendered they demanded proof, and French arranged for two of their number to be driven to Dublin, where Pearse told them to surrender.

Among the prisoners held in cattle pens at the grounds of the Royal Dublin Society was Seamus Grace, captured after his escape from 25 Northumberland Road. A Royal Army Medical Corps officer spoke quietly to him, telling him the rebels had surrendered, the city was in the hands of the Empire. At the end of a week of death, of fear and of inevitable defeat, Grace broke down and wept.

The RAMC man said, Don't let them see you crying.

You can still serve your country, he whispered, by keeping a brave face.

Vinny Byrne, the fifteen-year-old who almost didn't get to turn out for the rising, asked the Franciscan priest at Jacob's factory, 'Is there no chance of getting out to the hills and fighting it out?'

'No, my son, and come along with me.'

The priest took Vinny and another boy to a low window in Bishop Street and they dropped out into the street. The usual crowd of abusive locals was waiting, but one woman intervened. She took the two boys into her house, brushed the flour off their coats and sent them home.

A young Volunteer, one of the Ryan family from Ballybough, hiding in a friendly house, ran out the back when the house was raided. He was caught at gunpoint by a British soldier in the garden.

The boy said, 'I'm Dublin, from Clonliffe Road.'

'I'm from Summerhill, myself,' said the soldier.

Run out under the hedges, he told the boy.

One of the Volunteers from the fighting in Church Street walked away when the surrender came. The British, however, had barricades everywhere, searching everyone, checking identification. He was standing in East Arran Street, where passers-by were stopping to look at bodies being laid out at the Daisy Market, when he saw an old girlfriend.

Can you help me get away?

Her new boyfriend was a British soldier, on duty at a barricade at Mary's Lane. She went to the boyfriend, had a word, and he let the Volunteer through.

An elderly Citizen Army man was arrested with his son. He had once been in the Royal Artillery and feared he'd be shot if that was found out. He came up with a story.

He and his son, the story went, had been strolling down Sackville Street on the first day of the rising. They'd just come back from the races at Fairyhouse. Suddenly, there was shooting. They took cover in a doorway. As the shooting got worse they moved further into the building. Which happened to be the GPO. And once they were inside it became too dangerous to come out.

He stuck to his story. He stuck to it even after he and his son were sent to Wakefield Prison. After some days the authorities decided he was telling the truth and released them both.

Some had no wish to escape. At Grattan Street, as he and his comrades were marched into captivity, Andy McDonnell was getting used to the booing from the bystanders on the crowded pavements. A big woman, wearing a white apron, spotted the diminutive McDonnell and cried, 'Lord, look at the child going to be shot!'

She stepped into the road, picked McDonnell up in her arms and dragged him into the crowd. Furious at being taken from his comrades, McDonnell kicked her until she dropped him, then he ran to catch up with his unit.

One group of captive Volunteers, being marched past the Coombe Maternity Hospital, acquired the company of a couple of drunken men. The pair insisted on joining the ranks of the prisoners. They were thrown out. They moved elsewhere along the column and got back in. They were thrown out again, got back in again. Two weeks later they were spotted in the exercise yard at Knutsford Prison.

The public response was overwhelmingly abusive. The College of Surgeons garrison, having surrendered and been taken into captivity, was attacked by a mob on Grafton Street. The British officer told his rearguard to turn and face the crowd, rifles at the ready. He then forced the mob to disperse, threatening to give the order to fire.

Here and there, tokens of support appeared. A soldier took Sean MacDermott's cane and Harry Boland had to help him stay upright as he limped all the way to Richmond Barracks. Bystanders cheered as they passed. On a street corner, an old man stood to attention and saluted.

Oscar Traynor, on the long march to Richmond Barracks, experienced a barrage of condemnation.

'Murderers!'

'Starvers of the people!'

At the gates of the barracks Traynor saw an elderly Capuchin priest, tears in his eyes. The priest was aware that it was safer not to provoke the British soldiers with an open display of sympathy for the captives. The old man murmured over and over to the prisoners as they passed him on their way into the barracks: '*Misneach, misneach* . . . Courage, courage . . .'

Take that cigarette out of your mouth, Boss Shields was told, as he and Charlie Saurin stood in ranks in the barrack square of Richmond Barracks. 'Do you know where you are, do you?'

Detectives from G Division, responsible for keeping an eye on nationalists, moved around the square, scrutinizing the prisoners, picking out those they thought might be a leader or senior officer for assessment and possible trial.

Willie Pearse was picked out and there was some excitement among the detectives when they learned his name – which died down when they realized it was not Patrick Pearse but his brother. Sean MacDermott, not as prominent as Pearse and Clarke, escaped their attention.

For a moment it seemed that Boss Shields was to be singled out – possibly because his glasses gave him an intellectual appearance. But after a few questions they moved on.

Prisoners sprawled where they could, as the hours passed. Major John MacBride sat on the floor, his legs crossed tailor-fashion. A young Volunteer, Michael Lynch, sitting nearby, inched along the floor and tapped him on the arm.

'Are you Major John McBride?'

'I am.'

'I'm Michael Lynch, Jim Lynch's son. I met you when I was a little boy.'

MacBride shook his hand warmly. They exchanged details of where they had been during the insurrection and what they thought of the fight. MacBride didn't disguise his feelings.

'Listen, Michael – all my life I've waited for the week that's just gone by. I spent it shut up like a rat in a trap in Jacob's factory, and I never fired a shot. I wanted MacDonagh to get out several times, but he wouldn't.'

MacBride was resigned. 'However, it doesn't matter, it's all over now.'

Young Lynch would live to fight again, MacBride said. 'And, when next you fight, don't let anyone shut you up like a rat in a trap. Get a rifle, a few hundred rounds of ammunition, and get out under God's blue sky. And shoot until they get you, but never let them lock you up.'

Some days later, a large number of the Volunteers, having been vetted and deemed to be of no special importance, were paraded in the barrack square. They were given cocoa to drink, a couple of biscuits and some bully beef. When they asked what was happening a British soldier told them they were about to march down to the Dublin docks, to the cattle boats, to be sent to internment in Britain.

As they moved off, two detectives, Johnny Barton and Daniel Hoey, walked alongside the column. On the first day of the rising, Sean MacDermott had vehemently objected to Hoey's proposed assassination.

The detectives stopped the column and took MacDermott out of the ranks. 'Sorry, Sean, but you can't get away that easy,' said Hoey.

*

Sean MacDermott hadn't been foolish enough to identify himself to the British as a leader of the rebellion, but once Hoey did that job MacDermott was resigned to being shot. Such sacrifices were now necessary, he believed, to take the struggle on to the next stage.

'I'll be shot,' he told his companions at Richmond Barracks, 'and it'll be a bad day for Ireland that I'm not. You fellows will get an opportunity, even if in years to come, to follow on where we left off.'

MacDermott and his comrades had an unlikely ally in ensuring that would be the case.

General Sir John Maxwell was taking charge of the mopping up. Under his plenary powers of martial law he made decisions on life or death, liberty or imprisonment.

The Irish Parliamentary Party, led by John Redmond – eager to stress its loyalty to the Empire – began its blunder into oblivion. Redmond condemned the rising in gross terms: 'Germany plotted it, Germany organised it, Germany paid for it . . . it was a German invasion of Ireland, as brutal, as selfish, as cynical as Germany's invasion of Belgium.'

That wasn't true. The Volunteers bought guns where they could get them – as did the unionists. The German generals allowed guns to be sold to anyone who might cause trouble for the British.

Redmond's claim gave Maxwell licence to charge the rebels with being part of a German plot, an invasion of British territory – and that was treason, justifying execution.

Redmond asked that 'undue hardship' not be shown to the great mass of rebels, whose guilt was less than that of 'the instigators'. The message was clear – not too many executions, but the British generals should feel entitled to do pretty much as they thought best.

Redmond's colleague John Dillon had more understanding of the danger. He pleaded with Maxwell not to impose a harsh regime, as it might backfire.

Maxwell, however, had decided to crush any last ember of dissent. He told Dillon: 'I am going to ensure that there will be no treason whispered – even whispered – for a hundred years.'

He believed that the execution squads would fire the last shots of the 1916 rising. But he was wrong. As Clarke, Pearse and MacDermott hoped, General Maxwell's guns would fire the first shots in the war of independence.

Part Eight

Victory in defeat,
defeat in victory

30

At about six o'clock on a lovely morning in late August 1916 – four months after the rising – the ferry from Holyhead arrived at Kingstown. There was, as usual, a committee of Dublin unionists waiting at the end of the gangway, ready to greet and look after soldiers from the British Army home on leave from the front.

Down past this welcoming committee came Charlie Saurin, Boss Shields, Seamus Daly, Harry Colley and a range of other Volunteers, released from custody after four months in English jails.

The bulk of the internees would be released by Christmas 1916, and sentenced prisoners by the summer of 1917. When the best-known prisoners came home they were welcomed by massive crowds.

Saurin, Shields and Daly couldn't resist a visit to the city centre, to look in awe at the blackened ruins of the GPO, to retrace their steps along Henry Street and Moore Street. The evidence of the rising was everywhere, and the evidence of the awesome power of the Empire's response.

They got the tram to Clontarf. The conductor was a dour little man who had never shown the Volunteers any civility before the rising – now, he and the driver were shaking their hands and wishing them a warm welcome home.

When Saurin and his friends got off at Clontarf there were people shouting, 'The boys are coming home!'

Harry Colley had spent several weeks in hospital, recovering from the multiple bullet wounds he received in his charge on the barricade at Gloucester Street. After that, he'd been sent to internment in England. Now, in the summer of 1916, he passed some weeks in Wicklow, resting. One lung was in a bad way, his left shoulder was four inches lower than his right.

Colley was surprised and delighted by the way people now spoke about the rising, as something that was right and necessary.

Within weeks, the British had managed to turn the rebels' total defeat into the first stage of a victory. And they did so with a speed and thoroughness that not even Clarke and Pearse could have imagined.

After the surrender, General Maxwell, with the nervous backing of the politicians, set about suppressing what he termed the 'dangerous Sinn Feiners'. There were members of Sinn Fein involved in the rising, but as an organization it was relatively timid and completely uninvolved. Sinn Fein's aim was a dual monarchy – an idea originally proposed by British Prime Minister William Gladstone, in which Britain and Ireland would become two self-governing countries under one king, with fiscal and foreign policy agreements and a single army.

Sinn Fein had been a passive-resistance movement and in the wake of the rising it initially sought to distance itself from those violent fellows with their loutish Mausers. Despite all this, lazy journalists had long attached the generic name of 'Sinn Feiner' to all nationalists, and Maxwell didn't know any better. Despite a busy intelligence operation, the British didn't seem to understand the nature of the insurgency they faced, its strengths or its weaknesses.

Although there were about 1,200 people involved at the beginning of the rising, with perhaps another 300 joining in by the end, Maxwell rounded up 3,400 suspects. Of those, 183 were deemed of special interest and tried by secret court martial. Almost half of those tried were sentenced to death.

Maxwell personally decided which of the condemned should die and which should have their sentences commuted to jail terms. Over a period of ten days, he had fifteen people killed.

If Tom Clarke had been organizing the reprisals in a manner most likely to swing the public mood in favour of the rebels, he couldn't have done a better job.

Maxwell was not sadistic; he was seeking to extinguish an idea. If he stamped down hard enough, the very notion of Ireland as an independent country would be snuffed out by a wave of fear.

And he had the support of the establishment on both sides of the Irish Sea. The *Irish Times,* newspaper of the southern unionists, said: 'The surgeon's knife has been put to the body of Ireland, and its course must not be stayed until the whole malignant growth has been removed.' The newspaper demanded that sedition 'must be rooted out of Ireland once and for all'. This required 'a severity which will make any repetition . . . impossible for generations to come'. The newspaper chimed precisely with Maxwell's intentions.

The executions began at dawn on Wednesday, 3 May 1916.

Pearse, Clarke, MacDonagh.

Sometime in the hours before he was due to be killed, Tom Clarke said he'd like to see Ned Daly, commandant of the Four Courts garrison. Daly was the younger brother of Clarke's wife, Kathleen.

The army brought Daly from Richmond Barracks to Kilmainham Jail. As Daly arrived he was told it was too late, Clarke was about to be executed.

Daly said he'd still like to see Clarke, dead or alive.

After the killings, the bodies of Pearse, Clarke and MacDonagh were wrapped in army blankets and left in a shed. They were to be taken away to be buried anonymously in quicklime, without coffins, at an undisclosed place. There must, Maxwell said, be no martyrs' shrines to indulge Irish nationalist sentimentality.

Ned Daly was allowed to go out to the shed. He stood to attention in front of the three bodies and saluted. Then he took off his cap, knelt and prayed for a moment. He put on his cap, saluted again and returned to his escort.

Daly was taken back to Richmond Barracks. Later that day he was convicted by court martial and sentenced to death. The following morning, Thursday, 4 May, he was brought back to Kilmainham and shot dead, his body wrapped in a blanket, stored in the shed and buried anonymously.

Joe Plunkett and Willie Pearse were shot with Daly – and Michael O'Hanrahan, who two weeks earlier had told his friend Frank Henderson, 'Yes, we're going out. And not coming back.'

Daly had been in charge at the Four Courts garrison; Plunkett was a signatory to the Proclamation. O'Hanrahan, however, was a junior officer at Jacob's factory, where the action was negligible. There's no evidence he fired a single shot. Willie Pearse was executed because he was Patrick's brother.

There was little logic to it, other than to carry through General Maxwell's promise to terrorize nationalists so fiercely that they wouldn't raise their heads for a hundred years.

Friday, 5 May, John MacBride was killed.

The firing squads took the weekend off.

The Cumann na mBan prisoners at Kilmainham were taken to the prison church on Sunday morning for Mass. They were seated in the gallery, the male prisoners down below. All the women could see from their position was the altar and the front pews, where the congregation included such prominent rebel officers as Eamon Ceannt, Mike Mallin, Con Colbert and Sean Heuston. These four received Holy Communion.

Rumours flew around Dublin. Names were suggested for who would be next; others claimed there had been a reprieve, that there would be no more executions. Aware of the distress of the families of the condemned, Capuchin priest Fr Augustine went that weekend to a house on the North Circular Road and sent in a query to General Maxwell. Is it true that the executions are over?

The general sent out a reply: 'No, there is no truth in that statement. The executions are going to take place.'

Monday, 8 May: the four communicants of the previous day, Ceannt, Mallin, Colbert and Heuston, were killed.

Aine Ceannt, widow of Eamonn, set out with her sister-in-law to buy mourning clothes. They had no problem finding the appropriate black outfits. As a result of the European war there were a great many young widows and black clothing was in constant demand and plentiful supply.

The public didn't know where this was going. Would it go on and on, would there be dozens shot, or hundreds? Was it true that the British were digging mass graves?

Prime Minister Herbert Asquith was being peppered with pleas and warnings – politicians, writers, people who had some grasp of how this would affect the Irish public. And he hesitantly tried to suggest to Maxwell that it was possible to go too far.

Tuesday, 9 May: Volunteer Tom Kent – convicted of killing a policeman during a gunfight that followed a raid on his home – was executed down in Cork.

British politicians were worried about the legality of the executions. The military – from the soldiers in the Guinness factory to Captain Bowen Colthurst – seemed to believe that the declaration of martial law gave them the right to kill anyone, at any time, for any reason or none. General Maxwell's powers of life and death added to the impression of god-like authority.

Asquith, fearing an international backlash, wanted a legal basis to the killings.

To give the appearance of legality, the Crown lawyers seized on a letter Patrick Pearse wrote to his mother from his cell. Pearse added a postscript: 'P.S. I understand that the German expedition which I was counting on actually set sail but was defeated by the British.'

This reference to a non-existent 'German expedition' was taken as proof that Pearse was guilty of 'assisting the enemy' in time of war – although the British had to know that they had defeated no such expedition, because it didn't exist.

As a legal excuse for executions it was a bit of a stretch, and it wasn't evidence against any of the others sentenced to death. But you work with what you've got.

The *Irish Independent*, newspaper of the southern

Catholic middle class, intervened. Be careful, it warned the government, on Wednesday, 10 May – after six days of executions – you risk creating revulsion. But, before you stop, it's important that 'the worst of the ringleaders be singled out and dealt with as they deserve'.

Next day, John Dillon of the Irish Parliamentary Party told the House of Commons: 'It is not murderers who are being executed, it is insurgents who have fought a clean fight, however misguided. And it would be a damned good thing for you if your soldiers were able to put up as good a fight as did these men in Dublin.'

In reply, Asquith conceded, 'I agree as regards the great body of the insurgents that they did not resort to outrage. They fought very bravely. They conducted themselves, as far as our knowledge goes, with humanity.'

Dillon said that he and his colleagues had risked everything to convince Irish people to support the Empire. And for the first time ever, when war threatened England, a great majority within Ireland had supported that Empire. 'It is the first rebellion that ever took place in Ireland where you had a majority on your side. It is the fruit of our life work, and now you are washing out our whole life work in a sea of blood.'

At which point the *Irish Independent* editorialized: 'certain of the leaders remain undealt with . . . Are they, because of an indiscriminate demand for clemency, to get off lightly while others who were no more prominent were executed? If so, leniency will be interpreted as weakness.'

Will you shave me, in the morning?

Corporal Sheehan told the very ill James Connolly he would, of course.

Sheehan, from the 18th Royal Irish, had been assigned

to supervise the dozen soldiers guarding Connolly while he awaited his fate. Like the other executions, it was scheduled at sunrise, around 3.45am – first Sean MacDermott, then James Connolly.

Captain Stanley, of the Royal Army Medical Corps, supervised Connolly's transfer from Dublin Castle to Kilmainham Jail. Connolly was taken on a stretcher to a military ambulance. Captain Stanley sat beside the driver, Corporal Sheehan sat in the back, along with Connolly and two Capuchin priests, Fr Aloysius and Fr Sebastian.

When the ambulance arrived at Kilmainham, Captain Stanley came around to the back and quietly ordered Sheehan to use the blindfold.

I'm going to have to blindfold you, the corporal told Connolly.

'All right.'

Connolly's wounds had been treated, but he was in pain, feverish, the wounds having become gangrenous. He might not have lived long, even had he not been sentenced to death.

He was carried from the ambulance on a stretcher.

There was a wooden kitchen chair in the prison yard. A common type, with a curved, U-shaped piece of wood at the back.

I'm going to lift you, now, so you can stand on your uninjured leg.

Corporal Sheehan did so, then gently moved the blindfolded Connolly back until he touched against the kitchen chair.

'What's this?'

'It's a chair for you to sit on, Mr Connolly.'

Sean MacDermott had just been shot in this yard. The priest who attended him, Fr Eugene McCarthy, was standing behind the firing squad. Fr Aloysius and Fr Sebastian stood beside him.

Connolly sat down.

Blindfolded, lying back in the chair, he very deliberately held his head high. Behind his back one hand gripped the U-shaped back of the chair.

When the bullets hit him his hand jerked and ripped free the piece of wood.

Fr McCarthy crossed the yard and anointed Connolly's body.

Like the other leaders, Connolly was taken to an anonymous grave. He was buried with his hand still clutching the piece of wood.

The owner of the *Irish Independent*, William Martin Murphy, long an enemy of Connolly, would be forever linked to this execution, although he was in London at the time. It appears that it was journalists and management, anxious to print what they imagined would please the newspaper's owner, who decided to encourage Connolly's killing.

Nothing the newspapers said mattered. Prime Minister Asquith wanted to end the executions, General Maxwell wanted a final pair of examples to terrorize anyone with treasonous thoughts.

Worried now about the backlash in Ireland, Asquith paid the country a visit to make soothing noises about Home Rule. This didn't have the effect he hoped. Here was the prime minister, confirming for many that it was armed force that made the British state offer concessions.

He visited Richmond Barracks, where he talked to some prisoners and told them they were fine fellows who had fought a clean fight.

As a coda to all this, and in case public revulsion might be in danger of dying down, three months later Roger Casement – who had been on his way home to Ireland to argue against the rising, given its certainty of failure – was found guilty of treason and hanged.

The executions were just the most dramatic part of an overall policy of suppression of separatism as an idea.

Although the rising was in Dublin, the 3,400 people arrested were from all over Ireland, ensuring that the reaction would be widespread. Anyone who might be a suspect was pulled in. Even Professor Eoin MacNeill, who had tried to stop the rising, was arrested.

The harassment of nationalists didn't stop with arrests. Although the Gaelic Athletic Association dissociated itself from the rising, the military imposed a ban on all GAA games. Gradually, this was relaxed, though the police could cancel games that didn't have a permit. Under emergency powers, travel was tightly controlled, and special trains to GAA matches were cancelled. This had a drastic effect on income at Croke Park.

Then, as the shock of the executions lingered, terrible stories emerged about the killings of Frank Sheehy-Skeffington and others. And about the abuse of prisoners on the night of the surrender.

Forced to lie in the open all night, hundreds of Volunteers had shivered on a small patch of grass in front of the Rotunda Hospital, without food or water. Some of the soldiers jeered at them, others shared their water. One British officer, Percival Lea-Wilson – assigned to light duties in Dublin after being wounded in France – distinguished himself by his sneering and his threats.

The prisoners were crushed against one another in the small space, unable to lie down properly, physically

attacked if they stood. There were no toilet facilities. If
you were caught relieving yourself on the grass you got a
smack of a rifle. Some of the men were upset that three
or four women, including Winifred Carney, were kept in
those conditions.

Lea-Wilson's cruelty to Tom Clarke angered many.
Witness accounts vary – some saw him physically abuse
Clarke, ordering him to strip. When Clarke was slow
taking off his jacket, because of his stiff, wounded arm,
Lea-Wilson wrenched the jacket off, causing the older
man pain.

Michael Collins told the Volunteers to pass the word.
'We'll get that fella's name.'

Frank Thornton swore to a comrade, 'If that fella lives
through the war, I'll search for him and I'll kill him for
this.'

They lay there hungry, thirsty, wet. British snipers
in the hospital tower fired intermittently through the
night. The maternity patients shrieked inside the wards.
Lying cramped on the ground outside, Frank Henderson
thought they must be going out of their minds.

Stories that enraged many emerged from the fighting
at North King Street, where British soldiers – angered
by the intensity of the fighting and the loss of comrades
– murdered civilians. The most poignant detail was
probably the plea of sixteen-year-old Christopher Hickey:
'Oh, don't kill father!' But they killed his father and
they murdered him, too. Fifteen innocent people were
murdered in a small area – some of them buried in their
neighbours' cellars.

General Maxwell said of these well-documented killings, 'Possibly some unfortunate incidents which we
should now regret may have occurred.' It was, he said,
'the inevitable consequence of a rebellion of this kind'.

He told the *Daily Mail*, 'A revolt of this kind could not be suppressed with velvet glove methods.'

All of this, on top of the prolonged series of executions, produced a sense of grievance, but that was not the primary effect. More significantly, the cruelty and injustice bolstered the image of two nations, one dominating the other – separate in politics and aspirations and in culture. And, when challenged, the dominant nation proved ruthless and unaware of the realities of the nation it was oppressing, and the consequences of that oppression.

Michael Breen was in charge of the electrical department in Dockrell's builders' providers store, on South Great George's Street. As Captain Breen of the Irish Volunteers, his familiarity with electrical equipment had been useful at the Reis building, where Fergus O'Kelly's team laboured to broadcast news of the rebellion. Now, released from internment, Breen returned to his civilian job.

At once, the store's department heads came together and decided this would not do. They went to the owner, Sir Maurice Dockrell, and told him there was a rebel working on the premises and they wouldn't stand for it.

Dockrell was a passionate unionist. He and other employers had organized recruitment drives to urge Dublin men to defend the Empire. In 1913 he had pursued the Lockout ruthlessly and presented framed certificates to policemen who had been especially helpful in strike-breaking. He awarded silver cups to those in Trinity College who helped put down the rising.

Dockrell told the department heads that Michael Breen fought according to his colours. If you don't want to work in the same firm as Breen, he said, well, you know your way out.

*

A supporter of John Redmond, very pro-Empire, wrote an angry letter to the British Foreign Office from New York. He'd sought to advance Redmond's cause among the Irish in America – but, he wrote, as a result of the executions the separatists in the USA 'swept every active and passive Irishman into their net. Meetings are held daily everywhere.'

There were twenty thousand at a meeting he attended in Madison Square Garden, 'and practically all were Irish and bitterly incensed Irish'. In Philadelphia, thirty thousand attended a meeting. Tens of thousands of dollars were being collected. Irish recruitment to the Canadian Army collapsed. The executions, he wrote, created 'an anti-English movement of much menace here', as well as 'an anti-Imperial movement in the Colonies'.

The 1916 leaders had two goals. The overall objective was to get the British out – and they knew that was extremely unlikely to be achieved by the rising. The immediate aim was to shatter the culture of Empire within which the people of Ireland accepted their role as subjects in a poorly governed province, and thereby consolidate the belief in Ireland as a separate nation.

And, in a very short time, that second aim had been achieved among large sections of the population – largely through the ruthless British reaction to the rising.

Pretty soon, recognizing the consequences of the repression, the British began to release prisoners.

About 450 people died violently during the rising. The figure is approximate. In a disrupted city, burial was haphazard over those few days. Some were buried without coffins, many in mass graves.

Of those killed, about 250 were civilians – at least thirty of them children.

There were 132 dead soldiers and policemen.

There were 64 dead rebels.

Around 2,500 people were wounded.

In the war of independence, about 2,000 people were killed.

John Redmond's Parliamentary Party denounced the violence of 1916. At the same time, it urged Irish men to join the British Army to fight in the Great War. This would ensure that Britain's promises on Home Rule, the peaceful road to independence, would be honoured.

About 200,000 Irish men fought in the Great War. Of them, around 27,000 were killed. We will never know how many Germans and others those 200,000 Irish killed.

31

September 1916, five months after the rising, Gertie Colley, sister of Harry, put an advert in the *Evening Mail*. She was looking for a hall somewhere in the Fairview area to hold sewing classes. The best offer she got was a converted coach-house at the back of Clonliffe Road.

Soon the hall was hosting sewing classes, dancing classes and meetings of a social club – great fun being had by all. They had Irish and old-time dances every Wednesday and Sunday, with a packed house every time.

Gertie Colley was a front for Cumann na mBan. Behind closed doors in what became known as Clonliffe House, the 2nd Battalion began meeting again, in its various units.

When F Company met in Clonliffe House, sixteen men turned up. Charlie Saurin and Harry Colley were elected 1st and 2nd lieutenant – temporary positions until the former officers got out of prison.

Within a few months, F Company had about 160 members.

November 1916, the Abbey Theatre staged a one-act play titled *Partition*, by D. C. Maher, 'a satirical imagining of the prospect of a divided Ireland'. It was set in the fictional village of Ballynadurgh, half in Leinster and half in Ulster. When Home Rule is introduced and partition enforced, all sorts of allegedly hilarious developments ensue.

Sixth on the cast list, playing 'Long Reilly', was Arthur Shields. Third from the bottom was Charlie Saurin, making his first and last appearance on the Abbey stage, playing 'Home Rule Constable'.

The two friends would take separate paths from here, with Saurin deepening his involvement in the national struggle, while Shields concentrated on his acting career. They would remain lifelong friends.

By July 1917, Frank Henderson and Oscar Traynor were home from prison. Before the rising, Henderson had twice rejected offers to join the IRB. Now, he decided to accept.

He and Traynor rejoined F Company and were elected to their old officer positions, captain and lieutenant. Now with over two hundred men, F Company was back in business.

As the Great War chewed up a generation of English, Scottish and Welsh men, the Empire badly needed cannon fodder. The British insisted on conscription in Ireland. In a country in which nationalism had been so recently re-awakened, the demand brought a fierce response, creating even greater support for the separatists.

In the December 1918 general election, Sinn Fein – which the separatists took over and used as a ready-made political vehicle – wiped out John Redmond's Irish Parliamentary Party. Of 105 seats, Sinn Fein won 73.

The unionists won 22.

And Redmond's party won 6 (down from 74 in the previous election). Within four years, the Irish Party vanished.

The Sinn Fein MPs refused to go to Westminster. The following month, they set up a parliament in Dublin, the Dail.

Under Michael Collins, the reorganized IRA, successor to the Volunteers, waged a ruthless guerrilla war of independence. This brought the British to the negotiating table in 1921. There, the British and the Irish tried to square the old triangle – the competing needs of British imperialism, Irish nationalism and Irish unionism – and came up with a treaty that satisfied no one.

On the first day of the rising, Easter Monday, Joe Plunkett, Patrick Pearse and Desmond FitzGerald had a conversation during a quiet period inside the GPO. How, they asked one another, would it all work out if there's a miracle and we win?

Among other consequences, Pearse and Plunkett reckoned that Germany might provide a monarch acceptable to the Irish. They had in mind twenty-six-year-old Prince Joachim Franz Humbert of Prussia, youngest son of the German Kaiser. The notion of importing a foreign monarch didn't originate in that discussion – it had been considered by MacDonagh and Plunkett over a year before.

Sinn Fein was a monarchist party. And here, at the heart of the republican insurrection, leading republicans such as Pearse and Plunkett were considering the viability of an Irish monarchy, based on an imported foreign king.

To the nationalists, the word 'republic' didn't mean what it means to us today – a country governed by an elected parliament responsible only to the people, without the trappings of aristocracy and inherited position.

For many, the word 'republican' was interchangeable with 'nationalist' – if there was a difference it was that the republicans considered themselves more steadfast nationalists. It was often just a way of indicating that you supported complete separation from Britain – as opposed to Home Rule within the Empire.

To James Connolly, and to Citizen Army members such as Vincent Poole, a republic had a social and political meaning, beyond kicking out the British. But, despite the laudable promises of the Proclamation, 'the Republic' that was declared that Easter Monday was a vague entity.

The actual form of a future government – republic, monarchy, whatever – wasn't agreed within the rebel forces. What would happen after getting rid of the British was another day's work.

In the treaty, the British insisted on keeping Ireland within the Empire, with a parliament in Dublin that would swear loyalty to the king. An area controlled by northern unionists would remain within the kingdom.

Led by Michael Collins, the pro-treaty faction pointed out that the new state would have its own government, army and police, and would be a stepping stone to greater freedom.

Led by Eamon de Valera, a substantial section of the IRA recoiled. It was 'the Republic' or nothing.

The British wanted an immediate answer, or they would resume the war.

For a pragmatist like Collins, the determining factor was that the IRA was by now in too poor a shape to continue an effective war against the British. To fight on was to throw away what had been conceded, with no chance of victory.

The failure of the nationalists to agree beforehand on what 'the Republic' consisted of meant that when the debate blew up it did so in circumstances where the choices were narrow and frustrating and a decision was urgent. Under such feverish conditions, each side accused the other of betraying a republic they had never bothered to define.

The apparent defeat of the 1916 rising had carried within it the seeds of the victory that followed, as the British overplayed their hand.

Now, the apparent victory of the war of independence carried within it the seeds of the short, brutal, pathetic civil war that followed, the partition enforced by the treaty, and the creation of a tribal division among nationalists that would dominate politics for decades.

The differences between the opposing sides don't today seem large enough to justify a civil war, but the urgency of the circumstances worked against any kind of feasible compromise.

And when the civil war began it was fought even more ruthlessly than the war of independence. It lasted less than a year, but took over a thousand lives and involved each side in atrocities. The new government ordered many blatant murders.

Like the movement of which it was part, F Company split.

Frank and Leo Henderson went with the anti-treaty side. As did Oscar Traynor, Harry Colley and Harry Boland, who broke with his close friend Michael Collins.

Charlie and Frank Saurin went with the pro-treaty side, as did Seamus Daly.

Apart from Boland, all survived the civil war.

The anti-treaty side (the 'republicans') evolved into Fianna Fail and the pro-treaty side (the 'Free Staters') evolved into Fine Gael.

The debate on the nature of the new Ireland was

postponed indefinitely. Instead, tribal bitterness and arguments about who betrayed the heroes of 1916 prevailed. Things that mattered, that affected how people lived, and how they died, were considered of secondary importance, when they were considered at all.

32

In 1936 the *Irish Press* published a series of articles and photographs that revealed the extent of slum life in Dublin, twenty years after the 1916 rising. Thirteen years of government by Irish politicians had left the tenements more squalid than ever. There were even more people crushed into single-room dwellings than there had been under the British.

The newspaper chronicled the unsanitary conditions, the overcrowding, the vermin. It told of the premature deaths of children living in such unhealthy conditions – five dead in one family.

The fact that things were as bad as ever, or worse, under an Irish government was not a result of new policies tried and failed. The prevailing political view on social and economic matters was indistinguishable from that of the departed British regime.

William Cosgrave was president of the Executive Council – prime minister – between 1922 and 1932. He was a dominant force in setting the political priorities of the state in the first decade of independence. He was a 1916 veteran.

Here he is in 1930, commenting on the international crisis that would become the Great Depression, boasting

to a British film camera crew of how Ireland was a model
of how things should be done: 'We here in this country
. . . have, by reason of our economic structure, some
advantages which other nations may possibly envy and
may subsequently come to emulate'.

The notion of Ireland as different from, superior to, the
countries in the outside world was one that would under-
pin decades of ineffectual social policies.

This delusional nonsense didn't flow from ignorance of
the slums. Cosgrave was aware of them, but the people in
them were not of his species.

In May of 1921, Cosgrave wrote the following in a
letter to a colleague, Austin Stack:

> People reared in workhouses, as you are aware, are no
> great acquisition to the community and they have no
> ideas whatsoever of civic responsibilities. As a rule their
> highest aim is to live at the expense of the ratepayers.
> Consequently it would be a decided gain if they all took
> it into their heads to emigrate. When they go abroad they
> are thrown on their own responsibilities and have to work
> whether they like it or not.

It wasn't just snobbery, it wasn't just callousness. It
was a political view, widely held among conservatives –
a form of 'social Darwinism', the fittest prospered, the
unworthy got what they deserved. Mass poverty was due
to personal weakness, rather than political and social
conditions. The causes of the slums – the economic down-
turns and famines of the nineteenth century, the flight
of the poor to Dublin, the wealthy abandoning the inner
city, the greed of slum landlords, the political corruption
that allowed this – were all ignored.

Instead, Cosgrave and his class saw the slums as the

old regime had seen them – the result of the inevitable failings of an underclass, that other species.

Nothing could be done – except hope they might emigrate.

It was likewise seen as natural that there should be a permanent pool of cheap, desperate labour. Such labour was beneficial to those higher species with the entrepreneurial initiative to take advantage of it.

Anyone expecting a more ambitious policy from the other wing of the triumphant nationalist movement – Fianna Fail – was disappointed. In 1928, in a Dail speech, Eamon de Valera explained that Ireland was like a servant in a big mansion who 'was displeased with the kicks of the young master and wanted to have his freedom'. Having left the big mansion, the servant 'must remember that he cannot have in the cottage the luxuries around him which he had when he was bearing the kicks of the young master'.

It was a bizarre vision of Ireland as a nation of servants who quit their jobs in the Big House and were now condemned – without the guiding hand of the master – to live frugal lives.

The two wings of the same conservative movement, Fine Gael and Fianna Fail, squared up to each other, determined to fight and refight their bitter and meaningless quarrel – at its heart, the issue of who best represented the spirit of 1916.

Decades of stagnancy lay ahead.

By 1960, 40 per cent of private dwellings didn't have piped water – one in three didn't have an indoor toilet.

On Saturday, 17 June 1939, twenty-three years after the 1916 rising, the president of Ireland held his first garden party. For some it was a really big deal.

It was sixteen years since the founding of the new state.

That first decade and a half of the new Ireland was known to the social elite of the time as 'the grey days'. Civil war, unrest in the army, the murder by the IRA of a government minister – it had not been a time for pomp and ceremony.

Besides, pomp and ceremony were associated with the old regime.

But, in 1939, the state's new constitution was two years old. The presidency was one year old. Now, the elite were ready to preen a little.

The garden party was held in the grounds of the old Vice-Regal Lodge, which had become Aras an Uachtarain – House of the President.

Over two thousand invitations were sent out. The guest list defined the social elite.

The invitations didn't specify a dress code. Which is why, in a ruling class still insecure about such matters, some turned up in tweeds and others wore top hats. The photos of the occasion might well have been taken thirty years earlier, in any corner of the Empire. Military men with swords, gents with monocles, and women with big, big hats.

Two army bands provided music. The food – supplied by Lawlor's Hotel, of Naas – included brioche lobster and chicken and assorted petit sandwiches, savouries and French pastries. White-jacketed boys passed among the crowd with baskets, handing out ice creams.

For entertainment, according to a press report, guests were allowed to 'view the trees planted in the gardens by different royal personages in the past'.

As a special treat, guests could visit 'the grave of King Edward's pet dog'.

The president, Douglas Hyde – impeccably nationalist,

to reflect the politics of the state; impeccably Protestant, to demonstrate its tolerance – was seated under a portico, on a red leather chair.

His feet on a red footstool, the seventy-nine-year-old greeted the queue of cold, tired guests. All two thousand of them. Each guest handed the invitation to an official, who passed it to a second official, who passed it to a third, who read aloud the names inscribed thereon. President Hyde smiled, bowed to each guest. At ten seconds per guest, that's the guts of three hours, provided they came in pairs.

Irish Press journalist Anna Kelly described the 'hat-clutching wind which threw dust in the eyes and swirled the red and black and purple robes' of a nuncio, a cardinal and an archbishop.

Kelly gently chided the elite and noted that the band played the Soldiers' Chorus from *Faust*, in which 'the men of old' fight with 'courage in heart and a sword in hand'. She implied that the men and women of old who had created the state mightn't have been impressed.

Her article was denounced in the Dail. In response, a grovelling *Irish Press* hurriedly proclaimed that the garden party symbolized how far Irish society had travelled to 'capture the stronghold of alien power and culture'.

Top civil servants opened a 'personal file' on Kelly, noting her 'attitude'. She was to be barred from future presidential functions.

That wasn't enough. Political pressure was put on the *Irish Press* and Kelly was sacked.

Kelly was no respecter of position (she referred to the *Irish Press* editor as 'Lo' and to his assistant as 'Behold'). She was vigorously involved in the fight for independence. She'd worked alongside Michael Collins, she'd known de Valera for over twenty years, and she'd followed him in opposing the treaty. She had served jail time in 1923.

Words were spoken quietly in certain ears and Kelly got her job back.

It was a suitable coming of age for the new Ireland. Aping the pomp of the departed Empire, and reacting viciously to humorous comment on the new pomposities.

And then backing down as connections and reputations forged in the struggle against the Empire trumped the hurt feelings of the chaps with monocles and the ladies with big, big hats.

Above it all, the sad image of the social and political elite of the brave new Ireland gathering to visit the tombstone of a dead king's dog.

In the absence of any vision of the future, the country turned in on itself. The two wings of nationalism competed in asserting their Irishness, their Catholicism.

The South was to be a ferociously Catholic state. Without any sense of irony, its leaders denounced the North for becoming a ferociously Protestant state.

One of the first efforts of the new state was a Committee on Evil Literature. The Local Government (Temporary Provisions) Act of 1923 designated unmarried mothers to be 'offenders'. They were consigned to dreadful state 'homes' run by nuns, or sent to work in the Magdalene Laundries. Their children were declared 'illegitimate' and taken from them. And one in every three of those 'illegitimate' children born alive in 1924 died within a year of its birth – often from deliberate neglect by the state, or by paid foster parents.

The Catholic Church and its partner the state later concealed the existence of 'illegitimate' babies by selling them on the American adoption market.

The censorship of books ruthlessly limited access to stories and ideas that helped other societies examine themselves and develop. O'Connor, O Faolain, O'Flaherty, Clarke, Macken and Beckett had books banned. From outside, everyone from Graham Greene to Hemingway to Robert Graves, Balzac, Gide and Proust had a turn at being declared too obscene for Irish eyes. A single innocuous sentence could and did get a book banned.

It was a small step to, in 1931, barring a Protestant from taking a job as a public librarian, in Mayo, for fear she might introduce dangerous books.

The leading 'republican' of the time, Eamon de Valera, veteran commandant of 1916, supported such bigotry. It was not, however, a bigotry imposed from above. As in the North, it was a bigotry in tune with the fears and prejudices of the wider society.

The GAA banned from attending its games anyone playing or even attending foreign sports, such as soccer. When the country's first president, Douglas Hyde, attended an international soccer match in 1938 the GAA dismissed him as patron. Oscar Traynor – former professional goalkeeper, still a passionate soccer fan, now a government minister – believed it wrong to use sport to relegate sections of society to a lesser status. He opposed the GAA and lost that fight.

It would take until the 1970s, and the dying off of the 1916 generation, before some of the bizarre aspects of the Irish Catholic state began to be dismantled.

Pressure for change in the North brought a violent reaction, followed by thirty years of brutality.

Certainly, the seeds of the South's inward-looking, sectarian culture were sown in the struggle for independence – but, they were not the only seeds sown in that period. They were merely the conservative ones that won out.

Other seeds – visions of a different, better society – survived in the memories of some of those who took part in the rising. And died along with some of those who perished in the struggle.

Epilogue

What became of the survivors?

This is a section of a photograph taken at the Mansion House, Dublin, in June 1917, following the general release of convicted prisoners. Top left, Eoin MacNeill has his arm around Eamon de Valera. Some never forgave the man who undermined the rising, but de Valera, taking on a leadership role, believed reconciliation was necessary as the struggle entered a new phase. At bottom right is Vincent Poole.

Charlie Saurin

Charlie Saurin and Boss Shields were together in Frongoch internment camp, in Wales. At Frongoch, connections were made, friendships were formed, experiences discussed and lessons learned. The Empire obligingly brought into one place, from all over Ireland, activists who proceeded to put together the guerrilla army that a few years later would carry through the war of independence.

Charles Saurin in uniform, later in life

On Friday, 2 June 1916, Boss Shields's sister Madeline – known as Lini – visited the camp. She brought gifts for Boss and Charlie. Three days later, Saurin wrote to Boss's older brother, Will Shields. He thanked him for the gift of a book that Lini delivered. 'Books – that's what we missed most.' And he wrote of Lini: 'She has rather a small body (don't say to her that I said that) & I'm just wondering how her soul & spirit fits into it. I suppose the way it is, they float all around her in a big invisible cloud.'

At the age of twenty, Charlie Saurin had a war of independence and a civil war ahead of him. He was released from internment in August 1916 and immediately returned to F Company. He was involved in election work in 1918 and then in the war of independence, serving as a staff officer with 2nd Battalion and later as brigade adjutant. He was interned again in December 1920 and released a year later. In the civil war he was pro-treaty, and served in the National Army.

Meanwhile, he married Lini.

Like many others, the 1916 rising altered the course of his life. Saurin abandoned his studies and made a career in the army. In May 1936, playwright Sean O'Casey wrote to Boss Shields: 'Will you give my congratulations to Major Saurin on his recent promotion. I am glad that intelligent and cultured fellows like him are being recognised as important gains to Ireland. Best wishes to him and Lini.'

Towards the end of his career, Charlie Saurin was appointed to the Bureau of Military History, in Cork, with the task of 'collecting and recording the history of the war of independence'. Among his duties was the collection of photographs of historic places and events. Along with a number of photos he accumulated, Saurin put the following two sketches into his Bureau files. They show the skirmish at North Strand and the shelling of the Metropole Hotel. The 'C.S. 1918' on the bottom right

of the North Strand drawing indicates Saurin drew the scenes two years after the events.

He retired in 1953 with the rank of lieutenant colonel. He died in 1964, at his home in Courtmacsharry, Cork, at the age of sixty-nine.

Saurin remained friends with Boss Shields, though occasionally complaining that Boss never bought him that copy of *Lorna Doone*.

Arthur 'Boss' Shields

The actor became a stalwart of the Abbey Theatre for twenty-five years, playing three hundred parts and directing nineteen plays. He acted in the first productions of several of his friend Sean O'Casey's plays.

In 1936 he went to Hollywood and played Patrick Pearse in John Ford's movie version of *The Plough and the Stars*. At the end

*Arthur Shields, in his
Abbey days*

of the thirties he broke with the Abbey Theatre, disappointed by its increasingly introverted repertoire.

He moved permanently to California, his reputation as a respected character actor prospered there and he appeared in dozens of movie and TV roles and at the same time made a name for himself as a talented theatre director. He died there in 1970.

On the final day of the rising, Boss Shields was in Moore Street, while a hundred yards away General Lowe was accepting the surrender of Patrick Pearse. Lowe was hosting a visitor to Dublin that weekend, his son John, a British officer on leave from the war in France. Lieutenant John Lowe later became an actor, changed his name to John Loder and moved to Hollywood. In 1941/42, Arthur Shields and John Loder featured in three movies together, *How Green Was My Valley*, *Gentleman Jim* and *Confirm or Deny*.

Will Shields

Boss's brother Will Shields also became an actor, changed his name to Barry Fitzgerald, worked at the Abbey Theatre, went to Hollywood and won an Academy Award as Best Supporting Actor for his role in the 1944 movie *Going My Way*. Both the Shields brothers appeared in John Ford's *The Quiet Man*.

Vincent Poole

The Citizen Army captain was tried and sentenced to death after the surrender. The sentence was commuted. Poole served time in Portland, Parkhurst and Lewes ('we broke up the prison there'). At Lewes he was one of the leaders of a hunger strike.

After one row with prison officers he was thrown into solitary. The warden tried to pay him a visit but Poole

wouldn't let him into the cell. The
warders were sent in to put him
in a straitjacket. He beat them
up. Some of the other prisoners
wanted to strike in sympathy with
Poole, but the Prisoners' Council
decided against it. It's doubt-
ful that Poole was surprised –
he'd never seen solidarity as the
Volunteers' strong suit.

Vincent Poole

He was released in June 1917.

At one stage, Poole reckoned
the National Aid Committee,
which distributed money to the needy dependants of
those killed in the rising, wasn't giving a fair share to
the Citizen Army veterans. He interrupted a meeting at
which Michael Collins presided, and produced a pistol.
Bill O'Brien persuaded him to put it away.

Poole had a point. Payments were made according
to the income of the deceased. Relatives of those with
middle-class jobs got significantly more than the families
of manual workers. The dependants of officers were on a
higher rate.

Poole left the dwindling Citizen Army and joined the
IRA in 1920. He fought in the war of independence
and went against the treaty, serving in the Four Courts
garrison in the civil war. Afterwards, he returned to his
old job at Dublin Corporation – sewer worker. His wage
in 1935 was just over £4 a week.

Poole received a state pension of £24 a year gross
(£16 a year after deductions), for his service in 1916 and
the war of independence. He was living at 22 Lower
Dominic Street, Dublin, when he died in June 1955,
at the age of seventy-four. He was predeceased by his

wife Annie and survived by his daughter, Margaret O'Neill.

Poole's name wasn't on the definitive roll of honour of those who served in the rising, compiled by the National Museum. Neither were the names of his brothers, who also served with honour: Kit and Patrick at Stephens Green and the College of Surgeons; and John at the GPO and City Hall. The list in *Dublin in Rebellion: a Directory 1913–1923*, by Joseph E. A. Connell, is more comprehensive and includes the Pooles.

Henderson on the day of his wedding

Frank Henderson

The captain of F Company played a major part in reorganizing the Dublin forces and was active in the war of independence. Although now a member of the IRB, and a senior member of the IRA, Henderson had problems of conscience with the ruthless tactics employed under Michael Collins – in particular the shoot-on-sight policy and street ambushes of policemen. He remained active throughout the struggle, but was sidelined into headquarters work – although he was recalled to active duty towards the end of the war. He served as adjutant of the Dublin Brigade, and was appointed OC when Oscar Traynor was arrested.

In later years, Henderson was troubled by his involvement in actions that disturbed his conscience – in particular the assassination policy that led to the shooting dead of Sean Hales TD.

Henderson married Josephine Ni Bhraonain and they had nine children, two of whom became priests. In the introduction to Henderson's memoir, *Recollections of a Dublin Volunteer*, the editor wrote that Frank annually, 'over a period of sixteen years asked his son to say a Mass for Hales'.

Later on, Henderson and Oscar Traynor started a printing company in Parnell Square. He became a member of the Fianna Fail National Executive, but unlike Traynor he never took to political life.

He was repeatedly involved in ensuring that old comrades were not denied the pensions due to them. His witness statement for the Bureau of Military History lacked any trace of glory-seeking or triumphalism – it was a plain, cautious recounting of what he remembered and thought fit for such a record. He died in 1959.

Oscar Traynor in 1922

Oscar Traynor

In the war of independence, the ex-footballer was brigadier of the Dublin Brigade and played a major role in the campaign, until he was captured and imprisoned. He went with the anti-treaty side in the civil war and played a prominent part in hostilities.

He became a Sinn Fein TD in the mid-1920s and in the 1932 general election he stood for Fianna Fail and won a seat. He became a Cabinet minister in the mid-1930s and was Minister for Defence when the Bureau of Military History was set up. He retired in 1961, at the age of seventy-five, and died two years later.

Close to Oscar Traynor Road in Coolock, Dublin, there's an Oscar Traynor Coaching and Development

Frank Henderson, Harry Colley and Oscar Traynor, at an F Company reunion

Centre, where young boys and girls train for junior-league football.

Harry Colley

Colley remained active right through the war of independence and the civil war, in which he took the anti-treaty side. He helped found Fianna Fail in 1926 and first stood for the Dail in 1943, when he won a seat in Dublin North East. Both he and Oscar Traynor held seats in that constituency until 1957 – Traynor retained his seat thereafter, but Colley was defeated by the young Charlie Haughey.

Harry Colley was elected to the Seanad. He retired in 1961 and died in 1972. His son George became a Fianna Fail TD and minister.

Seamus Daly

The fitter and bomb maker was released from internment in August 1916. He immediately became involved in reorganizing the Volunteers. He served in the war of independence, was interned, took part in a hunger strike, and was in the National Army, supporting the treaty, during the civil war. He continued on in the army, in the munitions branch, retiring in 1946 with the rank of commandant. He died in February 1966.

The Mystery of John Neale

The socialist who fought with the Citizen Army at Annesley Bridge and the Metropole Hotel remains an enigma. Reliable witnesses talked with him, fought alongside him, yet nothing is officially recorded.

His name was not on the definitive roll of honour compiled by the National Museum. Again, the list in *Dublin in Rebellion: a Directory 1913–1923*, by Joseph E. A. Connell, is more comprehensive and includes Neale.

The Sinn Fein Rebellion Handbook, compiled by the *Irish Times* shortly after the rising, lists a John Neal as being buried in Glasnevin Cemetery. The cemetery records show a John Neal, died 1916.

No one knows if Neale was his true name. There were references to a socialist from Norwich with a similar accent who served in the GPO. His name was reputed to be Arthur Weekes, or Neil Weekes, or Arthur Wicks, or Abraham Wix. There may well have been at least two such people. It hardly seems likely. Most probably they were the same man.

Some referred to him as the 'Cockney socialist' because of his accent, and trustworthy witnesses such as Charlie Saurin were sure he was English. Yet, the equally reliable Joe Good, who was himself born and raised in London and had a Cockney accent, assumed that Neale was American.

Referring without question to the same man (both saw him out on the Metropole Hotel parapet), Saurin describes Neale's 'youth', while Good refers to an 'older man'.

Whatever his name was, or his age, whether he was from London, Norwich, the USA or elsewhere, he was respectfully recalled by those with whom he fought. A random bullet shortened the life of an idealistic man who

– amidst a nationalist rising – upheld the principle that nationality is not the most important thing that defines us.

Michael Collins

Having played a minor role in the rising, Collins quickly came to the top of the leadership of the reorganized movement, the IRA. Instead of the set-piece approach of the old Military Council, he organized a guerrilla campaign, systematic and ruthless, and a plan of urban assassination. It made the country ungovernable and brought the British to the negotiating table.

Collins was very much aware that the war of independence had left the IRA worn out, reduced in numbers and in no condition to continue an open-ended struggle. He was hopeful that the treaty would eventually lead to a more extensive victory. A section of the movement, led by Eamon de Valera, held out for full separation.

The movement split over the treaty and a pointless, savage and brief civil war followed – during which, in August 1922, Collins was shot dead in an ambush, at the age of thirty-one.

Joe Good

Quiet and modest, the London-born electrician fought in the war of independence and spent the rest of his life in Ireland. He stayed out of the civil war until his friend Michael Collins was killed by anti-treaty forces – at which point he joined the pro-treaty side. He was wounded in an ambush and was about to be finished off when anti-treaty fighter

Joe Good in 1913

Dan Breen recognized him as 'a 1916 man'. Breen suggested that instead of being shot, Good should be allowed to drive into the nearest village to get a priest for those killed in the ambush.

Joe Good married, had four children and remained close friends with his old comrade and fellow electrician Blimey O'Connor. He worked as a maintenance electrician at the College of Science and died in 1962.

Good left behind a memoir, *Enchanted by Dreams*, based on his Bureau statement. It's a fascinating book. (It was republished in 2015 by O'Brien Press as *Inside the GPO 1916: A First-hand Account*.)

John 'Blimey' O'Connor

The young Cockney electrician was interned in Stafford Prison until Christmas 1916. He fought in the war of independence and after the truce he took the anti-treaty side. He was interned and spent twenty-three days on hunger strike.

John 'Blimey' O'Connor in 1913

He remained in Dublin when the conflict ended, worked for the Electricity Supply Board and died in 1979, at the age of eighty-three.

Although they took opposing sides in the civil war, Blimey O'Connor and Joe Good remained friends. In 1962, Blimey was on holiday in Kerry when he heard of Joe's death. He drove non-stop to Dublin to arrange a military funeral.

Mattie Connolly

After a month in jail, the sixteen-year-old was released, because of his youth. He was one of approximately 120 boys freed on the basis of their age.

Mattie Connolly immediately went to work with those reorganizing the Citizen Army. He was involved in the 1918 general election campaign and in the war of independence. In February 1920 he went to London, got work there and was active in nationalist politics. The Citizen Army, without James Connolly's socialist politics, and with a conservative leadership dominating the Labour movement, gradually leaked membership – including Mattie Connolly – to the IRA.

After spending some time in America, he returned to Dublin and in the 1930s was employed as a carpenter in the City Architect's Department. He later moved to the Office of Public Works. He worked with the OPW during the 1960s and was involved with the renovation of the GPO and other significant buildings in preparation for the fiftieth anniversary commemoration of the rising.

He died in July 1985.

Helena Molony

Helena Molony, marginalized and excluded

After her capture at City Hall on Easter Monday, Helena Molony was held in Kilmainham Jail and Mountjoy in Dublin. She tried to dig her way out of Kilmainham with an iron spoon. She was deported to Lewes and Aylesbury jails, in England, and released at Christmas 1916.

She remained involved with the Citizen Army and took part in the war of independence. She also served as a justice in the Republican Courts in Rathmines.

In 1930 Molony noted the experience of women hadn't changed much under an Irish government. Women had the right to vote, but they retained 'their inferior status, their lower pay for equal work, their exclusion from juries and certain branches of the civil service, their slum dwellings and crowded, cold and unsanitary schools for their children'.

Asked later what women did in the rising, she said: 'I feel they might as well ask me what did the tall fair haired men do in the wars and what did the small dark men do. My answer in both cases is the same: they did what came to their hands to do – day to day, and whatever they were capable of by aptitude or training.'

Active in the leadership of the Irish Women Workers' Union between 1929 and 1940, president in 1936 of the Irish Trade Union Congress, Helena Molony retained her radicalism as the unions and the Labour Party moved steadily to the right. She clung to a defence of the Soviet Union, despite its authoritarianism. Her involvement with the republican group Saor Eire saw her further isolated.

Historian Fearghal McGarry said of her: 'Marginalised by class, gender, religion and nationalism, awkward women like Molony were long excluded from the narrative of the independence struggle.'

She lived in poverty in her later years. In April 1966 she attended the opening of the Garden of Remembrance, in Dublin, on the fiftieth anniversary of the rising. She died in 1967, at the age of eighty-two. She left behind assets of less than £100.

Ernie O'Malley

The young medical student who came to Sackville Street on the first day of the rising to see what the fuss was about, and saw the children playing happily with looted toys, later became a leading IRA commander in the war of independence.

Leo Henderson

Adjutant to the Dublin Brigade, Leo Henderson fought in the war of independence, was arrested in October 1920 and interned until December 1921.

He, like his brother Frank, sided with the anti-treaty IRA. He was arrested by National Army forces in June 1922, while attempting to commandeer a number of cars at a garage in Baggot Street, Dublin. (The arrest was carried out by a somewhat embarrassed pro-treaty officer, Frank Thornton, who commanded the Volunteers in the Imperial Hotel during the rising.)

In response to Henderson's arrest, the anti-treaty side (based in the Four Courts) some hours later kidnapped Ginger O'Connell, assistant chief of staff of the National Army. (The kidnap was carried out by Ernie O'Malley.)

When the anti-treaty side refused to release O'Connell (as long as the pro-treaty side held Henderson), Michael Collins ordered the bombardment of the Four Courts – and the civil war killing was under way.

In later life, Leo Henderson worked in local government. He died in October 1973.

Rosie Hackett

The co-founder of the Irish Women Workers' Union was, with Helena Molony, one of a number of women activists who, on the first anniversary of the rising, defied the authorities

Rosanna 'Rosie' Hackett,
with fellow trade unionist Bill O'Brien

and hung a banner from the ruins of Liberty Hall: 'James Connolly Murdered 12 May 1916'.

She lived in Fairview and continued her trade union work throughout her life. She died in 1976, at the age of eighty-four. In 2014 a new bridge over the river Liffey was named in her honour.

Peter Folan

The second shot of the attack on Dublin Castle was fired at Peter Folan, head constable of the RIC, who watched from a second-floor window as the Citizen Army contingent stormed the gates and shot Constable James O'Brien. The bullet intended for Folan broke the window at which he'd been standing.

By 1918, Folan was weary of his role as a policeman, and thoroughly committed to the nationalist cause. He told a nationalist friend he was thinking of quitting his job. Instead, he was urged to stay in the RIC, and throughout the war of independence he supplied Michael Collins's intelligence unit with secret documents.

Harry Boland

Boland was elected to parliament in 1918, refused to take his seat and helped set up the Dail. He was active in the war of independence, was an envoy to the USA, and worked alongside both Michael Collins and Eamon de Valera.

In the civil war he broke with Collins and opposed the treaty. He was shot by members of the National Army in July 1922,

Harry Boland's Mass card

while unarmed. It was a 'shot-while-trying-to-escape' job. He died several days later, in hospital, at the age of thirty-five. Although he knew the man who shot him, Boland refused to name him.

Kathleen Lynn

The chief medical officer of the Citizen Army remained a feminist and labour activist all her life. In 1919, she founded St Ultan's Hospital for infants, and ran it with her partner Madeleine ffrench-Mullen. The hospital pioneered the BCG vaccine, catered for the children of the poor and was unique in that it was managed and staffed by women. It had a huge impact in reducing infant mortality.

Dr Kathleen Lynn

Lynn worked to the end, attending her final clinic at St Ultan's at the age of eighty. She died the following year, in September 1955.

Constance Markievicz

After the rising Constance Markievicz was tried and sentenced to death, but the sentence was commuted because she was a woman – a fact that irritated her. A lawyer from the court martial, an army officer, wrote twenty years later than she begged the court not to kill her. 'I am a woman, you must not kill me. Please don't kill me.' The official court record, released many years later, shows that to be a lie. Even those not over-fond of Markievicz conceded she behaved with courage.

She fought in the war of independence and took the

anti-treaty side, with de Valera. She was elected to the Dail several times and in 1919 became the first woman appointed to the Cabinet. The second woman to enter the Cabinet was appointed sixty years later.

She died in 1927, at the age of fifty-nine.

Seamus Grace

Captured after the battle of Mount Street Bridge, the comrade of Lieutenant Mick Malone was interned. He was released on Christmas Eve 1916. A few days later Grace stood in Glasnevin Cemetery, beside the grave of Lieutenant Malone, which had been opened for identification purposes. There, Grace got a last glimpse of his comrade, in a blood-stained olive-green uniform.

As the grave was closed – in a Dublin still on edge from the shock of the rising – Grace and a comrade from his company, Sean Cullen, fired three volleys into the air in salute.

Matt Stafford

About noon on 3 May 1916 – the day Pearse, Clarke and MacDonagh were executed – Matt Stafford's home in Drumcondra was surrounded by British troops. He quickly found his rifle, cut off the stock, broke the gun into parts and hid the pieces in nooks and crannies around the house. If they found the rifle and figured him for a sniper, he believed, they might well shoot him then and there.

Matt Stafford, Fenian

The house was searched, the rifle wasn't found and he was arrested. They let him go later that day.

The Fenian in his sixties, left out of the mobilization by Leo Henderson because of his age, was still alive thirty years later.

Taoiseach Eamon de Valera appointed Stafford to the Seanad four times, between 1938 and 1948. It was a way of honouring the old Fenian and giving him an income, which was how things were done in the new Ireland.

In his ten years in the Seanad, Stafford spoke twice. On 12 February 1941, on the Army Pensions Bill, he said: 'I propose that we take the Committee Stage of the Bill now.' And during a debate on the Finance Bill, on 6 December 1939, he said: 'Nonsense.'

Matt Stafford died in 1950, at the age of ninety-seven.

Margaret Skinnider

She survived her life-threatening wounds and later went to the USA, where she campaigned for support for Irish independence and published a memoir of the rising, *Doing My Bit for Ireland*. She took part in the war of independence; in the civil war she went against the treaty. Initially drawn to the separatist movement by revulsion at the Dublin slums, she was a strong feminist and social activist.

Margaret Skinnider, in Cumann na mBan uniform

She had a career as a maths teacher and became president of the Irish National Teachers Organisation, through which she campaigned for equal pay. She died in 1971.

M. W. O'Reilly

Michael William O'Reilly was interned after the rising. He became director of training of the IRA in 1917. The

The well-shaven M.W. O'Reilly

following year he was one of the founders of the New Ireland Assurance Collecting Society. Other veterans, such as Liam Tobin and Frank Thornton, joined the company. During the war of independence most of senior management, including O'Reilly, were in jail or on the run.

New Ireland blossomed into a major insurance company. The first premises of the company were in the building on the corner of Bachelors Walk where Joe Good and his comrades defended 'Kelly's Fort'.

O'Reilly became one of the most respected businessmen in the new Ireland. He died in 1971, aged eighty-two.

Sean T. O'Kelly

The networker who considered himself a 'nominal' captain in the Volunteers later became a founder of Fianna Fail, a TD, a minister and served two terms as president of Ireland.

President-in-waiting O'Kelly

Bill O'Brien

As a friend and trade union associate of James Connolly, O'Brien was one of those interned after the rising – despite his lack of involvement. On release he went back to trade union work and helped rebuild the Transport Union. He and his union were a significant force in the anti-conscription campaign. In 1922 he was elected to the Dail, and won seats twice more, in the twenties and thirties. He retired in 1946 and died in 1968.

Nora O'Daly shortly after the rising

Nora O'Daly

O'Daly was held in Kilmainham Jail for nine days, then released. She was active in the war of independence and became a judge in the North City Republican Courts. She dropped away from activity when the civil war began.

Frank Henderson believed O'Daly 'exhausted herself in the service of the IRA 1916–1921'. In later life she suffered serious health problems as a result. She was awarded a military service pension of £21 a year. When she applied for a disability allowance the stringent assessors would not accept that her crippling illness stemmed from her service, though Frank Henderson was in no doubt that was the case. She died in 1943.

Company Quartermaster Sergeant Robert Flood

The soldier who ordered the shooting dead of two British Army lieutenants at Guinness's brewery, along with two Guinness workers, was born in London and had been in the Royal Dublin Fusiliers for seventeen years. He was aged thirty-one when he ordered the killings – so, he was fourteen when he enlisted. He served in Egypt and India.

In June 1916 he was court-martialled for the killings. He and other soldiers solemnly swore that Lieutenant Algernon Lucas said, before he was shot, that he was just a poor farmer's son, and that he'd been led into the rebellion by others. They claimed that Flood had been attacked without provocation by Lieutenant Basil Worsley Worswick, who was then shot. The Guinness workers accompanying the lieutenants, William Rice and Cecil Dockeray, were shot dead because they were suspected of being rebels.

It was established beyond doubt that neither of the British Army officers, and neither of the Guinness workers, had any connection whatsoever with the rebels. It was clear that the evidence of Flood and his supporters was perjured.

Sergeant Flood was found not guilty. There was applause in court.

He was subsequently transferred to the Royal Berkshire Regiment and was later awarded the Good Conduct and Long Service Medals. He was killed in action in a failed offensive against the Bulgarian Army on the Salonika front in May 1917.

Sir Edward Carson

The resolute unionist leader, who organized armed groups in 1912 with the declared intent of resisting the will of parliament, consistently made it clear that any attempt to include Ulster in Home Rule would be met by civil war. Despite this, in 1915 he was appointed attorney general.

One of his co-conspirators, British Army veteran Frederick Crawford, had previously planned the kidnapping – at Brighton – of Prime Minister William Gladstone, who was proposing Home Rule. In 1921, Crawford received a CBE.

Meanwhile, Sir Edward Carson's armed defiance of parliament did his career no harm. He was made First Lord of the Admiralty in 1916.

He was made a member of the UK Cabinet in 1917.

He was made a judge in 1921.

He was made a life peer, Baron Carson, in 1921.

And when he died in 1935, the UK government gave him a state funeral.

Paul Galligan

Paul Galligan, epic cyclist

The Cavan man who made the epic bicycle journey from the GPO to Enniscorthy survived the rising and was sentenced to death. The sentence was commuted and he was released from prison in June 1917. He was elected an MP in 1918, was active in the war of independence, was shot once and jailed three times.

After the war of independence he went back to civilian life. Before the rising he had been a draper's assistant. From the 1930s to the 1960s he ran his own gentlemen's outfitters in Dublin, offering Irish-made shirts, pyjamas, flannels and hats. His sales slogan was: 'Outfitters to particular men'. The address of the shop was 1 GPO Buildings, Henry Street, Dublin.

Galligan lived in Churchtown and died on 15 December 1966, aged seventy-eight.

Antli the Finn

The Finn and the Swede who joined the fight at the GPO on Easter Monday didn't make their appointment to ship out on Thursday. They were stationed on the roof of the building and both survived the bombardment of the GPO and the bullets of Moore Street, and were taken captive.

The Swede, whose name is not known, was released from Kilmainham Jail almost immediately, after the intervention of the Swedish consul. The Finn's first name was probably Antli, and he was called 'Tony' by his GPO comrades. Makapaltis, the surname used in records of the time, was probably a garbled guess.

The Finn spent some time in the military prison at Knutsford before being released. According to Captain Liam Tannam, who originally accepted the pair's offer of support for the rising, Antli was 'not a Catholic. He had no English but before he left he was saying the Rosary in Irish.'

Kathleen Clarke

Her loss was heavy – she suffered the execution of her husband, Tom, and of her brother, Ned Daly. She lost the baby she was expecting, which would have been her fourth child. Clarke immediately plunged into the work of organizing support for the dependants of those who died in the rising.

She was involved with the Republican Courts during the war of independence and was against the treaty. She was active politically, standing for councils, for the Dail and the Seanad. She helped found Fianna Fail but later fell out with the party.

She died in 1972, at the age of ninety-four.

Desmond FitzGerald

The parsimonious keeper of food in the GPO was said to be 'heartily cursed in every jail in England where men were confined when, starving with hunger, they thought of the food they had left behind them in the GPO'.

FitzGerald was released from jail in 1918, became a Sinn Fein MP, supported the treaty and became a minister in the provisional government. He was later a Fine Gael TD and a senator, flirting with the Blueshirt fascist movement in the thirties. He retired from politics in 1943 and died in 1947, aged fifty-nine. His son Garret became leader of Fine Gael in 1977 and Taoiseach in the 1980s.

Mick Doherty
Incredibly, the Irish Citizen Army member survived the dozen machine-gun bullets that hit him as he ate a sandwich on the roof of the College of Surgeons. He lost an eye and an ear. He ended up in Knutsford Prison. Two years later, the flu pandemic of 1918 infected about five hundred million globally and killed about a tenth of those, including about twenty thousand people in Ireland. Among those who died was Mick Doherty. He was from Mayor Street, North Wall.

Joe 'Moggy' Murtagh (John O'Connor)
The young Fianna scout attached to F Company survived the rising and served in the war of independence, in which he was jailed. He was pro-treaty in the civil war and reached the rank of lieutenant. He was shot in the chest in Capel Street in 1922, during an ambush, and as a consequence was declared medically unfit and discharged from the army in 1924, with the rank of lieutenant.

Moggy was born to John and Mary O'Connor in January 1900. Within a week of his birth he was handed over to a Mary Murtagh, for reasons not recorded, and he was raised by her and was henceforth known as Joe Murtagh. In 1929 he officially reverted to his birth name, John O'Connor. He died in London in 1964.

Bulmer Hobson
Active since 1904, friend of Tom Clarke, Hobson had sworn Patrick Pearse into membership of the IRB. Founder,

Bulmer Hobson

with Constance Markievicz, of the Fianna, former member of the Supreme Council of the IRB, one of the founders of the Irish Volunteers, organizer of the Howth gun-running – his daily life revolved around the cause. Although he lived another fifty-three years, Hobson had no significant involvement in politics. And the precarious living he made from writing about political events was ended.

In the aftermath of the rising, some told lies in an effort to suggest he was a traitor to the movement. There was a suggestion that he should subject himself to some form of nationalist court martial. Hobson ignored it all.

Soon after the rising, he and Claire Cregan married. They had two children. Hobson made a living working in the printing department of the Revenue Commissioners.

After being married for over twenty years, Hobson and Cregan split up. Hobson lived alone in Connemara for the next eleven years, and died in 1969 at the age of eighty-six.

Professor Eoin MacNeill

Arrested, sentenced to life in jail, then released in 1917, the titular head of the Irish Volunteers won a seat in the new Dail after the 1918 general election.

One of his three sons, seventeen-year-old Niall, was after the rising 'court-martialled' by a three-person IRA court for failing to take part in the insurrection. Constance Markievicz was one of the judges. Niall was 'exonerated' on the basis that he was under his father's influence.

Eoin MacNeill supported the treaty, as did two of his

sons, Niall and Turloch. The third son, Brian, opposed the treaty. During the civil war Brian was captured by the National Army, along with three comrades, in Sligo. Having been disarmed, he and his comrades were murdered.

Subsequently, Eoin MacNeill took some marginal part in politics but returned to academic life after losing his Dail seat in 1927.

He died in 1945, at the age of seventy-eight.

Colthurst

Captain J. C. Bowen Colthurst

The killer of Frank Sheehy-Skeffington, Thomas Dickson, Patrick MacIntyre and others was court-martialled and declared insane. He was hospitalized until 1922 and on release he emigrated to Canada, where he became a farmer (or, according to some, a banker). He died in 1965.

There would not have been a court martial without the courage of Sir Francis Fletcher Vane, a major with the Royal Munster Fusiliers. A retired officer, a veteran of the Boer War, a supporter of the suffragettes, Vane was in Italy when the Great War started – he returned to England, aged fifty-five, joined up and was sent to Ireland. He was second in command of the defence of Portobello Barracks.

An army report on the killings concluded: 'Captain Bowen Colthurst seems to have carried out his duties with discretion.' In the face of an official cover-up, Sir Francis Fletcher Vane travelled to London and spoke to

Field Marshal Kitchener and the prime minister's private secretary. The political establishment knew then the cover-up was doomed.

The military establishment was made of harder stuff. In Dublin, General John Maxwell ignored a telegram from London ordering him to arrest Bowen Colthurst. Eventually, fearing that Vane was about to go public with the case, the authorities insisted on a court martial for Bowen Colthurst.

General Maxwell withheld a report in which Vane was 'mentioned in despatches' for leading an attack that helped rescue an ammunition column threatened by the rebels. Maxwell decided that Vane's services were no longer required by the military.

For his insistence on pursuing justice, Vane was forcibly discharged and his career abruptly terminated, although he continued in vain to volunteer to fight in the war against Germany.

In 1917, Vane wrote a book about the Easter rising but it was banned by the army censor. He published his autobiography in 1929, titled *Agin the Governments: memories and adventures of Sir Francis Fletcher Vane*, and died four years later at the age of seventy-three.

Bowen Colthurst was Irish. He had family in Cork. During the war of independence the IRA organized a boycott, intimidated the family and eventually burned them out. Had Sheehy-Skeffington lived he undoubtedly would have defended an innocent family against such an attack.

Hanna Sheehy-Skeffington

The wife of the murdered pacifist campaigned to expose the facts of his killing. She was offered £10,000 compensation

*Hanna Sheehy-
Skeffington*

for her husband's murder and turned it down. She went to the USA to make the case, at public meetings, for Irish independence and she was jailed in the UK for speaking against British militarism. She supported the anti-treaty side in the civil war. She died in 1946, at the age of sixty-eight.

Noel Lemass

The wounded teenager in the tenement on Gloucester Street, along with Brennan-Whitmore and his comrades, recovered from the gunshot injuries to his foot. Noel Lemass fought in the war of independence and served on the anti-treaty side in the civil war. He was reputed to have killed two Free State officers in an ambush.

He was jailed by the pro-treaty side, escaped and went to England. He returned to Ireland when the civil war ended.

On 3 July 1923, on the corner of Exchequer Street, Dublin, Lemass was kidnapped by men in plain clothes, believed to be army officers. After he was tortured and his arm broken, he was shot three times in the head at close range. His body was dumped in the Dublin Mountains, where it was discovered three months later.

His alleged killer, Captain James Murray of the National Army, was a sadistic thug who indulged in mock and real executions of those he considered enemies of the state. He was subsequently convicted of the murder of another republican. He was sentenced to death for that. The Cosgrave government commuted the sentence on condition he left the country.

Lemass's younger brother Sean, who was in the GPO in 1916, became Taoiseach in 1959.

Sergeant John McQuaid

The sergeant who acted as the 'pivot', the central figure in mobilizing members of F Company, fought in the GPO. After the rising, 'owing to difficulties at home', he joined the British Army. Years later, Frank Henderson described McQuaid as 'a splendid Volunteer'. He may have gone to Australia after the war.

Sir Maurice Dockrell

The unionist store owner who ensured that Captain Michael Breen kept his job remained an implacable enemy of nationalism. In the 1918 general election he won a unionist seat in Rathmines – and while the victorious nationalists set up Dail Eireann he sat in Westminster.

He died in 1929, at the age of seventy-nine. His son Henry was a prominent Fine Gael TD and held a Dail seat from 1932 to 1948. When Michael Breen died, Henry Dockrell sent a wreath and paid the funeral expenses.

Percival Lea-Wilson

In June 1920, Michael Collins sent an assassination team to Gorey, in Wexford, to kill Percival Lea-Wilson, the officer who mistreated Tom Clarke in front of the Rotunda Hospital on the night of the surrender. Lea-Wilson was by then a district inspector of the Royal Irish Constabulary.

On one occasion the assassination team were within sight of Lea-Wilson, but his wife was present and they were

Lea-Wilson

Dr Marie Lea-Wilson

under orders not to kill him in front of her. They waited for another day, caught him alone and shot him dead.

Lea-Wilson's wife, Marie, received counselling from a Jesuit priest, a Fr Finlay, and decided to take up medical studies at Trinity College Dublin. She graduated aged forty-one and became a highly regarded paediatrician.

On a visit to Scotland in 1921 she saw, liked and purchased a painting by seventeenth-century Dutch painter Gerard van Honthorst. In the 1930s, Dr Lea-Wilson gave the painting to Fr Finlay, in thanks for the help he had given her. For decades it hung in the Jesuit House in Leeson Street, Dublin. In 1991 it was recognized as a priceless lost painting by Caravaggio – *The Taking of Christ*. It now hangs in the National Gallery of Ireland.

Eddie Byrne

The fifteen-year-old put by his father under Charlie Saurin's protection during the rising went on to fight in the war of independence. During the truce, he died following the accidental discharge of a shotgun. He was twenty-one.

Prince Joachim Franz Humbert of Prussia

When Germany lost the war, the Kaiser was unseated by uprisings, abdicated and went into exile. His son Joachim faced life as a commoner. His marriage in ruins, his finances likewise, Prince Joachim shot himself in July 1920, at the age of thirty – unaware that Patrick Pearse and Joe Plunkett had considered him for a new job as King of Ireland.

Sir Thomas Myles

The surgeon and gun-running knight of the realm was praised by the British secretary of state for war for 'distinguished services rendered in connection with the war' against Germany. Sir Thomas rendered those services as a member of the Royal Army Medical Corps. Simultaneously, as an Irish nationalist, he did what he could to protect and hide rebel patients at the Richmond Hospital, where he carried out exhausting medical work during the week of the rebellion.

Later, in the war of independence, Myles again ensured that wounded Volunteers were hidden away from where the authorities might find them.

He died in July 1937, aged eighty.

Vinny Byrne

The fifteen-year-old who cried when he almost missed the rising became – four years later – a member of Michael Collins's execution team, The Squad. He was involved in the Bloody Sunday killings of eleven British intelligence agents, and many other similar killings, and was noted for the coolness and ruthlessness he

Vinny Byrne, third from left, with other members of The Squad

brought to his work. Borrowing the lingo of American western novels, he reminisced later about 'plugging' his targets. He served throughout the war of independence and went with the pro-treaty side in the civil war. He died in 1992.

Johnny Barton and Daniel Hoey

The two detectives from G Division who picked out Sean MacDermott for special treatment were regarded as highly effective in the fight against subversives. During the war of independence they became targets for Michael Collins's assassination team. Hoey was shot dead in Townsend Street in September 1919. Barton was shot dead in College Street two months later. One of those involved in the latter killing was Vinny Byrne.

Frank Saurin

Too young to join his brother Charlie in the fighting in 1916, Frank Saurin grew up fast. After the rising he was active in the reorganized F Company, and became its intelligence officer. He was soon transferred to the General Headquarters Staff of the IRA, reporting to Michael Collins on a daily basis.

He became known as the best-dressed Volunteer in Dublin – always wearing a good suit, sometimes wearing lavender gloves. He frequented restaurants and hotels such as Jammet's, the Wicklow, the Shelbourne, the Moira and the Central, identifying likely targets for Collins's gunmen.

He wasn't a member of The Squad, Collins's execution team, but he often went along with them, waiting until they killed their targets, then quickly searching a room or a body for documents that might prove useful. Like his brother Charlie, he sided with Collins in the civil war.

In civilian life, Saurin became an executive of the Irish Hospital Sweepstakes, right-hand man to the controversial Joe McGrath, a 1916 veteran who founded the Sweepstakes. Although set up to raise money for the public hospitals, the Sweepstakes was a private company that made a fortune for McGrath.

Frank Saurin died in 1957.

Douglas Hyde

Ten years after his first garden party, the first president of Ireland died, in July 1949, at the age of eighty-nine. A member of the Church of Ireland, his state funeral was held at St Patrick's Cathedral. The Catholic bishops forbade any Catholic from attending a non-Catholic service. So, members of the Cabinet, led by John Costello, went to the cathedral but stood outside the grounds, as did the leader of Fianna Fail, Eamon de Valera. Only Noel Browne, a socialist member of the Cabinet, went inside.

W. J. Brennan-Whitmore

After the rising, the anti-dancing officer from Wexford wrote two books, one about the internment camp at Frongoch, and one a memoir of the rising. He remained a controversial figure.

He retained his anti-Semitic bent and was active with the Blueshirts in the thirties. In 1940 he was part of the pro-Nazi fringe and sought to found a fascist outfit called 'Clann na Saoirse' ('Tribe of Freedom'). In his last years, in the face of protests against South African racism, he supported apartheid.

He died in 1977, at the age of ninety-one.

The Legend of the 1916 Radio Station

The Morse code broadcast from the Reis building, set up by Fergus O'Kelly's group – including Michael Breen, Blimey O'Connor, Liam Daly and Boss Shields – has survived in legend as the world's first radio broadcast. Up to then, radio transmissions were usually directed towards a specific receiver. The transmission from the Reis building was a 'broadcast', in that it was a signal sent out to whatever receivers could pick it up.

In 1949, the Bureau of Military History wondered if the Morse code broadcasts from the Reis building had been received, decoded and re-transmitted to other countries. In particular, had any of the Irish republican sympathizers in the USA received early word of the rising? The BMH asked the Department of External Affairs to enquire among prominent Irish-Americans if that was the case. The editors of the *Irish World* and the *Gaelic American* were approached, and in turn made enquiries among their own contacts.

Word came back – whoever might have heard the Morse code, no one had passed on a message to the Irish-Americans.

Blimey O'Connor, halfway up the mast on top of the Reis building, Liam Daly on a ledge, exposed to sniper fire, risking their lives to fix the aerial and spread the word of the new Republic. Boss Shields and his comrades staggering under the weight of primitive radio equipment as they crossed Sackville Street, with bullets hopping off the ground around them. None of them could know if anyone was listening. Under orders, they cast their dots and dashes upon the ether in the hope that there would be some advantage to their cause. They did what they thought they ought to do.

Sources

The Bureau of Military History is a fascinating online resource. The idea for the book and the vast bulk of the detail that makes up the narrative came from the hundreds of witness statements available at:
www.bureauofmilitaryhistory.ie/

The site also has online copies of *An t-Oglac*, the Irish Army newspaper, which around the tenth anniversary of the rising carried the recollections of a number of Volunteers and members of Cumann na mBan.

The Military Service Pensions Collection, online, was also invaluable, as was the 1911 census, online at the National Archives, and the online version of Hansard.

The National Library of Ireland has, in its Manuscripts Department, a folder of handwritten and typed statements by 1916 veterans: MS 10915.

The Shields family archive, held in the James Hardiman Library, NUI Galway, provided background material on Arthur Shields and his friend Charlie Saurin.

Books

1916 Rebellion Handbook, Mourne River Press, 1998

Berresford Ellis, Peter, *A History of the Irish Working Class*, Pluto, 1985

Brennan-Whitmore, W. J., *Dublin Burning: the Easter Rising from Behind the Barricades*, Gill & Macmillan, 1996

Campbell, Fergus, *Land and Revolution: Nationalist Politics in the West of Ireland 1891–1921*, Oxford University Press, 2005

Connell, Joseph E. A., Jr, *Dublin in Rebellion: a Directory 1913–1923*, Lilliput Press, 2006

De Burca, Marcus, *The GAA: a History of the Gaelic Athletic Association*, Cumann Luthchleas Gael, 1980

Doherty, Gabriel, and Keogh, Dermot (eds), *1916: the Long Revolution*, Mercier, 2007

Dudley Edwards, Ruth, *An Atlas of Irish History*, Routledge, 2005

Dudley Edwards, Ruth, *Patrick Pearse: the Triumph of Failure*, Taplinger Publishing Company, 1978

Farmar, A. and A. (ed.), *Findlater's: the Story of a Dublin Merchant Family 1774–2001*, published online, 2013

FitzGerald, Fergus (ed.), *The Memoirs of Desmond FitzGerald*, Routledge & Kegan Paul, 1968

Galligan, Kevin, *Peter Paul Galligan*, Liffey Press, 2012

Giffen, Sir Robert, KCB, *Economic Inquiries and Studies*, Vol. 1, Gordon Bell and Sons, 1904

Good, Joe, *Enchanted by Dreams: the Journal of a Revolutionary*, Brandon, 1996

Henry, William, *Supreme Sacrifice: the Story of Eamonn Ceannt*, Mercier, 2005

Hopkinson, Michael (ed.), *Frank Henderson's Easter Rising: Recollections of a Dublin Volunteer*; *Irish Narratives* series, Cork University Press, 1998

Hughes, Brian, *16 Lives: Michael Mallin*, O'Brien Press, 2013

Jeffery, Keith (ed.), *The Sinn Fein Rebellion As They Saw It*, Irish Academic Press, 1999

Kearns, Kevin C., *Dublin Tenement Life*, Gill & Macmillan, 1994

Laffan, Michael, *The Partition of Ireland 1911–1925*, Dublin Historical Association, 1983

Lynch, Diarmuid, *The IRB and the 1916 Insurrection*, Mercier, 1957

Martin, F. X. (ed.), *The Irish Volunteers 1913–1915: Recollections and Documents*, James Duffy & Co., 1963

McCoole, Sinead, *No Ordinary Women*, O'Brien Press, 2003

McManus, Ruth, *Dublin 1910–1940, Shaping the City & Suburbs*, Four Courts Press, 2002

Mitchell, Arthur, and O Snodaigh, Padraig, *Irish Political Documents 1916–1949*, Irish Academic Press, 1985

Moynihan, Maurice (ed.), *Speeches and Statements by Eamon de Valera 1917–1973*, Gill & Macmillan, 1980

Ó Maitiú, Séamus, *W&R Jacob: Celebrating 150 Years of Irish Biscuit Making*, Woodfield Press, 2001

O'Clery, Conor, *Phrases Make History Here*, O'Brien Press, 1986

O'Connor, John, *The 1916 Proclamation*, Anvil Books, 1999

O'Farrell, Mick, *The 1916 Diaries of an Irish Rebel and a British Soldier*, Mercier Press, 2014

O'Hegarty, P. S., *The Victory of Sinn Fein*, Talbot Press, 1924

O'Rahilly, Aodogan, *Winding the Clock*, Lilliput Press, 1991

Stephens, James, *The Insurrection in Dublin*, Maunsel & Co., 1916

The Irish Uprising 1914–21: Papers from the British Parliamentary Archive, uncovered editions (series ed. Tim Coates), HM Stationery Office, 2000

Articles and papers

Biddlecombe, Darragh, *Colonel Dan Bryan and the evolution of Irish Military Intelligence, 1919–1945*, NUI Maynooth thesis, 1999

Crowe, Catriona, 'Dublin 100 Years Ago: Death, Disease and Overcrowding', *Liberty*, SIPTU journal, Lockout Special, October 2013

Ferriter, Diarmaid, 'Report to the Commission to Inquire into Child Abuse', in Volume V of the Ryan Report, 2009

Hay, Marnie, 'Kidnapped: Bulmer Hobson, the IRB and the 1916 Easter Rising', *Canadian Journal of Irish Studies*, Spring 2009

Henderson, Ruaidhri, *Easter Week Rising: a Tabulated Summary of Events in Dublin*, 1945 (held at the Bureau of Military History)

Kennerk, Barry, 'Compensating for the Rising: the papers of the Property Losses (Ireland) Committee, 1916', *History Ireland*, March–April 2013

Kerrigan, Gene, 'Those lazy hazy days of insecurity and oh-so-stately garden parties', *Sunday Independent*, 23 May 2004

Kinealy, Christine, 'Food Exports from Ireland 1846–47', *History Ireland*, Spring 1997

McCarthy, Sam, 'Englishman who died for Ireland', *Liberty*, SIPTU journal, Vol. 11, No. 5, July 2012 – article on John Neale

McConway, Philip, 'TV Eye: A lost son', *History Ireland*, March–April 2013

McGarry, Fearghal, 'Helena Molony: a revolutionary life', *History Ireland*, July–August 2013

Millar, Scott, 'Not for fame or for name', *Liberty*, SIPTU journal, Vol. 12, No. 10, December 2013 – article on Vincent Poole and his brothers

Mooney, Joe, 'Mural revives legacy of East Wall evictions', *Liberty*, SIPTU journal, Lockout Special, October 2013

Owens, Rosemary, 'Votes for Ladies, Votes for Women', *Saothar 9: Journal of the Irish Labour History*, Irish Labour History Society, 1983

Scully, Seamus, 'Moore Street – 1916', *Dublin Historical Record*, Vol. 39, No. 2, March 1986

Websites

comeheretome.com knowledgeable blog, with a good sense of history

eastwallforall.ie community and local history site

irishcentral.com US-based news, business, culture and history site

irishhistory.blogspot.ie history site

irishmedals.org military history

irishvolunteers.org the Irish Volunteers Commemorative Society

knowthyplace.wordpress.com heritage site

richmondbarracks.ie history site – a Dublin City Council–Community Partnership

thecricketbatthatdiedforireland.com lively history site

theirishstory.com history site

wcml.org.uk website of the Working Class Movement Library, in Manchester – material on Sir Francis Fletcher Vane and other notables

Thanks

Over the years, I've been grateful to Julie Lordan and Cathleen Kerrigan for their support on various projects. On this occasion, the support was immeasurable – words will never be enough.

Thanks to Christine Shields (Arthur Shields's daughter), Stella Stoddart (Charlie Saurin's daughter) and to Siobhan Henderson (Frank Henderson's granddaughter).

Thanks to Professor Adrian Frazier of NUI Galway, to Catriona Crowe of the National Archives, to Margaret Hughes and the staff of the James Hardiman Library, NUI Galway, to Comdt Padraic Kennedy of the Military Archives, to Aoife Torpey of Kilmainham Museum and to the staff of the National Library's Department of Manuscripts.

Thanks to my agent Peter Straus and to Eoin McHugh of Transworld. Thanks to copy-editor Brenda Updegraff, without whose scrupulous work the book would still have more than its share of errors, repetitions and awkward sentences.

Thanks, yet again, to my friends Evelyn Bracken and Pat Brennan, who read an early draft and suggested improvements, as did my daughter Cathleen.

Picture acknowledgements

The two sketches by Charlie Saurin are used by permission of the Bureau of Military History.

The photos of Charlie Saurin and Arthur Shields are used by permission of the James Hardiman Library, NUI Galway.

The photos of Nora O'Daly, Vincent Poole, Joe Good and Blimey O'Connor are used by permission of the Kilmainham Museum Archive; as is the photo of MacNeill, de Valera and Poole on the title page of the Epilogue.

The photo of Frank Henderson is used by permission of his family.

The photo of Paul Galligan is used with the permission of Kevin Galligan.

The photo of Henderson, Colley and Traynor is used by permission of the family of F Company's Peter Doran; thanks to Tony Redmond.

The photo of Oscar Traynor is used by permission of the National Library of Ireland.

The front cover photo, of Volunteers and Citizen Army members inside the GPO, is used by permission of National Library of Ireland.

The back cover photo of the centre of Dublin in flames is used by permission of Getty Images.

Every effort has been made to obtain the necessary permissions with reference to illustrative material. We apologize for any possible omission or error and will be pleased to make the appropriate acknowledgment in any future edition.

Index

ABOUT THE AUTHOR

Gene Kerrigan is from Dublin, where he writes for the *Sunday Independent*. He is the author of eight other non-fiction books and four novels.